The Defamation Act 2013

BLACKSTONE'S GUIDE TO

The Defamation Act 2013

Edited By

James Price QC
and Felicity McMahon

Contributors

Nigel Abbas
Jonathan Barnes
William Bennett
Iain Christie
Jacob Dean
Patrick McCafferty
Richard Munden
Justin Rushbrooke QC
Yuli Takatsuki
Mark Warby QC

all at 5RB <www.5rb.com>

OXFORD
UNIVERSITY PRESS

OXFORD
UNIVERSITY PRESS

Great Clarendon Street, Oxford, OX2 6DP,
United Kingdom

Oxford University Press is a department of the University of Oxford.
It furthers the University's objective of excellence in research, scholarship,
and education by publishing worldwide. Oxford is a registered trade mark of
Oxford University Press in the UK and in certain other countries

Published in the United States of America by Oxford University Press
198 Madison Avenue, New York, NY 10016, United States of America

British Library Cataloguing in Publication Data

Data available

ISBN 978–0–19–966421–4

Printed in Great Britain by
CPI Group (UK) Ltd, Croydon, CR0 4YY

Preface

The Defamation Act 2013 combines codification and substantive reform to the law. When the Act comes into force (at the time of writing, expected to be towards the end of 2013) it will provide a new framework for those dealing with the law of libel. This Guide combines analysis of this new legislative framework and comment on what may change as the courts get to grips with the new Act, with copies of the Act, its explanatory notes, and the changes the Act makes to Schedule 1 the previous Defamation Act (1996).

There are some aspects of how the law will change which are as yet uncertain. At the time of writing no regulations have been made, or even circulated in draft, under s 5 (operators of websites). Section 5 is a framework provision, and as such the authors of Chapter 6 have analysed the wording of the Act, its history and what is expected to be included in regulations. However, much is left to those regulations, and precisely how the notice system envisaged by s 5 will operate remains to be seen.

The Parliamentary stages of the Bill which became the Defamation Act 2013 ran in parallel with the Leveson Inquiry into the Culture, Practices and Ethics of the Press. At the time of writing there remain two parallel proposals for a new system of regulation of the press, backed by a Royal Charter. What new press regulator will emerge, and what shape any arbitration scheme for claims (including defamation claims) against the press will take, again remains unknown at the time of writing.

This Guide was written by a team of expert barristers at 5RB. Each a specialist in libel law, and other related areas of media law, the contributors will be working with the new Act on a daily basis. Contributors have been involved in some of the most high profile libel cases of recent years, and so have been able to bring to this Guide a wealth of experience of this area of law and practice. We are grateful to each contributor for the time spent in analysing the provisions of the Act, the debates in Parliament, and in considering how the new Act may operate in practice, including how it may interact with the old law (that which survives the repealing provisions) and how it may be interpreted by the courts.

We hope that this Guide will be useful to practitioners, academics, members of the public interested in libel law and libel reform, and all those who come into contact with the law of defamation, whether as professionals, litigants, publishers or merely out of interest.

James Price QC
Felicity McMahon

Table of Contents

List of Contributors

Nigel Abbas
Jonathan Barnes
William Bennett
Iain Christie
Jacob Dean
Patrick McCafferty
Richard Munden
Justin Rushbrooke QC
Yuli Takatsuki
Mark Warby QC

All the contributors are barristers at 5RB www.5rb.com

Table of Cases

Table of Legislation

1

INTRODUCTION AND BACKGROUND

A. BACKGROUND TO THE ACT

The impetus for the present parliamentary process, which led to the Defamation **1.01**
Act 2013, can probably be traced to the enactment by various US legislatures
of statutes preventing enforcement of foreign, particularly English, libel judgments within their jurisdictions. This started with the State of New York,
which in 2008 passed the Libel Terrorism Prevention Act, and culminated
with the enactment by the US Congress of the Securing the Protection of our
Enduring and Established Constitutional Heritage Act 2010, known for short
as the SPEECH Act. What motivated these statutes, or indeed their remark-
able names, is beyond the scope of a Blackstone's Guide to a new Act, but was
explained by Lord Hoffmann in his Dame Ann Ebsworth Memorial Lecture
delivered on 2 February 2010. The principal concern of American legislatures
was so-called libel tourism, which involves—so it is said—foreign, particularly
American, defendants being sued in England by foreign claimants, based on
modest distribution of defamatory publications in this jurisdiction, in print
form or on the internet.

The American reaction to libel tourism struck a chord with some media in **1.02**
the UK and fuelled a campaign to reform English libel laws and, in particular,
to introduce a rule modelled on the US Supreme Court case of *New York Times*

v Sullivan,[1] which, in the case of a public figure—a concept upon which there is much jurisprudence—requires that the claimant should prove, to a strict standard, malice on the part of the defendant as a condition of establishing a cause of action for defamation.

1.03   The controversy about English libel law prompted three charities, English PEN, Index on Censorship, and Sense About Science to form a committee to assess the impact of English libel law on freedom of expression, both in the UK and internationally. Its report entitled *Free Speech Is Not for Sale* was published in 2009, and made far-reaching recommendations for reforming the law, so as to tilt the balance significantly away from the protection of reputation and in favour of the free exchange of ideas and information. The report gave powerful impetus to the media campaign for reform, and attracted controversy; see, for example, Lord Hoffmann's lecture referred to above and a January 2010 paper by Professor Mullis of the University of East Anglia and Dr Scott of the London School of Economics, entitled 'Something Rotten in the State of English Libel Law?'.

1.04   During 2009, the Culture, Media and Sport Committee of the House of Commons took evidence from a wide range of witnesses in the course of its inquiry into Press Standards, Privacy and Libel, and published its report on 23 February 2010. It made recommendations concerning, in particular, the burden of proof, which under common law is on the defendant to prove the truth of the publication complained of, and libel tourism. In the meantime, the Lord Chancellor established a Working Group on Libel, which reported on 23 March 2010, focusing on four areas: libel tourism, the role of public interest considerations in establishing a defence to libel, rules about multiple publication—the rule that each copy of a defamatory publication or each hit on a defamatory web page, gives rise to a separate cause of action—with particular reference to internet publications, and procedural and case management issues.

1.05   The press campaign, and consequent public interest in defamation law reform, led to all three of the main political parties committing to reform in their manifestos for the May 2010 General Election. The Coalition Agreement of 11 May included, at section 10, agreement 'to implement a full programme of measures to reverse the substantial erosion of civil liberties under the Labour Government and roll back state intrusion', including, among 12 bullet points, '[t]he review of libel laws to protect freedom of speech'.

1.06   On 26 May 2010, Lord Lester of Herne Hill QC introduced in the House of Lords a Private Member's Bill, the Defamation Bill, which served as the precursor to the Bill later published by the Ministry of Justice. In July 2010, the Ministry outlined plans to review the law of defamation, carrying out informal consultations with interested parties, with a view to publishing a draft Defamation Bill for consultation and pre-legislative scrutiny at the beginning of 2011.

---

[1] 376 US 254 (1964).

B. GOVERNMENT CONSULTATION AND DRAFT BILL

In March 2011, the Ministry published its Consultation Paper,[2] including, at 1.07 Annex A, the draft Defamation Bill. The Bill was slightly misleadingly entitled 'A Bill to amend the law of defamation', whereas it was, and remains, a mixture of codification and reform. A number of important issues were recognized in the paper, but not covered in the Bill, being left for consultation.

In April 2011, a Joint Parliamentary Committee on the Draft Defamation Bill 1.08 was established, a committee of both Houses of Parliament comprising six MPs and six peers. The Committee called for evidence to be submitted on the draft Bill, and indicated that it would take oral and written evidence, culminating in a report of recommendations to Parliament and Government.

The Joint Committee published extensive written evidence, and in the period 1.09 from April to July 2011, heard oral evidence from a wide range of people, including the Lord Chancellor and the Minister of State at the Ministry of Justice, present and former law officers, judges, academics, lawyers, representatives of the media, NGOs, internet service providers, and trade unions. The evidence served to confirm that the contents of the draft Bill, and the other issues for reform, were highly controversial, with views on either side being at opposite poles. The one side argued for significantly greater freedom for the press; the other for the most part supported the existing role of the law in enforcing media responsibility, and in protecting reputation from damage by defamatory and false publications. Reputation is a right protected under Article 8 of the European Convention on Human Rights, so that the UK is, as matters stand, bound to provide effective protection for it, both by treaty and under the Human Rights Act 1998.

On 14 November 2011, hearings began in the Leveson Inquiry into the 1.10 Culture, Practices and Ethics of the Press. The focus of the inquiry was on phone hacking, invasions of privacy, bribery of public officials, and other alleged inappropriate behaviour by the press, whether reporters or more senior members of media organizations. The inquiry and the development and passage of the Defamation Bill proceeded in parallel, with little apparent cross-fertilization, except at the end of the parliamentary progress of the Bill.

C. JOINT COMMITTEE ON THE DRAFT DEFAMATION BILL

The Joint Committee reported on 19 October 2011.[3] The report welcomed the 1.11 proposals, but described them as 'modest', urging more far-reaching reform, in particular in relation to the cost of libel litigation. The Joint Committee urged

---

[2] Ministry of Justice, *Draft Defamation Bill: Consultation*, Consultation Paper CP3/11, March 2011.
[3] HL Paper 203, HC 930-I, 19 October 2011.

the Government to take a strategic view as to how the law of defamation interacts with privacy and the costs of civil litigation generally. In the Committee's view, the draft as it stood did not always achieve the clarification of the law for which it aimed, with the law remaining largely inaccessible to the public. Striking a fair balance between protection of reputation and freedom of speech, and the difficulties of enforcing the law in the global, online sphere, were also highlighted as areas of concern. Four core principles influenced the report and the Committee urged that they remain central in forthcoming debate:

(1) The balance between freedom of expression and protection of reputation.

(2) Reducing costs.

(3) Accessibility.

(4) Adapting to the new online environment with its challenges of jurisdiction, anonymity, and wide dissemination of content.

1.12 Many of the Committee recommendations followed the same direction of travel as changes that were already under way in the common law. The proposal for a threshold test for what is defamatory builds on the existing jurisprudence as set out in cases such as *Jameel (Yousef) v Dow Jones & Co Inc*[4] and *Thornton v Telegraph Media Group Ltd*,[5] but also appeared to show a desire to strengthen this test, making it more of a genuine hurdle for claimants. In reality this seems always to have been the intended outcome of what became s 1 of the Act. It is worth noting that the Impact Assessment for the Bill as introduced into Parliament stated: 'Claimants will find it harder to bring defamation cases against material published'.

1.13 Similarly, in relation to costs, the defamation costs management pilot scheme was under way and remains so at the time of writing. It attempts to give the judge more control of the costs of libel litigation, including through requiring the parties to prepare budgets at an early stage. For the Committee, the high costs involved in defamation cases were seen as having a 'chilling effect'.

1.14 The Government took the position that attempts to reduce the costs of proceedings would primarily be pursued elsewhere, this being a Bill aimed squarely at the substantive law of defamation, not other, albeit related, matters. This was a change of position from that expressed by Justice Minister Lord McNally during the passage of the Legal Aid, Sentencing and Punishment of Offenders Act 2012 (LASPOA 2012), which included legislative provisions relating to the implementation of the Jackson Review of Costs in Civil Litigation. In response to debate in the Lords about how defamation proceedings should be dealt with, Lord McNally stated that he expected such matters would be dealt with in the Defamation Bill.

1.15 That costs would be dealt with elsewhere was ultimately accepted, but parliamentarians continued to express their serious concerns about high costs, and

---

[4] [2005] EWCA Civ 75, [2005] QB 946.
[5] [2010] EWHC 1414 (QB), [2011] 1 WLR 1985.

the effect that this has on free speech and access to legal redress for the ordinary citizen, at each stage of the passage of the Bill.

Promoting the use of alternative dispute resolution mechanisms, such as arbi- **1.16** tration, was a key Committee recommendation, the aim being to keep cases out of court where possible, thus keeping costs lower. The Committee recommended a requirement for strict adherence to the existing Pre-Action Protocol for Defamation claims and the introduction of a presumption of 'early neutral evaluation' by an independent third party.

The issue of how to deal effectively with online publication, particularly where **1.17** publication is not by more traditional actors in the field—for example, the online versions of newspapers—but rather by often anonymous bloggers and social media users whose location is unknown, is a growing area of concern and one which the Committee sought to tackle. The Committee's recommendations were fairly detailed and proposed a take-down notice procedure.

The protection of publishers of scientific and academic journals was also a **1.18** matter which the Committee recommended the Government should address. High-profile cases such as that of Simon Singh, sued by the British Chiropractic Association (which ultimately withdrew its claim after the Court of Appeal found the words complained of to be opinion),[6] had raised concerns over whether publication of public interest matters—such as criticism of certain scientific methods or medical treatments—was sufficiently protected. Although these cases did not relate to peer-reviewed journals, these were the focus of the Committee and the legislative proposals which followed.

The Committee also recommended that the Bill should deal with parliamen- **1.19** tary privilege, to clarify the position of the press when reporting statements which have been made in Parliament. The impetus for looking at this area arose from cases where MPs used parliamentary privilege to name those subject to court orders (the case relating to Ryan Giggs achieved particular notoriety). There were also concerns about whether communications between MPs and their constituents were protected under the law. Interest in the scope of parliamentary privilege had also been raised by the MPs' expenses scandal and some of the defences put forward (unsuccessfully) by implicated MPs.

D. GOVERNMENT RESPONSE TO THE JOINT COMMITTEE AND CONSULTEES

In February 2012, the Government issued a response[7] to both the Joint **1.20** Committee and the responses to its Consultation Paper and draft Bill, dealing with the Joint Committee's recommendations point by point.

---

[6] *British Chiropractic Association v Singh* [2010] EWCA Civ 350, [2011] 1 WLR 133.
[7] Ministry of Justice, *The Government's Response to the Report of the Joint Committee on the Defamation Bill* (Cm 8295, February 2012).

- The recommendation that the threshold test be changed to 'serious and substantial harm' was accepted in part. The Government agreed that the test should be strengthened and proposed 'serious harm'. Having the dual test was rejected. The Government argued that it might cause confusion and increase costs through parties arguing over whether a claimant had overcome one, none, or both of 'serious' and 'substantial'.

- The Government accepted that action should be taken to address the difficulties faced by a claimant when dealing with an online defamatory post by an anonymous person, and committed to work on the matter further. By the time the Bill was introduced into Parliament, a clause had been added, along the lines of part of what had been recommended by the Committee, to establish a framework for a take-down procedure, where a claimant does not know the identity of a person posting defamatory statements online anonymously. This became s 5 of the Act.

- The Government accepted that protection for peer-reviewed academic and scientific journals should be increased, and agreed to conduct further work on how this should be done. Again this matter had been added into the Bill by the time it was introduced into Parliament. This became s 6 of the Act.

- On alternative dispute resolution, the Government agreed to consider the early neutral evaluation proposal and strengthening of the Pre-Action Protocol. The Government also pointed to the Leveson Inquiry, which would be considering methods of redress as part of its consideration of how best to regulate the media. This issue would return to prominence at a later stage.

- On parliamentary privilege, the Government view was that it was a topic which should be dealt with separately, as there are many aspects to parliamentary privilege, which go far beyond the privileges attaching the statements made in Parliament. The Government promised a Green Paper on the issues, which was published for consultation in 2012. The law relating to parliamentary privilege is beyond the scope of this book. As it is found in a series of statutes of considerable antiquity, there were, and remain, calls for it to be clarified and brought up to date. However, there are also counterveiling concerns that doing so might put matters of Parliament within the jurisdiction of the courts. At the time of writing the Government is still considering whether there ought to be a Parliamentary Privilege Bill. No plans for such a Bill were announced in the Queen's Speech in May 2013.

E. THE DEFAMATION BILL IN PARLIAMENT

1.21 The Bill was introduced into the House of Commons on 10 May 2012 and had its Second Reading on 12 June. The stated aims of the Bill at introduction were:

- Rebalancing the law, so that whilst people who have been defamed are able to protect their reputations, free speech is not unjustifiably impeded by libel actions, whether actual or threatened.

- Ensuring scientific and academic debate is not impeded by threat of libel action, and encouraging responsible journalism.
- Reducing the potential for libel tourism so that the law of England and Wales is internationally respected.

The Bill was given very little time on the floor of the House of Commons and **1.22** it was explicitly acknowledged that much of the scrutiny of the Bill was being left to 'the other place' with a number of MPs expressing the hope that various issues could be resolved there. The Commons Bill Committee sat on three days in June 2012, and Report and Third Reading took place after the summer break on 12 September 2012. The Bill was sent to the House of Lords with only minor amendments.

The Bill progressed to the House of Lords on 8 October 2012. The parlia- **1.23** mentary timetable gave the Lords more time with the Bill. A number of Lords with particular expertise, including Lord Lester of Herne Hill (whose Private Member's Bill had been a precursor to the Bill before the House), Lord Black of Brentwood (Chairman of the Press Standards Board of Finance), Lords who had been active campaigners for libel reform, and former members of the Judicial Committee of the House of Lords, all contributed to the debates.

Concerns continued to be expressed about how the Bill would interact with **1.24** the outcome of the Leveson Inquiry, with Lord Lester going so far as to recommend that Lord Justice Leveson should release an interim report for the Lords to consider. Also revisited were the previous battlegrounds covered by the Joint Committee, on whose work the Lords drew during the debates.

On costs, which remained a key area of concern, Lord McNally at Second **1.25** Reading assured the Lords that the Civil Justice Council had been asked to consider procedural changes to deal with costs, in time for resulting changes to the Civil Procedure Rules to be implemented before the Bill would be due to come into force. He was reminded of his assurances during the passage of the LASPOA, but ultimately, the route of addressing costs through other means was accepted.

The public interest defence remained a key area of disagreement. The details **1.26** of this are outlined at Chapter 5. The Government agreed to keep an open mind and listen to the views of both Houses. Whether to keep some, or all, of the ten factors identified by Lord Nicholls in the *Reynolds*[8] case itself, the corresponding (as some saw it) inaccessibility of the defence, and whether the defence went far enough to protect freedom of speech were all topics of a great deal of debate. Some proposed the introduction of a free-standing public interest defence, without any the responsible journalism elements of the *Reynolds* defence under the existing law. The argument that some topics were so important that entirely free speech should be permitted, was countered with the view that misinformation of the public was not in the public interest and should not be protected even in relation to topics which are of themselves of the highest public interest.

---

[8] *Reynolds v Times Newspapers Ltd* [2001] 2 AC 127, [1999] 3 WLR 1010.

1.27   On Leveson, the Government made clear that although Lord Justice Leveson was considering related matters, this was a Bill on the substantive law of defamation, which it did not want to hold up because of the inquiry.

1.28   Lord Justice Leveson published his report on the Culture, Practices and Ethics of the Press on 29 November 2012. By the time the Defamation Bill reached Report stage in the House of Lords in February 2013, whilst Lord Justice Leveson's recommendations had been welcomed by all political parties, many felt that substantive progress had not been made. This led to calls for the inclusion of clauses in the Defamation Bill to implement some of the Leveson recommendations. The Bill was not a suitable vehicle for such legislation, if legislation there were to be. Recommendations such as the establishment of a press regulator went far beyond the scope of a Bill to change the substantive law of defamation, quite apart from the more fundamental objections to statutory regulation of the press.

1.29   Even those recommendations which could fairly be said to relate to media torts went beyond the scope of the Bill. First, 'media torts' in Leveson parlance included not just defamation, but also privacy and harassment. Secondly, the recommendations related not to the substantive law, but to procedural matters—key among them the recommendations that an arbitration body be established to allow individuals to resolve disputes with publishers (particularly newspapers). Calls for the Bill to address these more procedural matters—costs following the Jackson Review and encouragement of alternative dispute resolution, including arbitration as a way to avoid court action in defamation cases—were not new.

1.30   Nonetheless, frustration at the lack of progress on implementing the Leveson recommendations led a group of Lords—Lord Puttnam, Lord Mackay of Clashfern, Baroness Boothroyd and Baroness Scotland of Asthal—to propose amendments to the Defamation Bill which would have:

- established a statutory recognition body for a press regulator,
- established an arbitration service for defamation and related civil claims against publishers, and
- allowed the court to award exemplary damages and indemnity costs against publishers who failed to sign up to the regulatory regime or to use the arbitration service.

1.31   These Leveson amendments to the Bill become the key battleground of its latter stages. The Lords voted the amendments into the Bill, and the Commons voted to disagree. The Government would not countenance the Bill becoming law with the amendments in place. For some time the Bill was in danger of being lost. Campaigners for libel reform campaigned again to save the Bill, referring to the amendments as wrecking amendments. The issue was resolved when the Government published a draft Royal Charter, and amendments to the Crime and Courts Bill, in order to implement Leveson recommendations. Both Houses then agreed to the removal of the Leveson amendments from the Bill.

A further key battleground which appeared, or more accurately reappeared, **1.32** in the latter stages of the Bill, and which dominated debate during ping pong, was the question of whether companies should have to clear not only the 'serious harm' threshold test to be introduced by cl 1 of the Bill as it stood, but also a permission stage at which they would have to show that the serious harm they had suffered or were likely to suffer was 'serious financial loss'. The issue of whether or not to include such a requirement had been considered by those involved in the development of the Bill since the early stages. The Joint Committee on the draft Defamation Bill had recommended that corporations should be required to obtain the permission of the court to bring defamation claims. The court faced with an application for permission, the Committee recommended, should consider a range of factors including, in particular, whether the corporation had suffered substantial financial damage.

The mischief such a hurdle was intended to address was primarily seen as **1.33** the chilling effect on free speech constituted by threatening letters sent out by companies to individuals in response to negative publicity. The Joint Committee described this as 'a widespread tactic'. Whether the new subsection will affect how companies respond to negative publicity in terms of lawyers' letters and threats of litigation (as opposed to taking the further step of bringing litigation) remains to be seen.

When the issue re-emerged in the House of Commons, the focus was on public **1.34** interest stories which publishers might be reluctant to print, with the threat of an action for libel by the company involved hanging over them. Examples raised included that of tobacco companies in the 1950s potentially being able to sue over claims that smoking is linked to cancer.[9] Given that linking a product to cancer would seem highly likely to result in serious financial loss to the company making that product, it is not clear how the new subsection would address this.

The Government opposed such an amendment, but agreed to look at the mat- **1.35** ter. In the Commons, Sir Edward Garnier MP (former Solicitor General and libel practitioner) was very much the lone voice arguing strongly against it. In the light of the strong feeling expressed by MPs it was agreed that the proposed amendment would not be voted on and the Government would consider an amendment on the subject in the Lords. When the Bill returned to the Lords, Lord McNally, again expressing the Government's opposition, but noting the strength of feeling, tabled the Government amendment which became s 1(2) of the Act.

With the parliamentary session drawing to a close, and the Bill already hav- **1.36** ing been held up by the Leveson amendments, s 1(2) represents a compromise. The proposal for a separate permission stage for companies (rejected by the Government since 2011) was seen off, with the test being rolled up into the 'serious harm' test. However, with loss limited to financial loss, there remain concerns

---

[9] Peter Bottomley MP, *Hansard*, HC Deb, 16 April 2013, Col 278.

about how a company will prove sufficient financial loss, especially where what is claimed is likelihood of future financial loss, as will be the case in many instances where claimants are trying to minimize the potential loss through vindication. A company's goodwill and trading reputation may be quantifiable in accounting terms, but such loss can be difficult to prove, particularly in advance. Yet it is extremely important to a company, and is likely to be the key interest that may be damaged by defamatory statements. These points are considered in Chapter 2.

1.37   A related area of contention was whether the *Derbyshire*[10] principle, under which central and local government bodies are barred from bringing claims in defamation, should be codified in the Bill. There was strong support for this from the Opposition, who feared that certain public bodies would be able to bring claims, and noted that the lines between public and private were increasingly blurred with, for example, private companies running prisons. Ultimately, the Government view prevailed. *Derbyshire* was considered to be sufficiently clear in common law, and the ossification of the law which codification might bring was seen as sufficiently undesirable, that the relevant amendment was removed from the Bill.

F. CONCLUSION

1.38   The Defamation Act 2013 seeks to clarify and increase the accessibility of the law of defamation, as well as introducing substantive changes, including those such as s 5, which is designed to provide a framework for tackling defamation on the internet. At the time of writing, the regulations implementing s 5 have not been published, so that no full account can be given as to how these important provisions will operate. As discussed throughout this book, there remain a number of areas where the Act raises questions as well as providing answers.

1.39   Another question raised by a number of sections of the Act, that has particular resonance when it comes to the publication on a matter of public interest defence (s 4), is how the court will use the existing case law in interpreting the provisions of the Act. The common law defences are explicitly abolished, but the Explanatory Notes make clear that the courts are entitled, and indeed expected, to consider the existing case law and use it as guidance in interpreting the Act. In particular in relation to the public interest defence, whilst the *Reynolds* defence is abolished, s 4 is said to be intended to reflect the decision of the Supreme Court in *Flood v Times Newspapers*.[11] Ultimately, it may be the case that, in the short term, litigation will increase as the new law is tested, even in areas which had previously been fairly clear. The codification is not a complete one as other statutory provisions and areas of common law remain. In terms of

---

[10]   *Derbyshire County Council v Times Newspaper Ltd* [1993] AC 534, [1993] 2 WLR 449.
[11]   [2012] UKSC 11, [2012] 2 AC 273.

accessibility, codifying the defences which are now set out at ss 2–4 of the Act is clearly an improvement. In terms of clarity, the position is not so clear, and, in particular, the abolition of common law defences raises serious and difficult questions as to which rules of law belong to the common law defence, and so have been abolished, and which properly form part of some other area of the law, such as the law on ascertaining meaning, or procedural law, which have not been abolished and remain binding on courts. These questions are considered at paras 3.34–3.42.The discussion there, in the context of the truth defence, applies to ss 2–4 of the Act generally.

2

REQUIREMENT OF
SERIOUS HARM

A. INTRODUCTION

Section 1 of the Act creates a new threshold test for determining whether a state- **2.01**
ment is defamatory. It provides that a statement is not defamatory unless its
publication has caused or is likely to cause serious harm to the reputation of the
claimant. It creates a further threshold test for a body trading for profit, providing that harm to the reputation of such a body is not 'serious harm' unless it has
caused or is likely to cause serious financial loss. The section is intended to raise
the bar from the common law threshold tests expressed in *Thornton v Telegraph
Media Group Ltd*[1] and *Jameel (Yousef) v Dow Jones & Co Inc.*[2]

---

[1] [2010] EWHC 1414 (QB), [2011] 1 WLR 1985.
[2] [2005] EWCA Civ 75, [2005] QB 946.

13

B. THE PRE-EXISTING LAW

1. The threshold tests

(a) *Substantial adverse consequences*

2.02 In *Thornton*, Tugendhat J accepted the submission that whatever definition of 'defamatory' is adopted it must include a qualification or threshold of seriousness, so as to exclude trivial claims. The judge considered that that was in accordance with Lord Atkin's speech in *Sim v Stretch*[3] and with the decision of Sharp J in *Ecclestone v Telegraph Media Group Ltd*,[4] with which he agreed. He also thought it was required by the development of the law recognized in *Jameel (Yousef)* as arising from the passing of the Human Rights Act 1998, in particular regard for Article 10 of the European Convention on Human Rights and the principle of proportionality. The judge considered that the word that would impose the lowest threshold that might be envisaged is 'substantially'.

2.03 Tugendhat J observed that, since 1936, Lord Atkin's test in *Sim* has most often been used by judges in directing juries or themselves:

[W]ould the words tend to lower the plaintiff in the estimation of right-thinking members of society generally?

He noted, however, that the definition recommended by the 1975 Faulks Committee had also been used:

Defamation shall consist of the publication to a third party of matter which in all the circumstances would be likely to affect a person adversely in the estimation of reasonable people generally

and that this test and that of Lord Atkins had both been used together in one sentence by Sir Thomas Bingham MR in *Skuse v Granada Television*:[5]

A statement should be taken to be defamatory if it would tend to lower the plaintiff in the estimation of right-thinking members of society generally (*Sim v Stretch* [1936] 2 All ER 1237 at 1240) or would be likely to affect a person adversely in the estimation of reasonable people generally (*Duncan & Neill on Defamation*, 2nd edition, paragraph 7.07 at p. 32).

2.04 So far as concerns the threshold of seriousness arising from *Sim*, Tugendhat J traced that back to Lord Atkin's speech where he said:

That juries should be free to award damages for injuries to reputation is one of the safeguards of liberty. But the protection is undermined when exhibitions of bad manners or discourtesy are placed on the same level as attacks on character; and are treated as actionable wrongs.[6]

---

[3] (1936) 52 TLR 669 at 672, [1936] 2 All ER 1327 at 1242.
[4] [2009] EWHC 2779 (QB).
[5] [1996] EMLR 278 at 286.
[6] *Thornton v Telegraph Media Group Ltd* [2010] EWHC 1414 (QB), [2011] 1 WLR 1985 at [20].

Tugendhat J could see no reason for distinguishing business or professional def- **2.05** amation from other defamation. He held that there must be a similar threshold in all cases.

In the light of the analysis in *Thornton*, the common law definition of what is **2.06** defamatory in respect of any particular publication requires a tendency or likelihood of substantial adverse consequences for the claimant.

(b) *Real and substantial tort*

In *Jameel (Yousef)* the Court of Appeal struck out as an abuse of process pro- **2.07** ceedings brought over very limited publication of serious defamatory allegations. The court applied the same test in relation to the statements within the jurisdiction as it would have required to be satisfied before giving permission to serve out of the jurisdiction, namely: was there a real and substantial tort within the jurisdiction? Lord Phillips of Worth Matravers said:

Keeping a proper balance between the article 10 right of freedom of expression and the protection of individual reputation must, so it seems to us, require the court to bring to a stop as an abuse of process defamation proceedings that are not serving the legitimate purpose of protecting the claimant's reputation, which includes compensating the claimant only if that reputation has been unlawfully damaged.[7]

Questions of what has become known as '*Jameel* abuse' most commonly arise in **2.08** low publication cases. However, the doctrine has a universal application and has been applied more widely, for example in circumstances where the claimant had achieved vindication by other methods during the course of the claim: *Hays plc v Hartley*[8] and *Cammish v Hughes*,[9] and where the claimant had no reputation capable of protection: *Williams v MGN Ltd.*[10]

2. Corporate bodies

The common law position—that corporate bodies do not have to prove special **2.09** damage in order to sue for libel—is well settled.

Lord Keith, in *Derbyshire County Council v Times Newspapers Ltd*,[11] reviewed **2.10** the authorities and concluded that they:

clearly establish that a trading corporation is entitled to sue in respect of defamatory matters which can be seen as having a tendency to damage it in the way of its business. Examples are those that go to credit such as might deter banks from lending to it, or to the conditions experienced by its employees, which might impede the recruitment of the best qualified workers, or make people reluctant to deal with it.

---

[7] *Jameel (Yousef) v Dow Jones & Co Inc* [2005] EWCA Civ 75, [2005] QB 946 at [55].
[8] [2010] EWHC 1068 (QB).
[9] [2012] EWCA Civ 1655, [2013] EMLR 13 (p 292).
[10] [2009] EWHC 3150 (QB).
[11] [1993] AC 534 at 547.

2.11 In *Jameel (Mohammed) v Wall Street Journal Europe Sprl*,[12] the House of Lords declined the invitation to rule that trading corporations should not be entitled to sue unless they can prove financial loss. Lord Bingham gave two reasons for doing so:

> First, the good name of a company, as that of an individual, is a thing of value. A damaging libel may lower its standing in the eyes of the public and even its own staff, make people less ready to deal with it, less willing or less proud to work for it. If this were not so, corporations would not go to the lengths they do to protect and burnish their corporate images. I find nothing repugnant in the notion that this is a value which the law should protect. Nor do I think it an adequate answer that the corporation can itself seek to answer the defamatory statement by press release or public statement, since protestations of innocence by the impugned party necessarily carry less weight with the public than the prompt issue of proceedings which culminate in a favourable verdict by judge or jury. Secondly, I do not accept that a publication, if truly damaging to a corporation's commercial reputation, will result in provable financial loss, since the more prompt and public a company's issue of proceedings, and the more diligent its pursuit of a claim, the less the chance that financial loss will actually accrue.[13]

C. BACKGROUND TO S 1

1. Criticisms of the common law and reform proposals

2.12 It had been a perennial complaint of potential defendants to libel actions brought or threatened by corporate bodies that such bodies could only be hurt in their pockets and should therefore only be able to bring defamation proceedings if they could establish actual or likely financial loss. In Australia this issue has been addressed by providing that corporations trading for profit cannot sue for libel if they have ten or more employees. The Libel Reform Group[14] recommended in their 2009 report *Free Speech Is Not for Sale* that 'large and medium-sized' corporate bodies and associations should be exempt from libel law, leaving them to any claim they might have in malicious falsehood.

2.13 Clauses 11 and 12 of Lord Lester's Private Member's Defamation Bill [HL] 2010–2011 recommended enshrining in statute the *Thornton* 'substantial harm' test and requiring that a body corporate must show substantial financial loss if any libel claim was not to be struck out.

2.14 Clause 1 of the Government's draft Bill of March 2011 also sought to set out the *Thornton* 'substantial harm' test. It contained no proposals concerning corporate claimants.

---

[12] [2006] UKHL 44, [2007] 1 AC 359.
[13] [2006] UKHL 44, [2007] 1 AC 359 at [26].
[14] English PEN, Index on Censorship, and Sense About Science.

The report of the Joint Parliamentary Committee on the draft Bill rec- **2.15** ommended that the 'substantial harm' test be replaced 'with a stricter test, which would have the effect of requiring "serious and substantial harm" to be established'.[15]

In responding to the Government's consultation on the right of non-natural **2.16** persons to sue, the Joint Committee said that it favoured 'an approach which limits claims to situations where the corporation can prove the likelihood of "substantial financial loss"'. In its view the test of substantial financial loss should 'focus on whether there has been, or is likely to be, a substantial loss of custom directly caused by the defamatory statements' and that 'neither mere injury to goodwill nor any expense incurred in mitigation of damage to reputation should enable a corporation to bring a libel claim' and that a corporation should not be entitled to rely on a fall in its share price, since the loss is suffered by shareholders not the corporation itself.[16]

2. The Defamation Bill 2012: parliamentary history of s 1

(a) *The Bill*
Clause 1(1) of the Bill as introduced in the Commons on 10 May 2012 replaced **2.17** the requirement for 'substantial harm' in the draft Bill with one of 'serious harm'. The Explanatory Notes to the Bill and the Act (para 11) state that this 'raises the bar for bringing a claim so that only cases involving serious harm to the claimant's reputation can be brought'. There was nothing in the Bill as introduced concerning corporate claimants.

(b) *Commons debates*
The First Reading of the Bill was in the House of Commons on 10 May 2012. **2.18** At the Second Reading debate on 12 June 2012 the Bill's Commons sponsor, the Lord Chancellor Rt Hon Kenneth Clarke MP, said:

Our first priority has been to reform the law so that trivial and unfounded actions for defamation do not succeed. Clause 1 therefore raises the bar, by a modest extent...It must be a serious matter causing serious harm to their reputation. Any citizen against whom a serious and unfounded allegation of personal misconduct is made will probably be able to demonstrate that it has done serious harm to his reputation. The hurdle is raised a little, but I trust that it will not bar any plaintiff who has had serious problems as a result of publication.[17]

---

[15] HL Paper 203, HC 930-I, para 28.
[16] HL Paper 203, HC 930-I, para 115.
[17] *Hansard*, HC Deb, 12 June 2012, Cols 179–181.

2.19 Jonathan Djanogly MP, Parliamentary Under-Secretary of State for Justice, said:

> It is our view that the requirement to show serious harm represents a higher hurdle than the current law. It will be a matter for the courts to determine how the test should apply in individual cases, but we wish to nudge the threshold up to deter trivial claims.[18]

2.20 At the Committee stage in the Commons the Government rejected attempts to introduce hurdles for corporations to be able sue. Jonathan Djanogly MP said in response to one such proposed amendment:

> While corporations are therefore not mentioned in the Bill, we think the correct approach generally is to raise the bar to trivial claims, and the Bill's new test of serious harm, with clearer defences, will apply equally to companies.

> Corporations are already unable to claim for certain types of harm, such as injury to feelings. In order to satisfy the serious harm test, a corporation would in practice be likely to have to demonstrate actual or likely financial loss in any event.[19]

(c) *Lords debates*

2.21 Introducing the Bill at Grand Committee, Minister of State for Justice Lord McNally sought to 'explain as fully as possible the Government's thinking behind Clause 1'. He repeated that the Government's aim was 'to ensure that trivial and unfounded actions do not succeed'. He stated that the 'substantial harm' test originally included in the draft Bill was intended to 'reflect and strengthen the current law' as set out both in *Thornton* and in *Jameel (Yousef)*, and that the 'serious harm' test in the Bill as introduced was intended to 'raise the bar to a modest extent above the requirement of the current law'.[20]

2.22 He gave the example of *Mardas v New York Times*[21] as a case which the Government considered would have been decided differently under the 'serious harm' test. The allegations complained of in that case were that the claimant was a 'conman and a trickster', but only around 200 hard copy and online publications had taken place in this jurisdiction. Lord McNally made expressly clear that 'when considering whether a statement has caused, or is likely to cause, serious harm, the court will have regard to all relevant circumstances of the case, which may include the extent of publication'.[22]

2.23 At the Report stage in the Lords the Labour peer Baroness Hayter of Kentish Town moved an amendment which would have required corporate bodies and other bodies trading for profit to seek permission of the court before bringing actions. Under the amendment claims by such bodies would be struck out unless

---

[18] *Hansard*, HC Deb, 12 June 2012, Col 159.
[19] PBC (Bill 005) 2012–2013, Col 206.
[20] *Hansard*, HL Deb, 17 December 2012, Cols GC 422–423.
[21] [2008] EWHC 3135 (QB), [2009] EMLR 8 (p 152).
[22] *Hansard*, HL Grand Committee, 17 December 2012, Col GC 424.

the body could show that the publication had caused or was likely to cause substantial financial loss.[23]

Lord Ahmad, responding on behalf of the Government, repeated that the Government did not think such a provision was necessary because 'in order to satisfy the serious harm test, businesses are likely in practice to have to show some form of actual or likely financial loss'.[24] The Government was defeated on a vote and the Hayter amendment agreed by the House.

2.24

(d) *Commons consideration of Lords amendments*
On a Government motion the Commons removed the Hayter amendment in relation to bodies corporate. Helen Grant MP, Parliamentary Under-Secretary of State for Justice, repeated the Government's position that 'in order to satisfy the serious harm test, such bodies are likely in practice to have to show actual or likely financial loss anyway'.[25] She stated, however, that the Government was going to give further consideration to the issue.

2.25

(e) *Lords consideration of Commons reasons*
That further consideration led to the introduction by Lord McNally of what is now s 1(2) of the Act. He said '[t]he use of the phrase "serious financial loss" makes it absolutely clear that the financial loss required to meet the serious harm test must itself be serious'.[26]

2.26

(f) *Consideration of Lords message*
Despite further opposition by Sir Edward Garnier MP, the Lords amendment was accepted by the Commons the day before Royal Assent.[27]

2.27

(g) *Explanatory Notes*
The Explanatory Notes to the Act emphasize that the intention is that the section 'raises the bar' and that it builds on both *Thornton* and *Jameel (Yousef)*.

2.28

D. THE STATUTORY PROVISIONS

Section 1 provides as follows:

2.29

1 **Serious harm**
(1) A statement is not defamatory unless its publication has caused or is likely to cause serious harm to the reputation of the claimant.

---

[23] *Hansard*, HL Deb, 5 February 2013, Col 174.
[24] *Hansard*, HC Deb, 5 February 2013, Col 181.
[25] *Hansard*, HC Deb, 16 April 2013, Col 269.
[26] *Hansard*, HL Deb, 23 April 2013, Col 1366.
[27] *Hansard*, HC Deb, 24 April 2013, Cols 913–923.

(2) For the purposes of this section, harm to the reputation of a body that trades for profit is not "serious harm" unless it has caused or is likely to cause the body serious financial loss.

E. KEY FEATURES OF THE TEST

1. Section 1(1)

(a) *Serious harm to reputation*

2.30 The 'serious harm' test raises the bar from the common law 'substantial adverse consequences' test. What measure of harm amounts to serious harm will fall to be decided in individual cases.

2.31 The serious harm must be harm to reputation. Thus, it appears that a statement which merely passed the common law test for being defamatory, and caused serious distress or hurt feelings as a result, would not qualify as being defamatory under the Act.

2.32 The test omits any reference to any 'tendency' to cause serious harm, which Tugendhat J found to be part of the common law definition in *Thornton*. In answer to a question in Committee as to why 'likelihood' and not 'tendency' had been used in the Bill, Jonathan Djanogly MP said:

> Our core aim through the clause is to discourage trivial claims. Using a more abstract term, such as whether the publication has the tendency to cause serious harm, rather than focussing on whether the publication is actually likely to cause harm, could make it more likely that doubtful claims would be able to proceed.[28]

2.33 However, the omission of any reference to tendency, coupled with the fact that the test seeks to reflect both *Thornton* and *Jameel (Yousef)*, does not act simply to raise the bar for what is defamatory. It means that in considering the question of whether serious harm has or is likely to occur the court will have to look at all the circumstances of publication, not simply the words themselves, in order to decide whether the statement is defamatory. This is a major departure from existing law and practice, considered further below.

(b) *Likelihood to cause serious harm to reputation*

2.34 The second limb of s 1(1) does raise a notion of likelihood: if the publication of a statement has not yet caused serious harm, it will nevertheless be defamatory if it is 'likely' to do so. The use of the word 'likely' here is potentially ambiguous: it may refer to the possibility of some future event occurring, or it may be used to describe the situation where the statement itself is of the nature that it is likely to cause serious harm to the reputation of the claimant. As the latter interpretation is effectively a 'tendency' test, explicitly rejected by the Government, it appears it

---

[28] PBC (Bill 005) 2012–2013, Col 17.

is not the intended one, and indeed if that is how the second limb of s 1(1) was intended to operate it would probably render the first limb redundant.

The Explanatory Notes to the Act at para 10 say that this part of the provision **2.35** is to cover situations where the harm has not yet occurred at the time the action for defamation is commenced. So, the second limb would seem to contemplate the bringing of a defamation claim in relation to a published statement that has not caused any serious harm to the reputation of the claimant, but which the claimant can establish may later do so.

The degree of likelihood required is not specified. A decision similar to that in **2.36** *Cream Holdings Ltd v Banerjee*[29] concerning the meaning of 'likely' in s 12 of the Human Rights Act 1998 may be needed in order to determine where, on the spectrum from 'could' to 'more likely than not', likelihood under the Act falls. Nor does the Act specify the means by which the claimant will be required to establish the likelihood, whether by evidence, inference, legal argument or otherwise.

2. Section 1(2)

Section 1(2) provides that for the purpose of the definition of what is defamatory **2.37** in s 1(1) harm to the reputation of a body that trades for profit is not 'serious harm' unless it has caused or is likely to cause the body serious financial loss. The Explanatory Notes at para 12 say that this requirement for serious harm is consistent with the new serious harm test in s 1(1) and reflects the fact that bodies trading for profit are already prevented from claiming damages for certain types of harm such as injury to feelings, and are in practice likely to have to show actual or likely financial loss.

There is no indication in the Act, and there was little discussion in the parlia- **2.38** mentary process, as to what might amount to, or might be relied on in demonstrating, actual or likely serious financial loss.

The requirement that the body must 'trade for profit' means that bodies such **2.39** as charities, if they otherwise have a cause of action, are not required to demonstrate actual or likely serious financial loss.

F. DISCUSSION

1. The definitional approach

In the Third Reading debate Sir Edward Garnier MP made the following point: **2.40**

As drafted, the clause confuses what is defamatory and the consequences of a defamatory statement. I hope that by the time the Bill becomes an Act, the clause will read: 'A defamatory statement is not actionable unless its publication has caused, or is likely to cause, serious harm to the reputation of the claimant'. Many things are defamatory that

---

[29] [2004] UKHL 44, [2005] 1 AC 253.

might not cause much damage, and many things are not very defamatory but can cause disproportionate damage.[30]

2.41 The definitional approach does have some curious potential consequences. *Jameel* abuse considerations which may be unrelated to the meaning of the words themselves, such as the extent of publication, the extent to which vindication or an injunction is needed, and the pre-existing reputation of the claimant, now come into play in determining whether serious harm has or is likely to be caused, and thus whether a statement is defamatory.

2.42 It seems however that some of the traditional elements of the common law definition of 'defamatory' must survive the new approach. Thus a statement must surely still have the effect of lowering the claimant in the estimation of 'right-thinking members of society generally' if it is to be defamatory. The section is a bar, not a definition.

2.43 However, it is questionable whether statements which cause a claimant to suffer mere ridicule survive the new test. The court would have to determine whether the damage caused by such statements can properly be regarded as serious harm to *reputation*.

2.44 Equally so with allegations (such as of communicable diseases) which do not impute any moral discredit, but which cause a claimant to be 'shunned and avoided'. Although it seems that the intention of Parliament was not to exclude such statements completely from the ambit of defamation proceedings, as s 14(2) of the Act provides that the publication of a statement that conveys the imputation that a person has a contagious or infectious disease does not give rise to a cause of action for slander unless the publication causes the person special damage.

2. Establishing serious harm

2.45 It seems tolerably clear that evidence must now be admissible on the question of whether a statement is defamatory. Establishing the fact or likelihood of serious harm may not necessarily be a straightforward evidential exercise. During the passage of the Bill concerns were raised concerning costs. Jonathan Djanogly MP said the following on the Third Reading debate:

Hon. Members have expressed concern that the test might require detailed evidence to be presented. We recognise that the introduction of the test might involve some front-loading of cost, but we believe it is better to resolve this issue at an early stage so that only cases involving serious harm proceed.[31]

2.46 During the Commons Committee Stage Jonathan Djanogly MP said:

In many cases, the existence of serious harm will not be a matter of dispute. When it is, there will be a need for some evidence to be provided, but we believe that it is better for

---

[30] *Hansard*, HC Deb, 12 September 2012, Col 373.
[31] *Hansard*, HC Deb, 12 June 2012, Col 159.

this to be resolved at an early stage, and that only cases involving serious harm should proceed.[32]

The statement quoted immediately above also indicates the Government view **2.47** that disputed questions concerning the threshold tests under s 1 should be resolved at an early stage. The current regime under the CPR Part 53 for determining whether a statement is capable of being defamatory, or bearing any particular defamatory meaning, does not fit easily with the new section. Lord Ahmad said the following on behalf of the Government at the Report stage in the Lords:

... we will be bringing proposals for procedural changes before the Civil Procedure Rule Committee shortly.... those proposals will enable key issues—such as whether there is serious harm, what is the actual meaning of the words complained of, and whether they are a statement of fact or opinion—to be brought before the court at the earliest possible stage. We will also be encouraging the courts to be more pro-active in managing cases to ensure that a tight grip is kept on cases which proceed to trial.[33]

There has been a tendency in recent years, with the declining use of juries and **2.48** the emphasis in the CPR on proportionality, for the court to determine the question of whether words are in fact defamatory and what meaning they in fact bear by way of preliminary issue. It remains to be seen to what extent new rules will require, or allow for, such matters to be determined early in the proceedings. Because evidence may now be relevant on these issues, there is the potential for an early mini-trial to be necessary in order to resolve any disputes of fact.

Despite the reversal (by s 11 of the Act) of the presumption, there remains a **2.49** potential for jury trial in libel proceedings, particularly those involving public officials. The question whether a statement is defamatory or not is traditionally one for the jury, thus potentially the early mini-trial could require a jury evaluation of the evidence of reputation harm, and its seriousness.

3. Corporate claimants

In *Ratcliffe v Evans*[34] Bowen LJ held to the effect that the law presumes *some* **2.50** damage will flow in the ordinary course of things from the mere invasion of a claimant's absolute right to reputation. Under the common law this principle applied equally to corporations as it does to individuals.[35] The availability in principle at common law of general damages to corporate claimants is not

---

[32] PBC (Bill 005) 2012–2013, Col 16.
[33] *Hansard*, HL Deb, 5 February 2013, Col 182.
[34] [1892] 2 QB 524 at 528.
[35] *Jameel (Mohammed) v Wall Street Journal Europe Sprl* [2006] UKHL 44, [2007] 1 AC 359.

inconsistent with the European Convention on Human Rights. In *Steel v United Kingdom*,[36] the court said:

> However, in addition to the public interest in open debate about business practices, there is a competing interest in protecting the commercial success and viability of companies, for the benefit of shareholders and employees, but also for the wider economic good.

2.51   It seems likely that something more is now needed. It is not specified whether the 'serious financial loss' required by s 1(2) must necessarily be in the form of a claim for special damages that has arisen from the publication under consideration, or can be established by, for example, a trading company demonstrating a reduction in the value of the goodwill in its business arising from a damaging statement published about it. At the stage of issuing proceedings and pleading its case, for example, it may be in practice that a company will need to do no more than aver that a harmful statement published about it has damaged its trading reputation, with the result that it has suffered serious financial loss in the form of diminution in goodwill. There may be scope for expert evidence as to the deleterious effect which such diminution has had on the company's finances.

2.52   However, the challenge for the claimant may be more modest than even that, since s. 1(2) provides an alternative condition to be fulfilled that harm will be considered 'serious' if it is *likely* to cause the trading body serious financial loss. Whether in this section 'likely' is used in the sense of a tendency, or with reference to a prediction as to what might happen in the future, the point likely to be made routinely on behalf of company and similar claimants is that the reason they sue over corporate defamation is because of the tendency for it to cause serious financial loss to a business if it is left uncorrected. That point on its own may be sufficient to satisfy the test in s 1(2) for 'serious harm' in the case of a body that trades for profit, at least in a serious case, such as a statement which strikes at the root of a company's selling point, circulated widely, or where it is calculated to do most harm.

2.53   At the Committee stage in the Commons, Jonathan Djanogly, the Parliamentary Under-Secretary of State for Justice, said the following in expressing Government opposition to an amendment requiring corporations to demonstrate financial harm, which contained an express provision that a drop in share price did not amount to such harm:

> Corporations are already unable to claim for certain types of harm, such as injury to feelings. In order to satisfy the serious harm test, a corporation would in practice be likely to have to demonstrate actual or likely financial loss in any event. Given the potential effects on shareholders and management, we see no reason why there should be no redress for a defamatory action that has caused a fall in share price.[37]

---

[36] (Application No 68416/01) (2005) 41 EHRR 22 (p 403), [2005] EMLR 15 (p 314) at [94].
[37] PBC (Bill 005) 2012–2013, Col 206.

One of the reasons for which Tugendhat J struck out a claim for special dam- **2.54** ages based on a diminution in share price in *Collins Stewart Ltd v Financial Times Ltd (No 1)*[38] was that a verdict in favour of the claimant would restore the damage to reputation which had caused the diminution in the share price, and therefore there would be no loss.

A similar point was made by Lord Bingham in the passage from *Jameel* **2.55** *(Mohammed)* quoted above,[39] saying that 'the more prompt and public a company's issue of proceedings, and the more diligent its pursuit of a claim, the less the chance that financial loss will actually accrue'.

There would be circularity in arguing that serious financial loss is unlikely **2.56** because prompt issue and pursuit of proceedings is likely to forestall it. If effective vindication is achieved at an early stage of proceedings, it may no longer be proper to permit the proceedings to continue, but the claimant may be entitled to the costs of taking the action to that point, as in *Cammish v Hughes.*[40] Equally if, unless the company issues and pursues proceedings, financial loss is likely because serious harm to reputation would cause banks, trading partners or employees to deal less favourably with the company, it would be perverse to deny the company a cause of action in libel on the basis that vindication in the course of the proceedings would forestall any serious loss.

There is a narrow answer to this, namely that such an argument ignores loss **2.57** which may occur during the course of the proceedings before judgment. It may be, however, that words to the effect of 'should the defamatory statement not be corrected' need to be read in at the end of s 1(2).

---

[38] [2004] EWHC 2337 (QB), [2005] EMLR 5 (p 64).
[39] At para 2.11.
[40] At para 2.08.

3

THE NEW STATUTORY DEFENCE
OF TRUTH

A. INTRODUCTION

Section 2 of the Act establishes a new statutory defence of truth. This replaces **3.01** the common law defence of justification, which is abolished. Section 2 also repeals the one significant statutory provision that modified the common law, s 5 of the Defamation Act 1952. However, s 2 as a whole was intended 'broadly to reflect the current law while simplifying and clarifying certain elements'.[1] Thus, whilst s 5 of the 1952 Act is repealed, it is replaced by new wording, in subss (2) and (3) of s 2, which is 'intended to have the same effect as...section 5...but...expressed in more modern terminology'.[2]

---

[1] Explanatory Notes to cl 2 of the Bill, para 13.
[2] Explanatory Notes, para 17.

B. THE PRE-EXISTING LAW

1. The common law

3.02   It was long part of English common law that a defendant could defeat a claim in defamation by establishing that the imputation in respect of which he was sued was substantially true. Historically, this defence was called 'justification'. That label was described by *Gatley on Libel and Slander* as 'unfortunate' because, although well understood by lawyers, it could suggest to lay people that there had to be some good reason for publication. That was not so. It was sufficient to prove truth, regardless of the nature of the information conveyed, the impact of its publication, and the defendant's state of mind. There was no requirement, for instance, that the publication should serve any recognized public interest. As a rule, there was no cause of action for malicious publication of the truth. (Publication of spent convictions was the sole exception to this general rule.) For these reasons it was proposed as long ago as 1975 by the Faulks Committee that the defence of justification be renamed 'truth'. However, that recommendation was not taken up and until the present Act was passed in 2013 the label 'justification' remained.

3.03   Justification was always a defence, which the defendant was required to establish. A claimant in defamation was never required to prove falsity. However, a defendant was not required to prove the literal truth of every statement contained in the words complained of; it was enough to establish the essential or substantial truth of the central defamatory 'sting' of the words.[3] Thus, a plea of justification could succeed even if other, immaterial details in the offending statement were not proved to be true.

3.04   The common law authorities established a large number of detailed rules as to the pleading and proof of justification. These governed when it was legitimate for a defendant to plead justification at all; what imputations or meanings it was legitimate to seek to justify; what facts were and were not relevant to proving such meanings; and what was needed in order to prove the relevant facts and establish the defence. Linked to some of these rules were others, governing what was considered relevant and admissible for the purpose of mitigating damages, if liability was established.

3.05   Some of these rules were clearly rules of substantive law, and others equally clearly no more than procedural or case management rules. Which of these categories certain of these rules belonged to was the subject of some debate over the years. At least one such old-established rule (known as the rule in *Scott v Sampson*) was classified by the Court of Appeal in 2000 as a case management rule and, in the light of that classification, re-cast.[4] Two points are, however,

---

[3] *Chase v News Group Newspapers Ltd* [2002] EWCA Civ 1772, [2003] EMLR 11 (p 218).
[4] *Burstein v Times Newspapers Ltd* [2000] EWCA Civ 338; [2001] 1 WLR 579; see further para 3.15.

beyond doubt. First, that there was a close inter-relationship between the substantive and procedural rules. Secondly, that many of the rules in question were heavily influenced by the fact that defamation was one of the few causes of action that survived the general sweeping away of jury trials for civil claims that occurred in the second half of the twentieth century. Until s 11 of the present Act was passed there was a strong statutory presumption under s 69(1) of the Senior Courts Act 1981 that defamation actions would be tried by jury. Signs of judicial mistrust of juries could be detected in some of the older authorities, at least.

Full accounts of the relevant rules of the common law are given in the stand- **3.06** ard textbooks on libel and slander, and this is not the place to examine them in any detail. However, a short summary of some of the chief rules of significance is set out in the next nine paragraphs, in order to put in context the commentary on the Act which follows.

(a) *The key role of meaning*

First, meaning was central. Both the range of claims that a claimant could make **3.07** and the permissible scope of a defendant's plea of justification were held to depend critically on the meanings of the words complained of. The only meanings or (to use the term preferred in Australia) imputations of which a claimant could legitimately complain, or which a defendant could properly seek to justify, were meanings which were either (a) the natural and ordinary meanings of the words, or (b) 'true innuendo' meanings—those which a publishee (that is, a reader or hearer) would put on the words in the light of some facts known to the publishee, extraneous to the publication.

Secondly, the case law established rules as to the ascertainment of meaning. The **3.08** primary rule was the 'single meaning rule': the rule that for the purposes of the law of defamation a given set of words can only bear a single meaning. The second rule was that 'single meaning' was to be determined by deciding how the statement in question would be understood by a hypothetical ordinary reasonable reader, who was neither unduly naïve nor avid for scandal. A third key rule, established long ago, became known as the 'repetition rule'. This was that where a defendant published a statement that some third person had accused the claimant of some wrongdoing, it was not permissible to seek to justify that statement by proving merely that the third person had indeed made the accusation; the only permissible plea of justification would be that the third party's accusation was true. The reason was that, to an ordinary person, the natural meaning of a statement that a third party has made an allegation is the same as that of a direct accusation.

Thirdly, the case law arrived at a broad classification of defamatory meanings. **3.09** In *Chase*,[5] three main levels of defamatory meaning were identified, each distinct

---

[5] *Chase v News Group Newspapers Ltd* [2002] EWCA Civ 1772, [2003] EMLR 11 (p 218); see para 3.03.

from the other: that the claimant was guilty of some misconduct, that there were reasonable grounds to suspect him or her of that misconduct, and that there were grounds to investigate whether he or she was guilty of that misconduct. These became known as *Chase* Level 1, 2, and 3 meanings. This was not held to be an exhaustive taxonomy of the possible types of meanings that defamatory words could bear, but was considered to represent the main categories of meaning with which the courts were likely to have to deal.

(b) *How a meaning could be proved true*

3.10 Rules were also established as to what facts could serve to prove or disprove a given meaning. Thus, rules as to what facts could serve to prove or rebut a case of reasonable grounds to suspect the claimant of misconduct were set out by the Court of Appeal in *King v Telegraph Group Ltd.*[6] The most significant of these was the 'conduct rule', to the effect that a *Chase* Level 2 plea of justification must focus on some conduct of the claimant giving rise to reasonable grounds to suspect him or her.

(c) *Defendants' leeway on meaning*

3.11 There were important pleading rules which, though procedural in nature, could have a significant effect on the evidence which could be adduced at a trial, and on the use that could be made of it if so adduced. This was primarily due to the presumption in favour of jury trial, one effect of which was that the court could not, ordinarily, determine in advance of trial the factual question of what was the actual defamatory meaning of a statement complained of. Thus, although the nature and scope of the claimant's complaint had some bearing on what a defendant could properly justify, the defendant was allowed considerable leeway.

3.12 A defendant was not entitled to justify a meaning of the words which was 'wholly separate and distinct' from any imputation(s) complained of by the claimant. However, subject to that limitation, a defendant was allowed to justify any meaning which the statement complained of was *capable* of bearing, that is to say, any meaning which a reasonable jury properly directed could find to be the meaning of the statement.[7] That was so, even if the defendant's meaning was significantly different from the meaning(s) of which the claimant was complaining.

3.13 Accordingly, a defendant sued for imputing guilt to a claimant could properly seek to justify a *Chase* Level 2 meaning of reasonable grounds to suspect, provided that was a possible meaning of the statement complained of. In such a case it could well be the position that as a matter of fact the words meant guilt and nothing else, and did not bear the *Chase* Level 2 meaning. In that event, proof of the lesser meaning would in principle be no answer to the claim. However, in a case to be tried by jury, the actual meaning of the words complained of

---

[6] [2004] EWCA Civ 613, [2005] 1 WLR 2282.
[7] *Polly Peck v Trelford* [1986] QB 1000.

would not be determined until the end of the trial. The consequence was that evidence would have been adduced in an attempt to prove the *Chase* Level 2 meaning which was in fact no answer to the claim. Such a course was essential in case the jury accepted the defendant's (arguable) case that the words did not bear the meaning complained of by the claimant. In that event, the defendant's plea would be relevant and its evidence might be sufficient to defeat the claim. If the defendant's case on meaning was rejected, however, the question arose as to whether the evidence adduced by the defendant had any, and if so what, residual relevance.

(d) *Partial truth and the reduction of damages*

The cases held that the nature and extent of any plea of justification could, even if not established, have a significant impact on damages either upwards or downwards. On the one hand, the unsuccessful pursuit of a plea of justification would ordinarily aggravate (that is, increase) damages because of its hurtful impact on the claimant's feelings. On the other hand, facts proved in a failed attempt to prove justification could serve to mitigate damages. It was held that any fact 'properly before the jury' at the trial, for whatever purpose, could be taken into account in assessing damages, and might reduce them, perhaps even to vanishing point (the *Pamplin* rule, after *Pamplin v Express Newspapers*[8]). This was so, even though the general rule as to mitigation of damages was that in the absence of a plea of justification it was impermissible to seek to mitigate by proving facts which tended to justify the words complained of. In other words, proof of facts damaging to reputation was generally allowed only if undertaken as part of an attempt to prove the truth of the imputations, and not merely in order to reduce damages.   **3.14**

This state of affairs incentivized defendants to advance optimistic pleas of justification which fell short of meeting the 'sting' complained of, and were never likely to work as a defence to liability, but might be thought likely substantially to diminish an award of damages. In *Burstein*,[9] the Court of Appeal considered these issues. It emphasized that the court should carefully scrutinize pleas of justification to ensure that the freedom given to defendants in this respect was not abused. At the same time, it expanded the range of matters that could legitimately be proved in mitigation, even in the absence of a plea of justification, so that it came to embrace facts forming part of the 'directly relevant background context' to the publication in question. Later decisions explored and mapped out the boundaries of what can count as 'directly relevant background context' for this purpose.   **3.15**

---

[8] [1988] 1 WLR 116.

[9] *Burnstein v Times Newspapers Ltd* [2000] EWCA Crim 338, [2001] 1 WLR 579; see also para 3.05.

2. Statute

3.16 Section 5 of the Defamation Act 1952 dealt, on the recommendation of the Porter Committee Report of 1948, with one perceived flaw of the common law of justification: the lack of any defence of 'partial truth'. The section provided, in summary, that where a statement contains two or more distinct defamatory 'charges', and the defendant proves the truth of one or more, but not all, of these, the defence of justification could still succeed. It would do so if the court was satisfied that the 'charge' which was not proved true did 'not materially injure the plaintiff's reputation having regard to the truth of the remaining charges'.

3.17 The common law of justification has not otherwise been affected by any of the various legislative provisions that have been enacted in relation to defamation. The last piece of legislation, the Defamation Act 1996, did not touch on justification.

C. BACKGROUND TO S 2

1. Criticisms of the common law and reform proposals

3.18 Criticisms of the common law of defamation have been many and various, and have persisted for many years, but so far as the common law defence of justification is concerned, the chief criticism over recent years has been the fact that the burden of proving truth lies on the defendant. That was among the main criticisms of libel law made by the Libel Reform Group[10] in its 2009 report *Free Speech Is Not for Sale*. The Group's Recommendation 1 was that the burden of proof should be reversed, with the claimant required to prove both damage and falsity. That aspect of the law had and still has its defenders, however, and was left untouched by the 2013 Act. The Libel Reform Group did not criticize the substantive law of justification.

3.19 Aspects of s 2 have their origins in cll 4 and 5 of Lord Lester's Private Member's Defamation Bill [HL] 2010–2011. These clauses were said by Lord Lester to 'update and clarify the defence in significant respects'.[11] Clause 4 of Lord Lester's Bill proposed renaming justification as 'the defence of truth'. Clause 5(1) provided that this defence was made out 'if the words or matters complained of are substantially true'. Clause 5(4) would have replaced s 5 of the 1952 Act with similar provisions in updated wording. Clause 5(3) added a further provision to the effect that where a single allegation is not shown to be true, the defence may succeed if that which is not shown true 'would not materially injure the claimant's reputation having regard to the truth of what the defendant has shown to be substantially true'.

---

[10] English PEN, Index on Censorship, and Sense About Science.
[11] *Hansard*, HL Deb, 9 July 2010, Col 426.

Lord Lester's Bill did not receive a Third Reading, but was withdrawn. Clause   **3.20**
3 of the Government's draft Bill of March 2011 retained three features of Lord
Lester's Bill: the relabelling of the defence as 'truth' (cl 3(1) and (5)); the emphasis on 'substantial' truth; and the repeal and re-enactment in new wording of
the substance of s 5 of the 1952 Act (cl 3(2) and (3)). There was nothing corresponding to Lord Lester's cl 5(3). However, cl 3(4) of the Government's draft
Bill contained a new and radical proposal, not advanced by Lord Lester: to
abolish the common law defence of justification. There was then consultation
on the draft Bill, and a report from the Joint Parliamentary Committee on it.
Consultees provided a range of comments, and proposals for amendment. The
Joint Committee made two substantive recommendations for change, so far as
the defence of justification or truth is concerned: that Lord Lester's provision as
to what is required to prove the truth of a single allegation[12] should be included,
and that the court should have power to order the defendant to publish a reasonable summary of its judgment.

2. The Defamation Bill 2012: parliamentary history of s 2

(a) *The Bill*

The clause on truth as presented to Parliament was almost identical to that con-   **3.21**
tained in the draft Bill. Neither the Joint Committee's report nor its own consultation exercise convinced the Government that any change of substance was
required. In the Bill as presented in the House of Commons in June 2012 the
main provisions of the draft Bill were retained, in the same words, with the few
changes being purely formal in character.

(b) *Commons debates*

The Bill's First Reading was in the House of Commons on 10 May 2012. At the   **3.22**
Second Reading debate on 12 June 2012 the Bill's Commons sponsor, the Lord
Chancellor, the Rt Hon Kenneth Clarke MP, stated[13] that the objective was to
'simplify and clarify the defences', which had become 'unnecessarily complicated'.
Mr Clarke said,[14] as regards cll 2 and 3, that '[i]n our opinion, the revised approach
should simplify the situation, ensuring that the defences are available without so
many endless and costly disputes over detail and interpretation'. Jonathan Djanogly
MP, the Parliamentary Under-Secretary of State for Justice, stated that the purpose of the clause was to set out the key principles of the defence as clearly as
possible and to provide 'greater clarity and certainty' in defamation proceedings.[15]

Clause 2 was broadly welcomed by the House, and discussion of the clause was   **3.23**
limited. A number of MPs did, however, express some reservations. The chief

---

[12] See para 3.19.
[13] *Hansard*, HC Deb, 12 June 2012, Col 180.
[14] *Hansard*, HC Deb, 12 June 2012, Col 181.
[15] *Hansard*, HC Deb, 12 June 2012, Cols 259–260.

concern was that codification of the defence could lead to increased uncertainty and hence additional cost. Thus, David Lammy MP observed that '[p]utting the common law on a statutory footing will make it subject to much interpretation by the courts' and that certain areas, including the defence of truth, would 'need a lot of teasing out over the months and years ahead'.[16] Stephen Phillips MP warned that 'codification is not always successful in reflecting either the existing law or its nuances or flexibility'.[17] He further stated that '[a]ttempted codification can, through drafting error, lead to uncertainty, change and stultification, all of which can lead to increased costs for litigants'.[18]

3.24 In the Committee debates Robert Flello MP moved an amendment[19] to cl 2 which was similar in effect to cl 5(3) of Lord Lester's Bill:[20] Mr Flello was, however, persuaded to withdraw the amendment after Jonathan Djanogly MP stated that the Government's view was that whilst damages might be reduced by proof that a lesser imputation was true, it would be wrong to allow a defendant to succeed on liability where he was unable to establish the substantial truth of the imputation he had published.[21]

(c) *Lords debates*

3.25 The Bill's First Reading was on 8 October 2012. At the Second Reading debate on 9 October 2012 the Bill's Lords sponsor, Lord McNally, made clear[22] that it was a 'consolidation Bill, aimed at clarifying the law and putting it into a place where people can clearly understand it'. Lord McNally was responding to contributions from, among others, Lord Mawhinney who[23] agreed that it was in the interests of ordinary citizens to codify the defence to make it more understandable to all, and Lord Morris who[24] emphasized the 'vital distinction' between seeking to make changes of substance in the law and simply proposing to codify the common law, and the importance of making clear which objective was being pursued.

3.26 Clause 2 was agreed without amendment during the Committee stages in the House of Lords.[25]

---

[16] *Hansard*, HC Deb, 12 June 2012, Col 216.
[17] *Hansard*, HC Deb, 12 June 2012, Col 224.
[18] *Hansard*, HC Deb, 12 June 2012, Col 224.
[19] *Hansard*, HC Deb, 19 June 2012, Cols 28–29.
[20] See para 3.19.
[21] *Hansard*, HC Deb, 19 June 2012, Col 30.
[22] *Hansard*, HL Deb, 9 October 2012, Col 983.
[23] *Hansard*, HL Deb, 9 October 2012, Col 948.
[24] *Hansard*, HC Deb, 9 October 2012, Col 960.
[25] *Hansard*, HL Grand Committee, 17 December 2012, Col GC 468.

D. THE STATUTORY PROVISIONS

Section 2 provides as follows: **3.27**

2 Truth

(1) It is a defence to an action for defamation for the defendant to show that the imputation conveyed by the statement complained of is substantially true.

(2) Subsection (3) applies in an action for defamation if the statement complained of conveys two or more distinct imputations.

(3) If one or more of the imputations is not shown to be substantially true, the defence under this section does not fail if, having regard to the imputations which are shown to be substantially true, the imputations which are not shown to be substantially true do not seriously harm the claimant's reputation.

(4) The common law defence of justification is abolished and, accordingly, section 5 of the Defamation Act 1952 (justification) is repealed.

E. KEY FEATURES OF THE DEFENCE

The defence is labelled in simple and unequivocal English as 'Truth'. No longer   **3.28**
will lawyers use the label 'justification', with the potentially confusing connotations discussed in para 3.02. That defence has been abolished by s 2(4). Its essentials remain, however. The core features of the statutory defence are now set out in a single sentence, in s 2(1). This sentence was said in the Explanatory Notes to the Bill[26] to reflect the common law as established in *Chase*,[27] and this does seem to be correct.

Subsection (1) of s 2 uses terminology which differs from that of *Chase*, and   **3.29**
from that which English lawyers had been accustomed to using. People commonly spoke of 'the words complained of' rather than 'the statement complained of', and the word 'meaning' was more often used than 'imputation'. The new wording is clearly apt, however, it corresponds to that in use in a major Commonwealth jurisdiction (Australia), and it makes no change of substance. The requirement that a defendant should prove the truth of the 'imputation conveyed' by the offending statement maintains the importance which the common law attributed to meaning. The requirement of 'substantial' truth seems to reflect the common law precisely.

Whether the Explanatory Notes are right to assert[28] that the long-standing   **3.30**
common law 'repetition rule'[29] is 'incorporate[d]' by the wording of s 2(1) is

---

[26] Explanatory Notes, para 14.

[27] *Chase v News Group Newspapers Ltd* [2002] EWCA Civ 1772, [2003] EMLR 11 (p 218); see para 3.03.

[28] Explanatory Notes, para 15.

[29] See para 3.08.

debatable. The repetition rule may survive the Act, but if so that will not be because the rule is preserved by s 2(1), it is suggested. The repetition rule was a rule about how to identify the meaning of a statement or, to use the language of the 2013 Act, the imputation conveyed by the statement. Section 2 makes no provision about how to ascertain meaning. It simply provides that once the imputation conveyed has been identified, a defendant has a defence if he proves it to be substantially true.[30]

3.31   Subsections (2) and (3) of s 2 deal with one type of case of 'partial truth': the situation where the statement complained of contains two or more distinct imputations, and the defendant proves the substantial truth of one or more, but not all of them. The defendant will not lose if, having regard to the imputations that are shown to be substantially true, those that are not shown to be substantially true do not 'seriously harm' the claimant's reputation. The Explanatory Notes state[31] that these provisions are intended to have 'the same effect' as s 5 of the 1952 Act[32] expressed in more modern terminology. (Section 5 of the 1952 Act is abolished by s 2(4).)

3.32   It is worth drawing attention to one of the changes of terminology for the 'partial truth' defence, however. Whereas under s 5 a justification defence would still succeed so long as the unproved charge(s) did not 'materially injure' reputation, s 2(3) of the 2013 Act provides that the defence will succeed if the unproved imputations do not 'seriously harm' reputation. The shift from 'materially' to 'seriously' clearly makes it harder for a claimant to achieve success when some, but not all, charges against him or her have been proved true. As the Explanatory Notes[33] point out, however, this strengthening of the partial truth defence is necessary to ensure consistency with the new and higher threshold for liability in defamation generally which is established by s 1 of the Act. A claim will only succeed now if the statement has caused or is likely to cause 'serious harm' to the reputation of the claimant.

3.33   Subsection (4) of s 2 does away with the whole of the pre-existing law of justification, by abolishing the common law defence and repealing the 'partial truth' provisions of s 5 of the 1952 Act. The Explanatory Notes state[34] that in consequence a defendant 'would be required to apply the words of the statute, not the current case law'. In Committee on 19 June 2012, Jonathan Djanogly MP said:[35] 'That does not mean that in reality the case law will have no future impact, and it will ultimately be for the courts to decide'. Mr Djanogly also reiterated the point made in the Explanatory Notes[36] that: 'In cases where uncertainty arises, the current case law would constitute a helpful but not binding guide to interpreting how the new statutory defence should be applied'.

---

[30] See further para 3.40.
[31] Explanatory Notes, para 17.
[32] See para 3.16.
[33] At para 17.
[34] Explanatory Notes, para 18.
[35] *Hansard*, HC Deb, 19 June 2012, Col 35.
[36] At para 18.

F. DISCUSSION

The most striking feature of the legislative method adopted in s 2 is the abolition   **3.34**
of the common law defence of justification. This is an unusual technique, first
adopted in the draft Bill of March 2011.[37] Its stated rationale was to avoid a situation where defendants might seek to rely on the common law defence alongside,
or even instead of, the new statutory defence.[38] A further oft-repeated aim was to
'simplify' the law on justification, to increase accessibility. Both those aims can
be said to have been achieved, at least in part. However, it is open to question
whether s 2 was really necessary, and it is possible that it may create as many if
not more problems than it solves.

On the one hand, the law on truth as a defence to a claim in defamation is now   **3.35**
stated in a few short sentences of ordinary English, rather than in many pages of
textbook and law reports. Accessibility is thereby improved. On the other hand,
this aspect of the law was well settled and uncontroversial. It was not in real need
of restatement. At the same time, it is clear that this simple statement of the law
cannot claim to provide answers, still less comprehensive answers, to the many
legal and practical questions that arise in the course of litigation over the truth
of defamatory imputations. Moreover, there is a risk that additional confusion
will be sown by adopting the legislative technique of abolishing a specified part
of the common law, when the boundaries of that part of the law are not necessarily crystal clear.

There is certainly a need for rules as to what meanings are relevant for the   **3.36**
purposes of a defamation action, how many meanings a statement can have, how
the meaning of a statement is to be determined, and when and how the truth
of an imputation can legitimately be pleaded and proved. No such rules are to
be found in s 2 or anywhere else in the 2013 Act. The question arises of where
they are now to be found. The common law of defamation contained sophisti-
cated rules on all these topics. Not all of those rules received universal approval.
However, the Government did not choose to try to improve the rules, or even to
pick and choose between them. The Consultation Paper of March 2011 said that
it was 'not feasible' for the new defence to capture 'all the nuances of the existing case law', and rejected the approach of requiring the courts to take that case
law into account, on the grounds that this risked confusion. It was said that the
courts would examine the previous case law anyway. There is a risk, perhaps, that
this approach coupled with the abolition of the common law defence could lead
to the additional uncertainty, litigation over interpretation and extra cost that
were warned against by David Lammy MP and Stephen Phillips MP.[39]

---

[37] See para 3.20.
[38] Ministry of Justice, *Draft Defamation Bill: Consultation*, Consultation Paper CP3/11, March
2011, para 23.
[39] See para 3.23.

3.37   It seems that now, whenever any 'old' rule of law or practice that affects a defence of truth appears to be relevant in a particular case, the first question for decision will have to be whether that rule remains good law. That will depend on whether the rule counts as part of 'the common law defence of justification' within the meaning of s 2(4). If the rule does not fall within that wording, then it remains a rule of the common law and the authorities relating to it retain the value they had before the passing of the 2013 Act, and should continue to be followed and applied accordingly. On the other hand, any rule which does fall within the wording of s 2(4) has been abolished and in relation to that rule the second question will arise: whether that 'old' rule of the common law of justification should be adopted as part of the 'new' law of truth, following the 2013 Act. This second question will be one that the court can, and will have to, decide without reference to the doctrine of precedent, as the abolition of the common law rules will have freed the court in that respect.

3.38   At one end of the scale there are rules which do appear to be clearly part of 'the common law defence of justification'. The conduct rule[40] is one example. The merits of that rule may therefore be said to be available for re-evaluation at first instance in the wake of the 2013 Act. A first instance judge could now decide not to adopt and follow that rule, without regard to the fact that the authorities that established it were decisions of the Court of Appeal.

3.39   The same may be true of the rule in *Polly Peck* that a defendant is entitled to plead the truth of any meaning that the words complained of are capable of bearing,[41] although it might be argued that it is merely procedural rather than substantive. This rule is likely to be significantly affected by the fact that, as a result of s 11 of the 2013 Act, trial by jury will no longer be the norm in defamation cases, thus in principle freeing judges to determine the actual meaning of the statement complained of at the interim stage, perhaps before service of the defence. Once the 'imputation conveyed by the statement complained of' has been determined, there will be no occasion to seek to prove the truth of any other imputation. That may have a knock-on effect on the law as to the evidence admissible to mitigate damages.[42] The *Burstein* rule as to what may legitimately be proved in mitigation may well assume even greater significance.

3.40   There are some other rules, of which it could be said that they are not, on a proper analysis, rules of the common law defence of justification, but rules about meaning. Of these it could be argued that since the Act does not purport to abolish or alter the common law as to meaning, they survive. This argument might be advanced, for instance, with regard to the existing authorities about the ascertainment of the natural and ordinary meaning of a statement, the 'single meaning rule', the repetition rule, and the *Chase* levels of meaning.[43] There is real room

---

[40] See para 3.10.
[41] *Polly Peck v Trelford* [1986] QB 1000; see para 3.12.
[42] See paras 3.12–3.15.
[43] See paras 3.08–3.09.

for argument, however. The single meaning rule has been said, for instance, to be a rule about meaning *and* a rule that governs the pleading of justification.[44] The *Burstein* rule[45] would seem to be a rule of procedural law, concerned with mitigation of damages rather than justification, and hence unaffected by s 2(4).

3.41 As already noted, the technique of codification coupled with abolition of the common law is unusual. There are few historic examples to refer to, in attempting to gauge its likely effects. The considerations just discussed do, however, suggest that in the case of s 2 there may be some force in one of the arguments commonly advanced against codification: that it is liable to increase legal costs, as there is an increased need for litigants to take professional advice when a restatement of the law is first enacted. Codification certainly does not seem likely to result in any increased certainty or predictability, in this instance.

3.42 The codification of the defence of truth will present a huge challenge to the courts. There is likely to be uncertainty for some time over the extent to which the old common law rules relating to the pleading and proof of the defence will be retained. The courts will have to do their best to give effect to the express intention of Parliament to 'abolish' the common law defence. However, beyond that simple statement, there remains substantial scope for disagreement.

---

[44] *Shah v Standard Chartered Bank* [1999] QB 241.
[45] See para 3.15.

4

THE NEW STATUTORY DEFENCE
OF HONEST OPINION

A. INTRODUCTION

Section 3 of the Act establishes a new statutory defence of honest opinion. This **4.01** replaces the common law defence which was for most of its long history called 'fair comment' (though latterly sometimes labelled 'honest comment' or 'honest opinion'). The common law defence is abolished. The statutory defence is more generous in some respects.

The most notable reforms made by s 3 are: (1) the removal of the common **4.02** law's requirement that the comment must be on a 'matter of public interest'; the statutory defence is available in respect of an opinion on any fact or matter;

(2) the simplification of the law relating to the factual basis required if an opinion is to be defensible; it will now be enough if the opinion could be honestly held 'on the basis of any fact which existed at the time the statement complained of was published', or if the opinion could be honestly held on the basis of something 'asserted to be a fact' in an earlier privileged statement; and (3) the clarification and expansion of the categories of privileged report or statement which are capable of supporting an opinion defence.

4.03   Section 3 also repeals the one significant statutory provision that modified the common law defence, s 6 of the Defamation Act 1952. That provision, outlined at para 4.16, allowed fair comment defences to succeed, even if facts stated in the words complained of were not proved true, provided the facts that were proved true were enough to support the comment. A provision of that kind 'is no longer necessary in light of the new approach' as to the factual basis for an opinion.[1]

B. THE PRE-EXISTING LAW

1. Summary

4.04   At common law a defamatory statement could be defended as 'fair comment' if it was shown that it was a comment or expression of opinion on a matter of public interest, based on true facts (or privileged statements of fact) sufficiently identified in the offending statement, and a statement which an honest person could make on that basis. If these matters were established, the defence could nevertheless be defeated by proof of malice.

4.05   The matters required to establish the defence at common law are examined at paras 4.06–4.15. Paragraph 4.16 deals with the minor statutory modification of one of the five elements. Paragraphs 4.17–4.18 address the meaning of malice in this context.

2. The five elements of the common law defence

4.06   In *Joseph v Spiller*[2] the Supreme Court thoroughly examined and authoritatively restated the common law. The court held that there were five matters which a defendant had to establish in order to make out the defence of fair comment: (1) the statement must be on a matter of public interest; (2) it must be recognizable as comment, as distinct from an imputation of fact; (3) it must be based on facts which are true or protected by privilege; (4) it must explicitly or implicitly indicate, at least in general terms, the facts on which it is based; (5) it must be a comment which could have been made by an honest person.

---

[1] Explanatory Notes, para 28.
[2] [2010] UKSC 53, [2011] 1 AC 852.

(1) Statement on a matter of public interest

Since this requirement of the common law has now been abolished and not re-enacted, it is unnecessary to examine it in any detail. It played a limited role in practice. The concept of matters of public interest became very broad. Whilst it was not unheard of for a defence of fair comment to fail on the basis that the statement was a comment, honestly made on a sufficient factual foundation, but not on a matter of public interest,[3] it was an extremely rare occurrence.

4.07

(2) Recognizable as comment not a statement of fact

The common law defence could only protect a defamatory comment or opinion. Defamatory statements of fact had to be the subject of some other defence, such as justification (that is, truth) or privilege. The classification of a statement as factual or as comment has often been a disputed and difficult question. The principles are relatively easy to state. The Court of Appeal reiterated them in *Branson v Bower*,[4] stating that a comment is 'something which is or can reasonably be inferred to be a deduction, inference, conclusion, criticism, remark, observation, etc.'. In applying those tests, the court had to consider the context in which the statement appeared, and how the particular readers were likely to understand the statement. However, the classification of particular statements by reference to these principles can be hard, and has on occasion been controversial. *Branson v Bower* itself involved what many would see as a liberal approach. A statement imputing base motives to the claimant was held to be comment, and incapable of classification as factual. The reasoning was that it would be clear to a reader that the writer could not know for certain whether the claimant's motives were as he alleged, but must be drawing an inference. On the other hand, in *Telnikoff v Matusevich*,[5] the House of Lords held that a defamatory statement about the claimant contained in a newspaper article was one of fact, and could not be classified as a comment by bringing into account as context a letter written by the claimant and published on another occasion, which was in fact the basis for the defamatory statement.

4.08

A vivid illustration of how widely different conclusions can be reached in the application of established principles to particular facts is provided by the case of *British Chiropractic Association v Singh*.[6] A campaigning journalist wrote on the *Guardian*'s comment and debate page that the claimant association made claims for its treatments for which there was 'not a jot of evidence' and that it 'happily promotes bogus treatments'. At first instance, these were held to be factual allegations which could not be protected by the comment defence but would have to

4.09

---

[3] See, for example, *Andre v Price* [2010] EWHC 2572 (QB) where public statements about the claimant's relationship with the defendant's son were held not to be on a matter of public interest under both the common law and the Human Rights Act 1998.

[4] [2001] EWCA Civ 791, [2001] EMLR 32 (p 800).

[5] [1992] 2 AC 343.

[6] [2010] EWCA Civ 350, [2011] 1 WLR 133.

be justified. That ruling, which led to a media furore, was reversed by the Court of Appeal. It held that the critical question was whether there was any evidence to support the Association's claims, and that this was a matter of opinion, not one of verifiable fact.

(3) *The comment must be based on true facts or facts published on a privileged occasion*

4.10 The principal rule was that there had to be true facts to support the comment, and the common law held that the defence would fail unless the defendant proved the truth of all the facts he or she had referred to and relied on in the statement complained of: 'If the facts on which the comment purports to be founded are not proved to be true, the defence of fair comment is not available'. This is the common law position approved in *Spiller*, but it was subject to statutory modification. As explained in para 4.13, under the law before the 2013 Act, a fair comment defence could succeed provided the defendant proved a factual basis sufficient to enable an honest person to make the comment in issue. It was clear law that the facts relied on had to be in existence at the time of publication. In *Lowe v Associated Newspapers Ltd*,[7] it was held that it was also necessary for the defendant to know the facts 'at least in general terms' at that time, though it was not necessary for every specific detail to be known.

4.11 There was an alternative rule that, by way of exception, a comment could be defended if it had as its basis a statement of fact contained in a privileged report. It was held, for instance, that if a fair and accurate and therefore privileged report of parliamentary or legal proceedings was published, in which a false factual statement had been made, a newspaper could nevertheless make 'fair comment' based on the reported fact. However, it was held necessary for the published statement to incorporate the privileged report, along with the comment.[8] This version of the defence was rarely litigated. It was not settled whether the law would recognize fair comment based on defamatory factual statements protected by *Reynolds* privilege.[9]

(4) *The comment must explicitly or implicitly indicate the facts on which it is based*

4.12 This needed to be done only in general terms, however, so the Supreme Court held in *Spiller*. The requirement existed so that the reader could understand what the comment was about and the commentator could, if challenged, explain, by giving particulars of the subject matter of his comment, why he had expressed the views which he had. The court held that the commentator was not obliged to identify the matters on which the comment was based with sufficient particularity

---

[7] [2006] EWHC 320 (QB), [2007] QB 580.

[8] *Brent Walker Group plc v Time Out Ltd* [1991] 2 QB 33 (CA).

[9] That is, the privilege for reasonable and responsible journalism on matters of public interest (*Reynolds v Times Newspapers Ltd* [2001] 2 AC 127, [1999] 3 WLR 1010).

to enable the reader to judge for himself whether it was well founded. This had previously been held to be a requirement of the common law, and it was in this respect that *Spiller* effected one, modest, development of the law.

(5) *The comment must be one that could have been made by an honest person*
This was known as the objective test of honesty. The question was whether, on **4.13** the facts proved, an honest person could have held the opinion. Many of the common law authorities emphasized that this requirement was a generous and not a restrictive one. In order to be defensible it was not necessary for comment to be 'fair' in the ordinary sense of the word, or fair-minded, or reasonable. It could instead be the view of a crank. In *Spiller*, Lord Phillips described this requirement as 'bizarre and elusive' and said he was unaware of any case in which it had been litigated. The court, however, approved the following sum-mary: the comment must be one that an honest person could have made,

however prejudiced he might be, and however exaggerated or obstinate his views…It must be germane to the subject-matter criticised. Dislike of an artist's style would not justify an attack upon his morals or manners. But a critic need not be mealy-mouthed in denouncing what he disagrees with. He is entitled to dip his pen in gall for the purposes of legitimate criticism…[10]

Those being the principles, the name 'fair comment' was frequently said to be potentially misleading. In *Singh*, the Court of Appeal said that 'honest opinion' was a better label.

The objective test of honesty had to be applied to the meaning which the court **4.14** found the statement to convey. Using the language of the 2013 Act, the question was whether an honest person could have believed in the imputation conveyed by the statement complained of. That meaning or imputation was determined objectively by using the 'single meaning rule'.[11] The court resisted and rejected attempts to argue that the objective test should be applied to the words used, rather than their single meaning, and that the question ought to be whether an honest person could have used those words, having regard to the facts.

The flexibility of language being what it is, a consequence of this approach **4.15** was that a defendant, aiming to express one heartfelt and adequately founded opinion, might use words which inadvertently conveyed a different one, and that unintended meaning might be found by the court to be the objective 'single mean-ing' of the defendant's statement and to lack a sufficient factual basis. The Court of Appeal held that this situation could be dealt with by a rule, based on human rights law, that 'where a comment, honestly expressed in a media publication and grounded upon a sufficient factual basis, may reasonably be thought to carry an additional imputation which may not be so grounded, the defendant should not ordinarily be held liable for that imputation unless it was maliciously advanced'.[12]

---

[10] *Joseph v Spiller* [2010] UKSC 53, [2011] 1 AC 852 at [18].
[11] For which see para 3.08.
[12] *Lait v Evening Standard Ltd* [2011] EWCA Civ 859, [2011] 1 WLR 2973.

3. Statutory modification

4.16 Section 6 of the Defamation Act 1952 modified the common law's requirements as to the truth of the factual basis for the comment. At common law a fair comment defence would fail unless the defendant proved the truth of all statements of fact contained in or referred to in the words complained of as the basis for the published comment. Section 6 provided that a fair comment defence would not fail on that ground alone, but could succeed 'if the expression of opinion is fair comment having regard to such of the facts alleged or referred to in the words complained of as are proved'.

4. Malice

4.17 A person sued for a comment he or she made could not rely on the defence of fair comment if he or she made the comment maliciously. The onus of proving malice lay on the claimant. For this purpose, malice was ultimately held to have a narrower meaning than in some other contexts.

> Comment which falls within the objective limits of the defence of fair comment can lose its immunity only by proof that the defendant did not genuinely hold the view he expressed. Honesty of belief is the touchstone. Actuation by spite, animosity, intent to injure, intent to arouse controversy or other motivation, whatever it may be, even if it is the dominant or sole motive, does not of itself defeat the defence. However, proof of such motivation may be evidence, sometimes compelling evidence, from which lack of genuine belief in the view expressed may be inferred.[13]

4.18 The rule just outlined did not apply to cases of reported comment, that is, cases where a person, such as a newspaper, who was not the author of the offending comment was sued for reporting it. The most obvious example of such a situation was where a newspaper was sued for publishing a defamatory comment in a reader's letter. The common law had not adopted a settled position. It seemed clear that the publisher would not be liable just because he or she did not share the writer's opinion, nor just because the author was malicious. Quite what would suffice to make the publisher 'malicious' and hence liable was unclear.

C. BACKGROUND TO S 3

1. Criticisms of the common law and reform proposals

(a) *Duncan and Neill on Defamation*

4.19 The long-awaited appearance of the 3rd edition of this important textbook in 2009 included a considered and detailed critique of some aspects of the law of

---

[13] *Tse Wai Chun Paul v Cheng* [2001] EMLR 31 (p 777).

fair comment. The authors queried[14] whether *Lowe*[15] was right to hold that a commentator needed to know the facts later relied on to support his or her comment. They suggested[16] that the law as stated in *Brent Walker*[17] was unduly restrictive, and that publishers should be able to defend comments on the basis of facts set out in privileged reports published by others, 'at least where the comment was published contemporaneously with fair and accurate reports.... elsewhere in the media'. They submitted[18] that *Reynolds* privilege might be capable of extending to cover comments and opinions,[19] and[20] that in the case of reported comment[21] the publisher should only be held malicious if he or she knew the author did not hold the opinion expressed.

(b) *The Libel Reform Group*

The Libel Reform Group[22] was critical of the common law of fair comment, among other aspects of the law. Its report *Free Speech Is Not for Sale* was published in November 2009, between the first instance and Court of Appeal decisions in *Singh*.[23] Recommendation 7 of the report was that 'Comment is not free...Expand the definition of fair comment'. It called for recognition that 'robust debate is essential...and should be allowed to flourish'. It focused attention on the tests for what is comment and what is fact. It criticized judges for being 'overly analytical in their approach' and called for a 'broader and more relaxed definition', though it did not identify what that definition might be. The Group urged that 'courts should be looking at the context in which a piece is published in order to determine whether it is intended or likely to be read as a statement of fact, or one of comment'. 4.20

(c) *Lord Lester's Defamation Bill*

This dealt with comment in cll 2 and 3. When the Bill was given its Second Reading in the House of Lords on 9 July 2010 its sponsor explained the intentions behind it: to 'strip out unnecessary technical difficulties and make the defence user-friendly...[to] update and simplify, clarifying what the defendant must prove to establish a sufficient factual basis, and stating the elements of the defence in clear terms'.[24] Although it progressed no further, Lord Lester's Bill set the basic pattern for the legislative proposals that were to follow, and for the 4.21

---

[14] *Duncan and Neill on Defamation*, paras 13.31–13.36.
[15] *Lowe v Associated Newspapers Ltd* [2006] EWHC 320 (QB), [2007] QB 580; see para 4.10.
[16] *Duncan and Neill on Defamation*, para 13.41, n 4.
[17] *Brent Walker Group plc v Time Out Ltd* [1991] 2 QB 33 (CA); see para 4.11.
[18] *Duncan and Neill on Defamation*, para 17.26.
[19] See para 4.11.
[20] *Duncan and Neill on Defamation*, para 13.46.
[21] See para 4.18.
[22] English PEN, Index on Censorship, and Sense About Science.
[23] *British Chiropractic Association v Singh* [2010] EWCA Civ 350, [2011] 1 WLR 133; see para 4.09.
[24] *Hansard*, HL Deb, 9 July 2010, Col 426.

provisions eventually enacted, by following *Singh* in renaming the defence as 'honest opinion' (cl 2); by setting out (in cl 3) a series of conditions satisfaction of which would afford a defence, subject to malice; and by formulating (again in cl 3) statutory criteria to determine when a publisher will be liable for reported comment.[25]

(d) *Spiller v Joseph*

4.22 At the Supreme Court hearings in *Spiller v Joseph* on 25 and 26 July 2010, a number of developments or modifications of the fair comment defence were urged on the court. When it came to give judgment on 1 December of that year, however, the court made only the one modest adjustment of the law referred to at para 4.12. In that respect, the decision was in line with Lord Lester's Defamation Bill. The Supreme Court agreed with the Court of Appeal in *Singh*, and with Lord Lester, that the defence should be renamed, but it disagreed with their choice of name, preferring 'honest comment'. Declining to go further, and to adapt or develop the law in any other way, the Supreme Court explained that it saw a case for reform, but it suspected some of the reforms urged upon it would complicate rather than simplify, and did not consider in any event that the court was the appropriate body to carry out reform. It saw a case for examination of the law by the Law Commission or an expert body.

(e) *The Government's draft Bill*

4.23 Clause 4 of the draft Bill, published in March 2011, contained provision for a statutory defence of 'honest opinion' which had many similarities with cll 2 and 3 of Lord Lester's Bill.

4.24 However, there were four main differences between the two sets of proposals. First, the draft Bill introduced the novel idea of abolishing the common law defence of fair comment and repealing s 6 of the Defamation Act 1952. That was in line with the draft Bill's approach to the defence of justification or truth. As regards the defence of honest opinion based on privileged statements, the draft Bill prescribed that such statements had to be 'published before the statement complained of', and the Consultation Paper explained[26] that this version of the honest opinion defence was not intended to be available in respect of statements protected by the 'public interest' defence set out in cl 2 of the draft Bill (an antecedent of s 4 of the 2013 Act). Finally, under the draft Bill, the opinion defence for reported comment would fail if the claimant showed that the defendant 'knew or ought to have known' that the author did not hold the opinion.

4.25 There followed consultation on the draft Bill, and a Joint Parliamentary Committee reported upon it. Consultees' views varied widely. The Joint Committee supported the proposal to put the defence on a statutory footing and welcomed the removal of any requirement that the commentator should know

---

[25] See para 4.18.
[26] *Draft Defamation Bill: Consultation*, Consultation Paper CP3/11, March 2011, para 47.

the facts. The Committee recommended five amendments, however: (1) dropping the term 'public interest' as an unnecessary complication; (2) requiring the subject area of the comment to be sufficiently indicated; (3) requiring the court to take into account facts existing at the time of publication which undermine those relied on to support the comment; (4) requiring the statement to be recognizable as an opinion; and (5) 'the vague reference to "privilege" must be clarified to make it clear that this term is confined to the absolute or qualified privilege which presently attaches at common law or by statute to the fair and accurate reporting of various types of public proceedings or notices'. The Committee was concerned that the Bill as it stood would, read literally, 'protect comments expressed on wholly false statements contained in private communications where publisher and recipient have a common law defence of qualified privilege based on a reciprocal duty and interest', which it did not think could have been the intention.

2. The Defamation Bill 2012: parliamentary history of s 3

(a) *The Bill*

In the light of consultation, the Government accepted the Joint Parliamentary **4.26** Committee's first, second, and fifth recommendations. Clause 3 of the Government's Defamation Bill 2012 accordingly differed from the draft Bill in that (a) it omitted any requirement that the statement be on a matter of public interest; (b) it added in a requirement that the statement should indicate 'whether in general or specific terms', the basis of the opinion; (c) it modified the provisions as to opinion based on privileged statements, and contained a list of the 'privileged statements' which could form a basis for an honest opinion defence. That list was exhaustive, but it included not only various statements made with the protection of statutory reporting privileges, but also followed Lord Lester's Bill in encompassing statements privileged as amounting to responsible publication on a matter of public interest.

The Joint Parliamentary Committee's third recommendation (requiring the **4.27** court to take account of facts undermining the opinion) was deemed unduly complex by the Government. The Government agreed with the principle underlying the Committee's fourth recommendation (requiring that the statement be recognizable as opinion), but considered that it was adequately covered by the wording of the draft Bill, which was accordingly carried through into cl 3 of the 2012 Bill. No other changes of substance were made to the draft Bill.

(b) *Commons debates*

The explanation for both cl 2 (truth) and cl 3 (honest opinion) given by the **4.28** Bill's Commons sponsor, the Lord Chancellor, at the Second Reading in the House of Commons was that they were intended to 'simplify and clarify' the law.[27] The debates made clear that proof of true facts and proof of privileged

---

[27] See para 3.22.

publications were alternative means of demonstrating a basis for a comment. When, at the Committee stage, Robert Flello MP, Shadow Minister for Justice, sought to add the word 'or' to cl 3(4)(b),[28] the Minister responded, 'I can confirm that the defendant will succeed in the defence if they can show that either of the limbs is satisfied; they do not have to show that both are', and the amendment was withdrawn.[29] Mr Flello also sought to introduce an amendment to ensure that the proof of malice would defeat the defence; the Minister argued that the current drafting was sufficiently clear and that amendment was also withdrawn.[30]

(c) *Lords debates*

4.29 At the Committee stage on 19 December 2012, Lord Phillips of Sudbury proposed that a requirement should be inserted that the basis of an opinion be 'adequately' indicated by the offending statement. Lord Ahmad, responding for the Government, said[31] that the amendment was unnecessary as 'including the word "adequately"...would make no difference to how the provision would operate in practice'. Lord Phillips moved a further amendment to broaden the 'reported comment' defence to cover a case where the reported statement was 'substantially the same' as the original. Lord Ahmad responded[32] that: 'This would create uncertainty in the law, as it could be read as implying that the defence might be available in situations where the defendant has changed the statement by the author'. Both amendments were withdrawn.

4.30 At the Report stage on 5 February 2013, Lord Lester moved an amendment to alter the Bill's requirement that the 'basis' for an opinion should be indicated to one that required an indication of the 'subject matter'. The Minister, Lord McNally, confirmed[33] that the intention was to reflect the requirement approved in *Spiller*, and that the Government considered that aim was better achieved by the word 'basis'. Lord Lester was satisfied and, alluding to *Pepper v Hart*,[34] withdrew the amendment.[35] Lord Lloyd of Berwick had tabled a further amendment, which sought to reverse the decision in *Telnikoff*,[36] and to make it sufficient, if commenting on a letter or article that has appeared in a newspaper, to identify the subject-matter of the letter or article, and the date it appeared. This amendment had been debated on 19 December 2012, when Lords Scott and Woolf (the latter, like Lord Lloyd, a member of the Court of Appeal whose decision was reversed by the House of Lords) spoke in its support. On 5 February 2013 Lord McNally

---

[28] This was in the terms set out in para 4.32.
[29] *Hansard*, Public Bill Committee Deb, 19 June 2012, Col 36.
[30] *Hansard*, Public Bill Committee, 19 June 2012, Col 38.
[31] *Hansard*, HL Grand Committee, 19 December 2012, Col GC 528.
[32] *Hansard*, HL Grand Committee, 19 December 2012, Col GC 530.
[33] *Hansard*, HL Deb, 5 February 2013, Col 192.
[34] [1992] UKHL 3, [1992] 3 WLR 1032.
[35] *Hansard*, HL Deb, 5 February 2013, Col 193.
[36] *Telnikoff* v *Matusevich* [1992] 2 AC 343; see para 4.08.

explained[37] that the Government stood by the *Telnikoff* decision: 'We consider that it should be clear from the document in which the statement appears that the author is expressing an opinion, otherwise a reader cannot know that there is a judgment to be made'. The amendment was not moved.

(d) *Section 3 as enacted*

Section 3 of the Act as passed is in terms that are materially identical to those of cl 3 of the Bill. The single change effected during the passage of the Bill was the deletion of one word. Amendments to the name and definition of the new statutory defence for publication on matter of public interest (s 4) were reflected by deleting the word 'responsible' from cl 3(7)(a).[38]   **4.31**

D. THE STATUTORY PROVISIONS

Section 3 provides as follows: **4.32**

3 Honest opinion
(1) It is a defence to an action for defamation for the defendant to show that the following conditions are met.
(2) The first condition is that the statement complained of was a statement of opinion.
(3) The second condition is that the statement complained of indicated, whether in general or specific terms, the basis of the opinion.
(4) The third condition is that an honest person could have held the opinion on the basis of—
    (a) any fact which existed at the time the statement complained of was published;
    (b) anything asserted to be a fact in a privileged statement published before the statement complained of.
(5) The defence is defeated if the claimant shows that the defendant did not hold the opinion.
(6) Subsection (5) does not apply in a case where the statement complained of was published by the defendant but made by another person ('the author'); and in such a case the defence is defeated if the claimant shows that the defendant knew or ought to have known that the author did not hold the opinion.
(7) For the purposes of subsection (4)(b) a statement is a 'privileged statement' if the person responsible for its publication would have one or more of the following defences if an action for defamation were brought in respect of it—
    (a) a defence under section 4 (publication on matter of public interest);
    (b) a defence under section 6 (peer-reviewed statement in scientific or academic journal);
    (c) a defence under section 14 of the Defamation Act 1996 (reports of court proceedings protected by absolute privilege);
    (d) a defence under section 15 of that Act (other reports protected by qualified privilege).

---

[37] *Hansard*, HL Deb, 5 February 2013, Col 192.
[38] Report Stage, House of Lords, 5 February 2013.

(8) The common law defence of fair comment is abolished and, accordingly, section 6 of the Defamation Act 1952 (fair comment) is repealed.

E. KEY FEATURES OF THE DEFENCE

4.33 The defence is to be called 'honest opinion'. Lawyers will need to give up use of the label 'fair comment'. That common law defence has been abolished by s 3(8). It may nonetheless be argued that the new statutory defence is not very different from its common law predecessor. The Explanatory Notes to the Act say that the section 'broadly reflects the current law while simplifying and clarifying certain elements, but does not include the current requirement for the opinion to be on a matter of public interest'.[39] It is also true that, apart from the removal of the 'public interest' requirement, the law as enacted in s 3 does seem on the face of it closely to resemble the common law, as restated by the Supreme Court in *Spiller*,[40] at least when it comes to the 'core' case of an opinion based on facts, as opposed to facts asserted in privileged reports.

1. Opinion based on fact

4.34 In this 'core' case of honest opinion, the defendant has to satisfy conditions that reflect those identified in *Spiller*, other than the 'public interest' requirement. Shortly stated, the statement complained of must be shown to be (1) an expression of opinion which (2) indicates its factual basis and (3) could be held by an honest person on the basis of any fact that existed at the time. A 'fact' in this context is something the defendant must prove to be true. Whether the terms in which these conditions are expressed in s 3 makes any of them in any way significantly different from their common law counterparts is considered later in Section F of this chapter,[41] where it is suggested that it is well arguable that the section does alter the law as previously understood.

4.35 The defence will be defeated if the claimant proves that the defendant did not hold the opinion. It is a matter for debate how the law will deal with cases of honest people inadvertently conveying opinions which they do not hold.[42]

2. Opinion based on something asserted to be a fact in a prior privileged statement

4.36 When it comes to this 'non-core' defence of honest opinion the defendant still has to prove that the statement (1) was one of opinion and (2) indicated its basis. The

---

[39] Explanatory Notes, para 19.
[40] See para 4.06.
[41] See paras 4.41–4.53.
[42] See para 4.40.

defendant does not, however, have to prove the truth of the supporting fact(s). Instead, it is enough for the defendant to prove, first, that an honest person could have held the opinion on the basis of something asserted to be true in a report 'published before the statement complained of'; and, secondly, that the earlier report was a 'privileged statement' within the meaning given to that term by s 3(7). Whether these provisions reflect, or develop, the position as it stood at common law is considered in Section F of this chapter.[43] It is there suggested that the Explanatory Notes arguably understate the impact of this aspect of the legislation, and that the law has been extended, to an extent which is presently uncertain.

Again, the defence will be defeated if the claimant proves that the defendant **4.37** did not hold the opinion. As to the inadvertent expression of opinions not held, see the final sentence of para 4.35.

3. Opinion of another, published by the defendant

Such an opinion could in principle give rise to a 'core' defence of honest opinion, **4.38** or a 'non-core' defence, or both. Such a defence will not be defeated by proof that the defendant publisher did not hold the opinion in question. It will be defeated only by proof that the author did not hold the opinion, and that the publisher (1) knew this or (2) ought to have known it.

F. DISCUSSION

1. Abolition and repeal of the existing law

As with the defence of truth, the 2013 Act renders non-binding an extensive body **4.39** of case law, in so far as that case law forms part of the 'common law defence of fair comment'. As discussed in Chapter 3, however, this approach seems to give rise to a threshold question of whether any given legal rule is to be characterized as a rule of that common law defence, or as some other kind of rule, for instance a rule of the law as to meaning, or a procedural rule. If the former, the rule ceases to be binding. If the latter, it would seem to survive.[44]

One question that is likely to arise in this context concerns the 'single meaning **4.40** rule'. Put another way, how is the objective test of honesty which is now embodied in s 3(4) to be applied? Is it the right approach, as was held to be the position at common law, that the court should first determine the objective 'single meaning' of the published statement, and then ask whether an honest person could hold that opinion on the basis of the proven facts? Or may it be the case, under s 3, that (as argued in *Spiller*[45]) the question is whether, on the proven facts, an

---

[43] See paras 4.51–4.53.
[44] See the discussion in paras 3.36–3.42.
[45] See para 4.14.

honest person could have used the words employed in making the statement complained of? The third condition requires that an honest person could have held 'the opinion'. 'The opinion' is, clearly, the 'statement of opinion' referred to in the first condition, which, according to para 21 of the Explanatory Notes, 'embraces the requirement...that the statement must be recognisable as comment...on the basis of how the ordinary person would understand it'.[46] If that is right, it appears to follow that the opinion, which the honest person could have held, must be objectively determined as that which the ordinary person would have understood. In other words, the single meaning rule appears to be applicable.

2. The conditions

(a) *That the statement complained of was a statement of opinion*

4.41   The Explanatory Notes state at para 21 that this condition (in s 3(2)) is 'intended to reflect the current law', including the requirement that the statement be 'recognisable as' comment rather than fact. It is said to be 'implicit' that the assessment is 'on the basis of how the ordinary person would understand it'. It is not entirely clear, however, that the wording adopted is apt to achieve these aims. The question whether a statement 'was' a statement of opinion might be seen as a subjective question, depending on the intention of the maker of the statement rather than the interpretation put upon it by the reader or hearer.

4.42   Paragraph 21 of the Explanatory Notes states that an inference of fact 'would be encompassed by the defence'. This, presumably, would not always be so, but only if the inference was expressed in such a way that it appeared as an evaluative statement.

(b) *The statement complained of indicated, whether in general or specific terms, the basis of the opinion*

4.43   According to para 22 of the Explanatory Notes, this condition (now in s 3(3)), 'reflects the test approved by the Supreme Court in *Spiller* that "the comment must explicitly or implicitly indicate, at least in general terms, the facts on which it is based"'. As noted,[47] this was reiterated by Lord McNally in the House of Lords. It seems to be a fair statement, as does the assertion in para 22 of the Explanatory Notes that the wording is intended 'to retain the broad principles of the current common law defence as to the necessary basis for the opinion expressed'. The subsection thus appears to be merely restating an established principle of the common law. That can be said to aid accessibility.

4.44   It is a good deal less obvious that restating this general principle in statute will achieve the further aim identified by the authors of the Explanatory Notes: to

---

[46] See para 4.41.
[47] At para 4.30.

'avoid the complexities which have arisen in case law, in particular over ... the extent to which the statement must explicitly or implicitly indicate the facts on which the opinion is based'.[48] The difficulty is that, as the authors of the Explanatory Notes themselves point out, 'the facts that may need to be demonstrated in relation to an article expressing an opinion on a political issue, comments made on a social network, a view about a contractual dispute, or a review of a restaurant or play will differ substantially'. In other words, the application of the test approved in *Spiller* will inevitably be fact-sensitive. It may be a consequence of this that, as acknowledged in the Explanatory Notes, the 'case law has sometimes struggled to articulate with clarity how the law should apply in particular circumstances'. At any rate, it is a little hard to see how this subsection will help the courts in that task. It remains to be seen whether the 'complex and technical' common law rules referred to in the Explanatory Notes may reassert themselves.

(c) *An honest person could have held the opinion on the basis of any fact which existed at the time the statement complained of was published*

The intent behind this provision (in s 3(4)(a)) was, according to the Explanatory **4.45** Notes, 'to simplify the law by providing a clear and straightforward test', to 'retain the broad principles of the current common law defence' and 'avoid ... complexities over ... the extent to which the opinion must be based on facts which are sufficiently true'.[49] It is questionable whether the wording adopted achieves any of those aims. What the 'complexities' were is not explained in the Explanatory Notes. Many considered this aspect of the common law to be clear enough. If that is wrong, it remains to be seen whether, and if so how, the enactment of s 3(4)(a) will help. There is a risk that it might make things worse.

The wording in cl 3 of the draft Bill was identical, except that it spoke of 'a **4.46** fact', rather than 'any fact'. The Consultation Paper that accompanied the draft Bill explained[50] that the intention was to do enough to ensure that the defendant proves a sufficient factual basis for the comment. Focusing on 'a fact' was said to mean that it would not be necessary for the defendant to prove the truth of every allegation of fact set out in the statement complained of. If the fact was not a sufficient basis for the opinion, an honest person would not have been able to hold it.[51] It certainly does seem clear that this statement of the law makes s 6 of the 1952 Act redundant, and its repeal is logical. It is also clear from the wording of the Act that there is no requirement that the commentator should have known the facts relied on to support the opinion.[52]

---

[48] Explanatory Notes, para 22.
[49] Explanatory Notes, para 22.
[50] Ministry of Justice, *Draft Defamation Bill: Consultation*, Consultation Paper CP3/11, March 2011, para 45.
[51] See Explanatory Notes, para 23.
[52] See also *The Government's Response to the Report of the Joint Committee on the Defamation Bill* (Cm 8295, February 2012), para 33.

4.47   As to the interpretation of the phrase 'any fact', clearly this must mean a fact that was true at the time of publication, otherwise it can hardly be a fact which 'existed' at that time. The Explanatory Notes say that 'any relevant fact or facts will be enough',[53] which seems to allow a defendant to rely on any fact that was true at the time of publication irrespective of other (less convenient) facts. The Joint Parliamentary Committee recommended that the court should be required to take into account any facts that existed at the time of publication which so undermine the facts relied on that they are not longer capable of supporting the opinion, because a person may honestly express a defamatory opinion on the basis of a fact which, although once true, has by the time of publication wholly lost its validity because of a subsequent fact that may be unknown to the commentator. The Government's Response to the Joint Committee Report[54] was that such a provision would over-complicate the clause, and that any difficulty may in practice be resolved by the claimant using subs (5) to argue that the defendant must have known about the intervening fact. If and when this problem arises, it will have to be resolved by asking the question whether the fact which is put forward to support the opinion was true at the date of publication, having regard to any other competing facts.

4.48   The Explanatory Notes say that 'if the fact was not a sufficient basis for the opinion, an honest person would not have been able to hold it'[55] which suggests that the opinion must have some logical or rational basis, in the fact or facts said to support it. It seems very unlikely that the new defence will be held to have abrogated the common law position, that a comment may be honestly held, however prejudiced the commentator might be, and however exaggerated or obstinate his views.[56] The perennial problem of reconciling these propositions is certainly not made any easier by the Act.

4.49   Section 3 does not explicitly require there to be any link between the fact(s) indicated as the basis of the opinion in the statement complained of (condition 2), and the fact(s) that form the basis for defending it as honest opinion (condition 3). Thus, on the face of it, a person who has misstated all of the facts in a publication, and then expressed a defamatory opinion upon them, will now be able to defend the publication, if he or she can find some other fact upon the basis of which it would be possible for an honest person to express the opinion. This would be a significant change in the law.

4.50   It may be argued that the reference, in s 3(4)(a), to '*any* fact' as being available as support for the opinion on the part of an honest person, means what it says, and that the fact(s) relied on to support the opinion need not be the fact(s) indicated in the statement complained of as the basis of the opinion, or be linked to them in any way. It is, however, suggested that there must be *some* relationship

---

[53] Explanatory Notes, para 23.
[54] At paras 34 and 35.
[55] Explanatory Notes, para 23.
[56] See para 4.13.

between the fact(s) indicated as the basis for the opinion and the fact(s) relied on to support it. It cannot have been intended that an opinion expressed on wholly false facts can be supported on an entirely different basis. Otherwise, for example, a person could be accused of dishonesty, or of being a danger to the public, on the basis of some recent alleged, but entirely false, conduct in his or her public capacity, and the comment could be defended as one which could be held by an honest, but prejudiced, obstinate, etc person, on the basis of some conduct in a wholly different and private capacity, years previously. The change in the law would be a radical one, and it is significant that the parliamentary history of the provision, and para 22 of the Explanatory Notes, clearly suggest that condition 3 'is intended to retain the broad principles of the current common law defence'. There is nothing to suggest that the change from 'a fact' in the draft Bill to 'any fact' in the Act was intended to have this radical effect, rather than to reinforce the intention that not all of the facts indicated in the statement complained of as the basis for the opinion need be shown to be true. It is suggested that the position is made clearer when this point is considered in relation to s 3(4)(b): it cannot be the case that a defendant could publish an opinion based on wholly false facts, and then defend it as one which an honest person could have held on the basis of a privileged statement published perhaps years previously, and nowhere referred to or indicated in the statement complained of.

(d) *An honest person could have held the opinion on the basis of anything asserted to be a fact in a privileged statement published before the statement complained of*

Although, as noted above, the common law counterpart of this version of the honest opinion defence has been little litigated over the years, this may be the part of s 3 has the greatest potential to generate doubt and litigation. Section 3(4)(b), which sets out the essentials of this defence, is supplemented and explained by s 3(7), which contains an exhaustive list of statements to be treated as 'a privileged statement' for this purpose. The list encompasses only statutory privileges. It includes, however, not only the reports of proceedings and other matters which have traditionally had statutory protection, currently under ss 14 and 15 of the Defamation Act 1996, but also the two new categories of statutory privilege introduced by the 2013 Act. In that respect, the defence has been extended beyond its previous limits, and will surely be explored in some detail. **4.51**

Further, s 3(4)(b) evidently allows A to defend a statement as honest opinion based on a privileged report published by B, provided that A's statement complies with the second condition, and 'indicates' in some way that B's report is the basis for A's opinion. Section 3(7) provides that a statement is a 'privileged statement' if 'the person responsible for its publication would have one or more of' the specified statutory privilege defences, if they had been sued in respect **4.52** of it. This seems to be in line with the argument advanced by *Duncan and Neil on Defamation*,[57] but is certainly new law, and its implications will need to be worked out. Will it matter when B's privileged statement was published, and how extensively? Or will any ancient report, with limited circulation, be enough? If the privilege would have been qualified, what if B was malicious, and would therefore have lost the privilege? Will it suffice if B would have had a privilege defence at the time of first publication, or will it be necessary to show that such a defence would still be available? The answer may differ as the balance of public interest shifts over time, as demonstrated by such cases as *Qadir v Associated Newspapers Ltd*.[58]

4.53   Section 3(4)(b) requires the privileged statement to have been published *before* the statement complained of. This might be said to provide narrower protection than the previous law, which protected a publisher who, in a single article, reported fairly and accurately what was said in Parliament or the courts, and commented on the basis of the facts so reported. It is suggested that this places too literal a construction on 'before', which should be taken to embrace what is logically, as well as what is temporally, antecedent.

3. Lack of belief and negligence

4.54   The law as stated in s 3(5) appears to be identical to the common law of 'malice', as stated in *Cheng*,[59] as was the intention according to the Explanatory Notes. The provisions of s 3(6) are different. This area of the law lacked clarity, and the statutory provisions could be welcome in providing it. They do, however, give rise to some interesting questions.

4.55   The reason the honest opinion defence is needed by, say, a newspaper which publishes readers' letters is 'the repetition rule': the rule of defamation law that treats reported statements as equivalent to direct statements. For the purpose of assessing meaning, the publisher is treated as if he or she had made the assertion and not just reported it. But the repetition rule does not always reflect reality. There may be many situations in which the media report opinions expressed by third parties, whilst firmly believing that the third parties are insincere or lying in what they say. The political arena is just one in which reporting of that nature is common. The courts may have some work to do, interpreting and applying these provisions. What will be made, for example, of an article which reports the third party opinion and states that the newspaper does not believe it is sincerely held? Might the publisher be liable for the defamatory imputation? The answer is likely to be found in taking a proper view of the meaning to be attached to the

---

[57] See para 4.19.
[58] [2012] EWHC 2606 (QB).
[59] *Tse Wai Chun Paul v Cheng* [2001] EMLR 31 (p 777); see para 4.17.

report taken as a whole, bane and antidote together. Even in a case to which the repetition rule applies, it is still necessary to decide the meaning of the publication, read as a whole, as Lord Devlin indicated in *Lewis v Daily Telegraph Ltd.*[60]

4. General observations

Section 3 may be said to exemplify the dangers of attempting at the same time   **4.56** to codify and amend a complex part of the common law. A cottage industry may result, as the courts attempt to clarify the extent to which the existing law survives, and the law will scarcely be less complex than before, since many of the same questions will arise again, and will have to be resolved anew; and new questions are liable to flow from the wording chosen for the new provisions.

---

[60] [1964] AC 234 at 284.

5

PUBLICATION ON MATTER OF PUBLIC INTEREST

A. INTRODUCTION

Section 4 of the Act introduces for the first time a statutory defence of publica- **5.01**
tion on a matter of public interest, in circumstances where the publisher reasonably believed that the publication was in the public interest. It is intended to

reflect the common law, whilst strengthening freedom of speech by removing a perceived tendency on the part of the courts to rely on checklists and emphasizing the potential importance of editorial discretion.

B. THE PRE-EXISTING LAW

1. Introduction

5.02   The introduction in *Reynolds v Times Newspapers Ltd*[1] of a defence for the publication in the mass media of untrue defamatory allegations was a significant development in the common law, representing a major shift in favour of freedom of expression. Subsequent cases liberalized the law further, emphasizing the flexibility of the defence, giving a greater role to editorial discretion, and giving special protection to the neutral reporting of disputes on matters of public interest.

2. *Reynolds* and responsible journalism

(a) Reynolds v Times Newspapers
5.03   At the start of his speech in *Flood v Times Newspapers Ltd*[2] Lord Phillips observed:

> Put shortly *Reynolds* privilege protects publication of defamatory matter to the world at large where (i) it was in the public interest that the information should be published and (ii) the publisher has acted responsibly in publishing the information, a test usually referred to as 'responsible journalism' although *Reynolds* privilege is not limited to publications by the media: see *Reynolds v Times Newspapers Ltd* [2001] 2 AC 127.

5.04   What Lord Phillips described as 'the foundation of *Reynolds* privilege' is the following passage of Lord Nicholls' speech in *Reynolds*:[3]

> The elasticity of the common law principle enables interference with freedom of speech to be confined to what is necessary in the circumstances of the case. This elasticity enables the court to give appropriate weight, in today's conditions, to the importance of freedom of expression by the media on all matters of public concern.

> Depending on the circumstances, the matters to be taken into account include the following. The comments are illustrative only. 1. The seriousness of the allegation. The more serious the charge, the more the public is misinformed and the individual harmed, if the allegation is not true. 2. The nature of the information, and the extent to which the subject matter is a matter of public concern. 3. The source of the information. Some informants have no direct knowledge of the events. Some have their own axes to grind, or are being paid for their stories. 4. The steps taken to verify the information. 5. The status of the information. The

---

[1] [2001] 2 AC 127, [1999] 3 WLR 1010.
[2] [2012] UKSC 11; [2012] 2 AC 273.
[3] [2001] 2 AC 127 at 204–5.

allegation may have already been the subject of an investigation which commands respect. 6. The urgency of the matter. News is often a perishable commodity. 7. Whether comment was sought from the plaintiff. He may have information others do not possess or have not disclosed. An approach to the plaintiff will not always be necessary. 8. Whether the article contained the gist of the plaintiff's side of the story. 9. The tone of the article. A newspaper can raise queries or call for an investigation. It need not adopt allegations as statements of fact. 10. The circumstances of the publication, including the timing.

Lord Nicholls recognized that his 'list is not exhaustive. The weight to be given to these and any other relevant factors will vary from case to case'. **5.05**

(b) Jameel (Mohammed) v Wall Street Journal

The *Reynolds* defence next came before the House of Lords in *Jameel* **5.06** *(Mohammed) v Wall Street Journal Europe Sprl*.[4] Lord Hoffmann expressed the view that '*Reynolds* has had little impact on the way the law is applied at first instance. It is therefore necessary to restate the principles'.[5]

Lord Hoffmann said that the first question was whether the article as a whole **5.07** was on a matter of public interest. He then said this:[6]

If the article as a whole concerned a matter of public interest, the next question is whether the inclusion of the defamatory statement was justifiable. The fact that the material was of public interest does not allow the newspaper to drag in damaging allegations which serve no public purpose. They must be part of the story. And the more serious the allegation, the more important it is that it should make a real contribution to the public interest element in the article. But whereas the question of whether the story as a whole was a matter of public interest must be decided by the judge without regard to what the editor's view may have been, the question of whether the defamatory statement should have been included is often a matter of how the story should have been presented. And on that question, allowance must be made for editorial judgment. If the article as a whole is in the public interest, opinions may reasonably differ over which details are needed to convey the general message. The fact that the judge, with the advantage of leisure and hindsight, might have made a different editorial decision should not destroy the defence. That would make the publication of articles which are, *ex hypothesi*, in the public interest, too risky and would discourage investigative reporting.

The next stage for Lord Hoffmann was for the court to determine 'whether the **5.08** steps taken to gather and publish the information were responsible and fair' for which he used the shorthand of 'responsible journalism'.[7] He disagreed with the trial judge that the test of responsible journalism was too vague, saying 'the standard of responsible journalism is as objective and no more vague than standards such as "reasonable care" which are regularly used in other branches of the law'.

---

[4] [2006] UKHL 44, [2007] 1 AC 359.
[5] [2006] UKHL 44, [2007] 1 AC 359 at [38].
[6] [2006] UKHL 44, [2007] 1 AC 359 at [51]–[52].
[7] [2006] UKHL 44, [2007] 1 AC 359 at [53].

5.09 He then said the following in relation to the ten factors set out by Lord Nicholls in *Reynolds*:

They are not tests which the publication has to pass. In the hands of a judge hostile to the spirit of *Reynolds*, they can become ten hurdles at any of which the defence may fail.[8]

(c) Flood v Times Newspapers

5.10 The passage of the Bill was made more complicated by the fact that shortly before it was presented to the House of Commons (and after it had been drafted) the Supreme Court handed down the third in the trilogy of public interest journalism cases to reach the highest court: *Flood v Times Newspapers Ltd.*[9] The major effect of *Flood* was to emphasize and endorse the role which Lord Hoffmann gave to editorial discretion in *Jameel*.

5.11 Lord Mance[10] quoted with approval Lord Hoffmann's words in *Jameel* set out at para 5.07. Lord Dyson cited as an 'important principle' the following:

... although the question of whether the story as a whole was a matter of public interest must be determined by the court, the question of whether defamatory details should have been included is often a matter of how the story should have been presented. On that issue, allowance should be made for editorial judgment.[11]

5.12 The following passage from the speech of Lord Brown of Eaton under Heywood JSC in *Flood*[12] was cited by the Government as the test which s 4 was intended to reflect[13] and must be seen to be the best indication of legislative intention:

In deciding whether *Reynolds* privilege attaches (whether the *Reynolds* public interest defence lies) the judge, on true analysis, is deciding but a single question: could whoever published the defamation, given whatever they knew (and did not know) and whatever they had done (and had not done) to guard so far as possible against the publication of untrue defamatory material, properly have considered the publication in question to be in the public interest?

3. *Reynolds* and reportage

5.13 A series of cases beginning with *Al-Fagih v HH Saudi Research and Marketing (UK) Ltd*[14] sought to build on *Reynolds* to give protection to the neutral reporting of an existing dispute, which came to be known as 'reportage'.

5.14 Lord Phillips in *Flood* described reportage as follows:

Reportage is a special, and relatively rare, form of *Reynolds* privilege. It arises where it is not the content of a reported allegation that is of public interest, but the fact that the

---

[8] [2006] UKHL 44, [2007] 1 AC 359 at [56].
[9] [2012] UKSC 11, [2012] 2 AC 273.
[10] [2012] UKSC 11, [2012] 2 AC 273 at [132].
[11] [2012] UKSC 11, [2012] 2 AC 273 at [192].
[12] [2012] UKSC 11, [2012] 2 AC 273 at [113].
[13] See para 5.46.
[14] [2001] EWCA Civ 1634, [2002] EMLR 13 (p 215).

allegation has been made. It protects the publisher if he has taken proper steps to verify the making of the allegation and provided that he does not adopt it.[15]

Lord Phillips[16] cited with approval the description of the distinction between **5.15** mainstream *Reynolds* and reportage given by Lord Hoffmann in *Jameel*:

In most cases the *Reynolds* defence will not get off the ground unless the journalist honestly and reasonably believed that the statement was true, but there are cases ('reportage') in which the public interest lies simply in the fact that the statement was made, when it may be clear that the publisher does not subscribe to any belief in its truth.[17]

4. Discrete *Reynolds* issues

(a) *Meaning*

The so-called single meaning rule does not apply in *Reynolds* situations, rather **5.16** the range of meanings which a statement might reasonably be taken as bearing is relevant to the question of whether publication was responsible. Lord Phillips in *Flood*, following the decision of the Privy Council in *Bonnick v Morris*,[18] said:

When deciding whether to publish, and when attempting to verify the content of the publication, the responsible journalist should have regard to the full range of meanings that a reasonable reader might attribute to the publication.[19]

(b) *Public interest*

Lord Bingham's attempt at defining public interest in the Court of Appeal in **5.17** *Reynolds*[20] was cited with approval by Lord Phillips in *Flood*:

By that we mean matters relating to the public life of the community and those who take part in it, including within the expression 'public life' activities such as the conduct of government and political life, elections (subject to Section 10 of the [Defamation] Act 1952, so long as it remains in force) and public administration, but we use the expression more widely than that, to embrace matters such as (for instance) the governance of public bodies, institutions and companies which give rise to a public interest in disclosure, but excluding matters which are personal and private, such that there is no public interest in their disclosure.[21]

Lord Hoffmann said in *Jameel*[22] that in answering the question as to whether the **5.18** subject matter of the article was a matter of public interest 'one should consider the article as a whole and not isolate the defamatory statement'.

---

[15] *Flood v Times Newspapers Ltd* [2012] UKSC 11, [2012] 2 AC 273 at [77].
[16] *Flood v Times Newspapers Ltd* [2012] UKSC 11, [2012] 2 AC 273 at [78].
[17] *Jameel (Mohammed) v Wall Street Journal Europe Sprl* [2006] UKHL 44, [2007] 1 AC 359 at [62].
[18] [2002] UKPC 31, [2003] 1 AC 300.
[19] *Flood v Times Newspapers Ltd* [2012] UKSC 11, [2012] 2 AC 273 at [51].
[20] [2001] 2 AC 127, 176–7.
[21] *Flood v Times Newspapers Ltd* [2012] UKSC 11, [2012] 2 AC 273 at [33].
[22] [2006] UKHL 44, [2007] 1 AC 359 at [48].

(c) *Non-journalists*

5.19 The defence was available (at least in theory) not just to journalists, but to anyone who published material of public interest in any medium.[23]

C. BACKGROUND TO S 4

1. Criticisms of the common law and reform proposals

5.20 The Libel Reform Group[24] asserted in their 2009 report *Free Speech Is Not for Sale* that 'there is no robust public interest defence in libel law'. Their threefold criticism of *Reynolds* was 'prohibitive cost', 'misplaced burden of proof' and that it had 'not been applied widely enough beyond investigative journalism'.

5.21 Lord Lester's Private Member's Defamation Bill [HL] 2010–2011 sought to codify *Reynolds*, with a dual requirement that the matter published relate to an issue of public interest and that the defendant acted responsibly in making the publication. It provided that the court should have regard to all the circumstances in making the assessment of responsibility, setting out some, but not all, of the *Reynolds* factors. A version of the reportage defence was set out as one of the potential factors to be taken into account in assessing responsibility.

5.22 The draft Bill published by the Ministry of Justice broadly adopted the Lester approach. The Explanatory Notes stated that the clause was 'based on' *Reynolds*, whilst intending to introduce both clarity and flexibility. It was also intended to 'encapsulate the core of the law in relation to the "reportage" doctrine'.

5.23 The Joint Parliamentary Committee[25] broadly agreed with the proposals in the draft Bill, but recommended an additional requirement that 'when deciding whether publication was responsible, the court should have regard to any reasonable editorial judgment of the publisher on the tone and timing of the publication'. The Joint Committee also recommended that the common law defence should be abolished expressly.

5.24 In its Response to the Report of the Joint Committee the Government accepted the proposal that the common law defence should be abolished expressly. The Government rejected the proposal by the Joint Committee that there should be an express reference to editorial judgement. It also acknowledged concerns as to how reportage was dealt with in the draft Bill, and said it intended to consider whether there was a way of 'reflecting more accurately the current position'.

---

[23] *Jameel (Mohammed) v Wall Street Journal Europe Sprl* [2006] UKHL 44, [2007] 1 AC 359 at [54]; *Seaga v Harper* [2008] UKPC 9, [2009] 1 AC 1 at [11].
[24] English PEN, Index on Censorship, and Sense About Science.
[25] See para 1.08.

2. The Defamation Bill 2012: parliamentary history of s 4

(a) *The Bill*

The Bill as introduced in the Commons on 10 May 2012 sought in cl 4 to cod- **5.25**
ify and abolish the common law. The Explanatory Notes stated that the clause
was 'based on the existing common law defence established in *Reynolds v Times
Newspapers* and is intended to reflect the principles established in that case and
in subsequent case law'.[26]

The way in which the Bill did that was broadly similar to the Lester Bill and **5.26**
the draft Bill, in providing a public interest test and non-exhaustive list of factors to be taken into account in assessing responsibility. The concerns expressed
at the draft Bill stage about reportage led to a new formulation, which in the
words of the Explanatory Notes was (again) 'intended to encapsulate the core
of the common law doctrine of "reportage"'.[27] The way in which that was done
was in effect the same as that eventually found in the Act, providing that when
considering a report on a dispute to which the claimant was a party the court
must disregard any omission to verify.

The Explanatory Notes said the following in relation to the public interest test **5.27**
in the Bill (which remained unchanged in the Act):

...In relation to the first limb of this test, the section does not attempt to define what
is meant by 'the public interest'. However, this is a concept which is well-established in
the English common law. It is made clear that the defence applies if the statement complained of 'was, or formed part of, a statement on a matter of public interest' to ensure
that either the words complained of may be on a matter of public interest, or that a
holistic view may be taken of the statement in the wider context of the document, article etc in which it is contained in order to decide if overall this is on a matter of public
interest.[28]

(b) *Commons debates*

The First Reading of the Bill was in the House of Commons on 10 May 2012. **5.28**
At the Second Reading debate on 12 June 2012 the Bill's Commons sponsor, the
Lord Chancellor, the Rt Hon Kenneth Clarke MP, said:

Alongside the new defences of truth and honest opinion, we are introducing, for the first
time a statutory defence of responsible publication in the public interest. This is based
on the common law defence that has been developed by the courts in recent years following the case of *Reynolds v Times Newspapers* but expressed in clear and flexible terms. It
provides a defence where the defendant can show that the allegedly defamatory statement
is, or forms part of, a statement on a matter of public interest, and that he or she acted
responsibly in publishing it.

---

[26] Also in para 29 of the Explanatory Notes to the Act.
[27] Also in para 32 of the Explanatory Notes to the Act.
[28] Also in para 30 of the Explanatory Notes to the Act.

The relevant clause identifies specific factors to which the court may have regard in deciding whether the defendant has acted responsibly, based on current case law. However, we do not want those to be interpreted as a checklist or a set of hurdles for defendants to overcome, and the list is intended to set out factors in an illustrative, non-exhaustive way so courts will retain flexibility. It is not our intention to change the *Reynolds* defence; we have sought to set it out in statutory form in a way that we hope will help.[29]

5.29 David Lammy MP said the following during the Second Reading debate in the Commons, speaking about the Bill generally:

It is right to codify this area of law at this time, if only so that ordinary citizens who are not in public life—those who are not celebrities and are not famous—who find their reputations tarnished or damaged can, as a result of what we are doing today, at least go to a piece of paper and determine for themselves what the law looks like in Britain, without having to rely on costly lawyers to interpret several different cases in order to determine whether they have any kind of claim. That must be a good thing for the general public as a whole.[30]

5.30 During the debate various members complained, seemingly inspired by an article in *The Times* that morning, that cl 4, in codifying *Reynolds*, ignored *Flood*, and had the danger of setting up the stated factors as hurdles to be surmounted.

5.31 Jonathan Djanogly MP, the Parliamentary Under-Secretary of State for Justice, in closing for the Government, said:

Clause 4 is based on existing common law and the defence established in *Reynolds*, and is intended to reflect the principles established in that case and in subsequent case law. The essential test is whether the defendant has acted responsibly in a matter of public interest. That matches the case law and gives the court appropriate flexibility.[31]

5.32 A variety of amendments were tabled at the Committee stage in the Commons. Some continued the theme that the Bill ignored (or had come too late to take account of)—*Flood*. The first mention of 'editorial judgement' came from an amendment moved by Robert Flello, Junior Minister for Justice, suggesting that added to the list of factors should be:

the reasonable judgement of the author or editor having regard to what was known at the time of the decision to publish the statement.

5.33 In speaking to the amendment Mr Flello said:

In *Flood v Times Newspapers*, ... Lord Mance held that journalistic judgment and editorial freedom were entitled to weight when considering how much detail should be published. That is reflected in [the amendment] which adds reasonable journalistic judgment to the list of factors to which the court may have regard when considering whether the defendant acted responsibly in publishing a statement. It is an objective test by the court of what was

---

[29] *Hansard*, HC Deb, 12 June 2012, Col 181.
[30] *Hansard*, HC Deb, 12 June 2012, Col 216.
[31] *Hansard*, HC Deb, 12 June 2012, Col 260.

a reasonable decision for an editor to make in the circumstances, and is relevant, for example, to rolling news coverage where there is little chance for extensive checking.[32]

The response of the Government, through Jonathan Djanogly MP, Parliamentary   **5.34**
Under-Secretary of State for Justice, was as follows:

The question whether the defendant has exercised his judgement responsibly goes to the essence of the new defence, and it would be very difficult and potentially confusing to include a specific reference to editorial judgement in the clause, as the amendment would do. It would effectively be saying that in deciding whether the defendant had exercised judgement responsibly in publishing the statement, the court should have regard to the judgement of the defendant. There is also the need to ensure that the defence is clearly applicable in a wide range of circumstances beyond mainstream media cases, and focussing specifically on editorial judgement in this way might cast doubt on that.[33]

It is very unlikely that the courts will cease to consider and give weight to the existing case law in interpreting the new statutory defence where they consider it appropriate to do so, and as such we would expect that they will want to continue to have regard to the *Flood* judgment. In addition the explanatory notes accompanying the Bill explain that the court does not have to determine whether it would have acted in the same way as the defendant, but merely whether the defendant acted responsibly, and that this means allowance will be made for what has been referred to in the case law as 'editorial discretion'. That should, I believe, provide sufficient clarity and reassurance that editorial judgement will continue to be taken into consideration by the courts without the need for a specific provision.[34]

On reportage the Under-Secretary of State had the following to say: **5.35**

The hon Member for Newcastle-under-Lyme asked why the reportage provision applies only in relation to a dispute to which the claimant was a party, and not to any kind of dispute. We consider it right to ensure that the claimant was a party because, where he is a party, one can expect him to have the opportunity as part of the dispute to put his side of the story or say why what the other person has said is wrong. A fair and accurate report of that dispute would generally include the two sides and, where the claimant is a party to the dispute, there is a safety mechanism built in that does not exist where the claimant is not a party.[35]

At the Third Reading debate the (by then) Lord Chancellor and Secretary of   **5.36**
State for Justice, Chris Grayling MP, said that the Government recognized the concerns which had been expressed about cl 4 and that his team 'has come to these issues relatively freshly in the past few days' and was 'open to continuing discussions'.[36]

---

[32] PBC (Bill 005) 2012–2013, Col 63.
[33] PBC (Bill 005) 2012–2013, Col 78.
[34] PBC (Bill 005) 2012–2013, Col 79.
[35] PBC (Bill 005) 2012–2013, Col 81.
[36] *Hansard*, HC Deb, 12 September 2012, Col 368.

(c) *Lords debates*

5.37 Clause 4 of the Bill as brought from the Commons to the Lords was the same as introduced to the Commons. The Explanatory Notes were also the same. There was continued criticism during the Second Reading debate, at the end of which Lord McNally, Minister of State for Justice, indicated the Government's intention to look at cl 4 'in light of the *Flood* judgment'.[37]

5.38 Lord McNally then introduced the majority of what became s 4 of the Act in Grand Committee. This represented several radical departures from the original proposal.[38] The requirement in the Bill as originally introduced that 'the defendant acted responsibly in publishing the statement complained of' was replaced with the requirement that 'the defendant reasonably believed that publishing the statement complained of was in the public interest'. The much-criticized checklist was removed. The reportage part of the clause was revised to refer to the 'reasonable belief' test, but no change was made to its substance. And a clause was added requiring the court, when determining whether it was reasonable for a defendant to believe that publishing a statement was in the public interest, to 'make such allowance for editorial judgement as it considers appropriate'.

5.39 In relation to the new 'reasonable belief' test, the Minister said:

Consideration of whether a publication was 'responsible' involved both subjective and objective elements. 'Reasonable belief' also does this, but we believe that it brings out more clearly the subjective element in the test—what the defendant believed at the time rather than what a judge believes some weeks or months later—while retaining the objective element of whether the belief was a reasonable one for the defendant to hold. The courts will need to look at the conduct of the publisher in deciding that question.[39]

5.40 In relation to the new reference to editorial judgement, the Minister said:

This expressly recognises the question of editorial discretion which has featured in recent cases, in particular in the *Flood* judgment. Although this provision is likely to be most relevant in journalism cases, it has been drafted in a way that does not limit it to that context.[40]

5.41 Later he said: 'I can assure the Committee of our view that the term "editorial" is not limited to editors or newspapers'.[41]

5.42 In relation to the removal of the checklist, the Minister said:

This is a difficult issue. Although we do not believe that the courts would apply the list of factors, based on those in *Reynolds*, as a checklist, we have responded to strongly expressed concerns that the use of a list may be likely to lead in practice to litigants and practitioners adopting a risk-averse approach and gathering detailed evidence on all the factors listed, in case the court were ultimately to consider them relevant.

---

[37] *Hansard*, HL Deb, 9 October 2012, Col 984.
[38] *Hansard*, HL Grand Committee, 19 December 2012, Col GC 533.
[39] *Hansard*, HL Grand Committee, 19 December 2012, Col GC 534.
[40] *Hansard*, HL Grand Committee, 19 December 2012, Col GC 534.
[41] *Hansard*, HL Grand Committee, 19 December 2012, Col GC 558.

We recognise that in the short term removing the list may lead to some uncertainty as the courts consider how the new defence should be interpreted and applied. However, in the longer term, the position will clarify as case law develops and, on balance, we consider that it is preferable for there to be greater flexibility than a statutory list might provide. At the same time, in determining whether in all the circumstances the test is met, we would expect the courts to look at many of the same sorts of considerations as they have done before. We believe that these amendments improve the Bill and avoid an overly prescriptive approach, while at the same time maintaining an appropriate balance between the interests of claimants and defendants.[42]

He said later: 'It has always been on my mind [during the progress of the Bill] whether it is necessary to raise the hurdle a little in our defamation legislation. This is an attempt to do so without being over prescriptive'.[43]   **5.43**

An amendment along the lines of what became s 4(2), requiring the court to take account of all the circumstances of the case when considering whether it was reasonable for a defendant to believe that publishing was in the public interest, was proposed by Lord Browne of Ladyton. It was not moved, but Lord McNally said the following in relation to it: **5.44**

I will think about it. As a layman, I tend towards thinking that there is nothing intrinsically wrong in writing the bleeding obvious into a Bill.[44]

In responding to the debate on the clause Lord McNally again appeared to indicate that it was the Government's intention not simply to reflect, clarify, or simplify the common law but to strengthen it in favour of defendants. He said: 'Yes, we are lifting the bar or moving the goal posts...Clause 4 is a genuine attempt to strengthen freedom of speech and should be seen as such'.[45]   **5.45**

However, in the Report stage in the Lords, the Minister then stated that the intention of cl 4 was to *reflect* the current law, particularly as it had been articulated by Lord Brown in *Flood*, where he said that the key question was whether: **5.46**

whoever published the defamation, given whatever they knew (and did not know) and whatever they had done (and not done) to guard so far as possible against the publication of untrue defamatory material, properly have considered the publication in question to be in the public interest?[46]

The Minister said: 'my absolute intention is for this part of the legislation to embrace and reflect *Flood*'[47] and '[w]e think that we have got it right and that what we have reflects the view of the noble and learned Lord, Lord Brown'.[48]   **5.47**

---

[42] *Hansard*, HL Grand Committee, 19 December 2012, Col GC 534–535.

[43] *Hansard*, HL Grand Committee, 19 December 2012, Col GC 536.

[44] *Hansard*, HL Grand Committee, 19 December 2012, Col GC 557.

[45] *Hansard*, HL Grand Committee, 19 December 2012, Col GC 558.

[46] *Flood v Times Newspapers Ltd* [2012] UKSC 11, [2012] 2 AC 273 at [113].

[47] *Hansard*, HL Deb, 5 February 2013, Col 198.

[48] *Hansard*, HL Deb, 5 February 2013, Col 199.

5.48 In relation to the revised reportage clause the Minister repeated what had been said on previous occasions about it being 'intended to catch the core elements of reportage as articulated by the courts'.[49]

5.49 The final piece of s 4, requiring the court to have regard to all the circumstances, was put in place by an amendment moved in the Lords at Report Stage. Lord McNally said that it was in response to concerns expressed that 'the courts would simply invent a new checklist' and that 'on reflection' it was the Government's view that 'it would be helpful to send a signal to the courts and practitioners to make clear the wish of Parliament that the new defence should be applied in as flexible a way as possible in light of the circumstances'.[50]

D. THE STATUTORY PROVISIONS

5.50 Section 4 provides as follows:

4 Publication on matter of public interest

(1) It is a defence to an action for defamation for the defendant to show that—
 (a) the statement complained of was, or formed part of, a statement on a matter of public interest; and
 (b) the defendant reasonably believed that publishing the statement complained of was in the public interest.

(2) Subject to subsections (3) and (4), in determining whether the defendant has shown the matters mentioned in subsection (1), the court must have regard to all the circumstances of the case.

(3) If the statement complained of was, or formed part of, an accurate and impartial account of a dispute to which the claimant was a party, the court must in determining whether it was reasonable for the defendant to believe that publishing the statement was in the public interest disregard any omission of the defendant to take steps to verify the truth of the imputation conveyed by it.

(4) In determining whether it was reasonable for the defendant to believe that publishing the statement complained of was in the public interest, the court must make such allowance for editorial judgement as it considers appropriate.

(5) For the avoidance of doubt, the defence under this section may be relied upon irrespective of whether the statement complained of is a statement of fact or a statement of opinion.

(6) The common law defence known as the Reynolds defence is abolished.

---

[49] *Hansard*, HL Grand Committee, 19 December 2012, Col GC 563.
[50] *Hansard*, HL Deb, 5 February 2013, Col 198.

E. KEY FEATURES OF THE DEFENCE

1. Section 4(1)(a): statement on a matter of public interest

The first of the two elements required to make good the defence under s 4(1) is **5.51** that the statement complained of was, or formed part of, a statement on a matter of public interest. Public interest is deliberately left undefined in the Act, but the Explanatory Notes suggest that it 'is a concept which is well-established in the English Common law'. It seems likely that Lord Bingham's approach quoted at para 5.17 will remain a fair guide as to the public interest for the purposes of s 4(1)(a). Other attempts at defining the public interest may also retain their influence. Lord Hoffmann in *Jameel*[51] considered that the Press Complaints Commission Code of Practice could provide 'valuable guidance' on responsible journalism generally. The Code provides that:

The public interest includes, but is not confined to:
i)   Detecting or exposing crime or serious impropriety.
ii) Protecting public health and safety.
iii) Preventing the public from being misled by an action or statement of an individual or
     organisation.

The Code also recites that '[t]here is a public interest in freedom of expression itself'.

It will be noted that the statement which is complained of does not itself have **5.52** to be on a matter of public interest, as long as it 'formed part of' a statement that was. The Explanatory Notes say that this is designed to allow the court to take a 'holistic' view of the article or other material in which the statement appears in its wider context.[52] It is clear that this question under s 4(1)(a) is a matter for the court to decide. The court is not directed by subs (4) to make allowance for editorial judgement in answering this question.

2. Section 4(1)(b): the defendant reasonably believed that publishing the statement complained of was in the public interest

There are two aspects to this second element of the defence. First, the defend- **5.53** ant must have 'believed' that publishing the statement was in the public interest. This subjective requirement was not present in *Reynolds*. The onus of proof is on the defendant, and it may require every defendant relying on the public interest defence to lead evidence from someone who took, or was involved in taking,

---

[51] *Jameel (Mohammed) v Wall Street Journal Europe Sprl* [2006] UKHL 44, [2007] 1 AC 359 at [55].
[52] Explanatory Notes, para 30.

the decision to publish. That in turn may give the claimant an opportunity to cross-examine that person on his or her stated belief, incorporating an interrogation of whether or not it was in truth held, by reference to its reasonableness (or otherwise). With its emphasis on the state of mind of the publisher, this may lead to a greater role for 'malice'-type arguments, which were rarely found in *Reynolds* cases. Indeed, in the early *Reynolds* case of *Loutchansky v Times Newspapers Ltd (Nos 2–5)*,[53] Lord Phillips MR giving the judgment of the Court of Appeal observed:

> ...in *Al-Fagih*, when deciding that verification may well not be necessary or even appropriate in a case of neutral reportage, we concluded that the reckless form of malice could not run. Although that left outstanding the claimant's plea of malice on the basis that the publisher's dominant motive had been to injure him, it may be doubted whether in truth there remains room for such a principle in a case of *Reynolds* privilege. Once the publication of a particular article is held to be in the public interest on the basis of the public's right to know, can the privilege really be lost because the journalist (or editor?) had the dominant motive of injuring the claimant rather than fulfilling his journalistic duty? It is a surprising thought.[54]

5.54　The second aspect is that the defendant must have 'reasonably' believed that it was in the public interest to publish the statement complained of. This appears to conflate the second and third stages of Lord Hoffmann's tests as set out in *Jameel*.[55] His second stage was whether the inclusion of the statement in the article (or other accompanying material) was justifiable as part of the public interest story. It is that decision which Lord Hoffmann considered required due respect to be given to editorial discretion.

5.55　　However, with no separate requirement of responsible journalism being set out in the Act, it is the reasonable belief test that must now bring in factors relevant to the previous common law test. The extent to which editorial judgement is relevant at that stage is less clear, particularly with Lord Hoffmann's statement in *Jameel* that the standard of responsible journalism was an 'objective' matter.

5.56　　It seems that, in effect, an element requiring that there has been objectively responsible journalism will remain. As Lord Mance said in *Flood*:

> It will not be, or is unlikely to be, in the public interest to publish material which has not been the subject of responsible journalistic enquiry and consideration.[56]

The Explanatory Notes to the Act make it clear that 'the intention in this provision [s 4(1)] is to reflect the existing common law as most recently set out in *Flood v Times Newspapers*'.[57] Ministerial statements upon introduction of the revised wording of s 4(1) in the Lords show clearly that the publisher's conduct before

[53] [2001] EWCA Civ 1805, [2002] QB 783.
[54] [2001] EWCA Civ 1805, [2002] QB 783 at [34].
[55] As to which, see paras 5.07–5.08.
[56] *Flood v Times Newspapers* [2012] UKSC 11, [2012] 2 AC 273 at [123].
[57] Explanatory Notes, para 29.

publication, including the steps taken to guard against publication of untrue defamatory material, will be highly material to the question of the reasonableness of belief that publication was in the public interest.[58]

F. DISCUSSION

1. 'Public interest'

It is important to keep in mind that the words 'public interest' in s 4(1)(b) have a very different role to those in s 4(1)(a). The question for the second limb of the defence relates to whether it was in the public interest to publish the defamatory statement in question, which brings in all the relevant circumstances.[59] But as to the first limb, the inquiry is directed towards the subject matter of the statement and/or of the article in which it appeared: was it a matter of public interest, or to paraphrase Lord Nicholls' second point in *Reynolds*, was the subject matter of public concern? **5.57**

2. Section 4(2): all the circumstances of the case—what will they be?

The court's duty under s 4(2) is to have regard to all the circumstances of the case in determining whether the defence under s 4(1) has been made out. That is subject to subss (3) and (4), considered below, in which specific statutory provision is made concerning reportage and editorial judgement. **5.58**

As alread.y noted, s 4(2) emerged following parliamentary criticism of the proposed checklist approach, with the stated purpose for its introduction being to prevent a judge-made checklist from springing up. One of the complaints about *Reynolds* was that it was difficult in practice to advise defendants (or claimants) pre-publication whether it would be effective as a defence. However, the existence of the 'checklist' did at least enable some structure to be given to an analysis of what should be done to enable publication at as low a risk a possible. Without guidance from the courts on which circumstances might be relevant and what their relevant weight might be, advising pre-publication is likely to become less certain again, at least in the early years of the defence. **5.59**

Nevertheless, it seems clear that Lord Nicholls's ten non-exhaustive factors listed in *Reynolds*[60] will continue to be relevant circumstances, in many cases some of them highly relevant, to which the court must have regard under s 4(2). The concern in Parliament about a checklist was that a list of relevant considerations might end up being treated as a list, backed with the authority of statute, of hurdles, each of which has to be surmounted in every case.[61] Lord Nicholls' **5.60**

---

[58] See paras 5.39 and 5.46–5.47.
[59] See further paras 5.58 et seq.
[60] See para 5.04.
[61] See paras 5.30 and 5.42.

list will continue to be useful as a reminder of the principal factors which *may* be relevant in particular cases, without being in any way exhaustive. For example, it will often be necessary to consider questions concerning the seriousness of an allegation that has been made (Lord Nicholls' first point), its context within the words complained of taken as a whole (see *Jameel*), the tone of an article and whether or not allegations have been adopted as statements of fact (Lord Nicholl's ninth point, which resonates with the subsequently developed law on reportage). These points also particularly require, as emphasized in *Flood*, due allowance to be made for editorial judgement. Then there will very probably have to be consideration of the source of any information used in the publication, the quality of any relevant human source's knowledge of events and the source's partiality or impartiality, the steps taken to verify the information, the status of the information and whether there have been any previous or related investigations, whether comment has been sought from the claimant and whether or not the words complained of contained the gist of the claimant's side of the story (see Lord Nicholls' third to fifth, seventh and eighth points). Although the timing of any publication will also be a 'circumstance' (see Lord Nicholls' tenth point), that, and indeed the urgency of the matter (Lord Nicholls' sixth point), have not featured prominently as decisive factors in the *Reynolds* cases decided under the common law. It seems doubtful, therefore, that timing considerations will take on any greater significance under the Act.

5.61   One circumstance which may, however, now come into play more than before is the nature and status of the publisher, to reflect the complaint about *Reynolds* that it was a counsel of perfection only available to those with the deepest pockets. Yet, the Act clearly requires a defendant to satisfy himself that publication is in the public interest, and the fact that he may not have the resources to do so does not relieve him of the requirement. The objective standard is, however, reasonableness, and the practicality, difficulty and expense of verification are no doubt circumstances to which the court must have regard under s 4(2), provided that verification was, in all the circumstances, sufficient to support reasonable belief that it was in the public interest to publish. 'No public interest is served by publishing or communicating misinformation.'[62]

3. Section 4(3): reportage

5.62   The extent to which reportage was distinct from mainstream *Reynolds*, and how it interacted with the repetition rule, was a matter of debate at common law. Cases such as *Jameel* and *Flood* had elements of reportage and elements of mainstream *Reynolds*. The open-textured nature of *Reynolds* allowed reportage elements of a statement to be taken into account along with other relevant factors. However, this part of the section contains prescriptive and mandatory

---

[62] *Reynolds v Times Newspapers Ltd* [2001] 2 AC 127 at 128B (Lord Hobhouse).

elements: it dictates, in reportage cases which are covered by the subsection, that the court's consideration of 'all the circumstances of the case' under s 4(2) must be skewed in what is only ever likely to be in favour of a defendant.

If the qualifying tests are met, namely that the statement, (a) was or formed **5.63** part of a statement on a matter of public interest, and (b) was or formed part of (c) an accurate and (d) impartial (e) account of a dispute (f) to which the claimant was a party, then the court *must* disregard any omission of the defendant to take steps to verify the truth of the imputation conveyed by it. The section does not leave a court with any scope even to investigate the circumstances of any relevant omission: it must simply disregard it.

There is a danger that this part of the section may absolve the publisher, on **5.64** the basis that bare denials have been made, from making any attempt to verify the truth of serious allegations before they are published. A *disagreement* about a matter of public interest can, for example, be generated deliberately by a false accuser, if the accused then denies the allegations. Whether that is a 'dispute' for the purpose of the Act, is almost a metaphysical question: in one sense it is, in another it does not seem to be what the subsection is aiming at. The more significant point is that the publisher must show that it was reasonable for him to believe that publishing an accurate and impartial account of the dispute was in the public interest. This will not be so if the 'dispute' is a mere Trojan horse to cover publication without verification of seriously defamatory accusations. The reason why the statute excludes consideration of the publisher's failure to verify is that it can be in the public interest to publish impartial reports of disputes on matters of public concern, and in such cases, verification is not merely unnecessary, but beside the point. For the publisher to try to decide which side is in the right means relinquishing impartiality with respect to the dispute.[63]

The Explanatory Notes to the Act say: 'Subsection 3 is intended to encapsulate **5.65** the core of the common law doctrine of "reportage" (which has been described by the courts as "a convenient way to describe the neutral reporting of attributed allegations rather than their adoption by the newspaper")'.[64] This suggests that 'reportage' is, following the Act, confined to the factual situation described in subs (3), neutral reporting of disputes. Ministerial statements in Parliament suggest the same thing.[65] But, the public interest defence involves a spectrum, with pure reportage at one end, and factual allegations made or adopted by the publisher, which require verification, at the other. In between are cases where a greater or lesser degree of suspicion is reported, of which some verification, tailored to the nature of the report, is required.[66]

---

[63] See on this Simon Brown LJ in *Al-Fagih v HH Saudi Research and Marketing (UK) Ltd* [2001] EWCA Civ 1634, [2002] EMLR 13 (p 215) at [49]–[52].

[64] Explanatory Notes, para 32.

[65] See paras 5.35 and 5.48.

[66] See Lord Mance in *Flood* at [158].

5.66   It is not inconceivable that there may be cases, not involving reporting of any dispute, in which it would be in the public interest to report an unverified accusation against another, made, for example by a politician or a politician's wife. Most such cases are covered by the privilege for reports contained in s 15 of the Defamation Act 1996 (amended by s 7 of the 2013 Act), but there might be others. It is suggested that the law of reportage should not be treated as in effect ossified by s 4(3), so as to be incapable of covering such a report. Section 4(3) contains the single example of a class of reportage in which verification is statutorily irrelevant. That does not mean to say that there may not be other classes of reportage, in which, in the result, the court may hold that the defendant reasonably believed that publishing was in the public interest, notwithstanding his omission to take steps to verify it. In such a case the omission to verify may be relevant, but not in the result decisive.

4. Section 4(4): editorial judgement

5.67   Whereas subs (3) concerning reportage could not be stronger in directing a court in its consideration of 'all the circumstances of the case' under s 4(2), subs (4) could not be less prescriptive in inviting the court 'to make such allowance for editorial judgement as it considers appropriate'. The Explanatory Notes say: 'This expressly recognises the discretion given to editors in judgments such as that of *Flood*, but is not limited to editors in the media context'.[67] It appears to involve no change from the common law.

5. Section 4(5): fact or opinion

5.68   Section 4(5) does no more than restate the common law in saying that the s 4(1) defence may be relied upon irrespective of whether the statement complained of is a statement of fact or a statement of opinion. Incidentally, it is difficult to envisage circumstances in which a defamatory statement of opinion would be protected by the public interest defence but would not also be protected by the honest opinion defence.

6. Section 4(6): abolition of the common law

5.69   The comments in Chapter 3[68] concerning the impact of the abolition of the common law of justification as part of the introduction of the new defence of truth have some resonance in relation to the similar approach adopted in the new public interest defence: see s 4(6). In the debate on the Lester Bill, Lord Hoffmann

---

[67] Explanatory Notes, para 33.
[68] See para 3.34.

welcomed the fact it did not adopt the American public figure defence, as some had called for, but said the following:

> But I am slightly puzzled by what it does do—which is to take the public interest defence, as laid down by your Lordships' House in *Reynolds* and *Jameel*, and restate it in its own language. I am always nervous, speaking as a former judge, about legislative attempts to restate rules of common law. They lead to expensive litigation over whether or not Parliament intended to change things. As the *Jameel* case appeared to be generally welcomed by the press and has been followed by the Canadians, I should have thought that there was a case for leaving well alone.[69]

However, *Reynolds* was a recent innovation in the common law. There is much **5.70** less encrustation around the central principles and thus less room for argument about what has and has not survived. Moreover, despite Lord Nicholls' hope in *Reynolds* that 'over time, a valuable corpus of case law will be built up',[70] the significant developments in the common law in this area have tended to seek to reduce reliance on the detail of previous decided cases, in favour of statements of general principle.

One thing that is clear from Hansard and the Explanatory Notes, is that **5.71** although by s 4(6) the *Reynolds* defence is abolished, Parliament did not intend to change the general principles for the availability of a public interest defence along *Reynolds* lines, such as that most recently articulated in *Flood*.

---

[69] *Hansard*, HL Deb, 9 July 2010, Col 432.
[70] *Reynolds v Times Newspapers Ltd* [2001] 2 AC 127 at 205.

6

THE NEW DEFENCE FOR
OPERATORS OF WEBSITES

A. INTRODUCTION

Section 5 of the Act provides an entirely new defence for 'operators of websites', **6.01**
who did not 'post' the statement complained of. The defence is unconditional in
respect of comments by identifiable authors, save where the operator has acted
with malice. In respect of unidentified authors, the defence is conditional upon
compliance with regulations, which have yet to be made. Many of the key terms
are left to be defined by the courts. As such it is difficult to assess the difference that the new defence will have in practice. It does not affect any of the
pre-existing statutory and common law defences for website operators, which
already provide protection in respect of the majority of complaints.

B. THE PRE-EXISTING LAW

1. The common law

(a) *Liability as publishers*

6.02 The general law of defamation is that any person involved in the publication of a defamatory statement is liable as a publisher, including, for example, the editor, publisher, printer, distributor, and retailer.[1] In respect of internet publications, court rulings on the question of whether persons other than authors or editors involved in internet publications are prima facie liable as publishers have not been consistent, at least as regards the period prior to notification of the existence of the statement. An internet service provider (ISP) providing its subscribers with access to Usenet discussion forums was held to be a distributor in the same class as booksellers and libraries in *Godfrey v Demon Internet Ltd.*[2] However, in *Tamiz v Google Inc*,[3] although the host of a blogging platform and website was held to be a publisher (at least arguably) after the point at which it received notice of the defamatory statement, the Court of Appeal's reasoning, based on *Byrne v Deane*,[4] suggests that the defendant was not a publisher prior to notification. Whichever is correct, a website operator will almost always be able to avail itself of a defence—under the common law or the statutes discussed below—prior to notification of the defamatory statement complained of.

(b) *Defence of innocent dissemination*

6.03 At common law persons involved in the publication of a defamatory statement only as a distributor, such as a printer, a retailer, or a library, are prima facie liable as a publisher, but will have a defence if they can establish that (1) they did not know that the material that they were distributing contained the libel complained of; (2) they did not know that the material was of a character likely to contain a libel; and (3) their lack of knowledge was not through their own negligence, ie that there was no reason that they should have known of the defamatory statement: *Vizetelly v Mudie's Library.*[5] Subject perhaps to establishing (2), this would provide operators of websites with a defence in respect of most complaints, at least prior to notification of the defamatory statement (in *Metropolitan International Schools Ltd v Designtechnica Corp*,[6] Eady J rejected the suggestion that the defendant needed to know that the statement was libellous, ie that it was defamatory *and* that there was no substantive defence available). However, the defence has largely been superseded by the statutory defences discussed later in this chapter.

---

[1] See, for example, *Gatley on Libel and Slander* (11th edn, 2010) para 6.4.
[2] [2001] QB 201 at 208–9.
[3] [2013] EWCA Civ 68, [2013] EMLR 14 (p 308).
[4] [1937] 1 KB 818 (CA).
[5] [1900] 2 QB 170 (CA).
[6] [2009] EWHC 1765 (QB), [2011] 1 WLR 1743 at [70].

2. Statute

(a) *Section 1 of the Defamation Act 1996*

Section 1 of the Defamation Act 1996 provides a defence to a person who is not **6.04** the author, editor, or publisher of a defamatory statement. An 'editor' for the purposes of the section is a person 'having editorial or equivalent responsibility for the content of the statement or the decision to publish it', while 'publisher' means a 'commercial publisher' whose 'business is issuing material to the public, or a section of the public' and who issues the material containing the statement 'in the course of that business', both of which may apply to (and thus exclude from the protection of the defence) website operators who operate a proactive moderation policy on user-generated content or profit from issuing material on their websites.

Section 1(3) sets out categories of those who are not to be taken as authors, **6.05** editors, or publishers and states that these may be applied by analogy to other situations. Two of these categories will include many website operators, namely persons who are only involved 'in operating or providing any equipment, system or service by means of which the statement is retrieved, copied, distributed or made available in electronic form'[7] or 'as the operator of or provider of access to a communications system by means of which the statement is transmitted, or made available, by a person over whom he has not effective control'.[8]

Once a defendant has established that he is not an author, editor, or pub- **6.06** lisher for the purposes of the section, the defence is established if he shows that he 'took reasonable care in relation to the publication of the defamatory statement'[9] and that 'he did not know, and had no reason to believe, that what he did caused or contributed to the publication of a defamatory statement'.[10] Under s 1(5), in considering whether the defendant took 'reasonable care' or knew or had reason to believe the matters in s 1(1)(c), regard must be had to 'the extent of the defendant's responsibility for content of the publication', 'the nature or circumstances of the publication', and 'the previous conduct or character of the author, editor or publisher'. This requires a potentially fact-sensitive investigation by the court and as such will in some cases rule out the possibility of summary determination in the defendant's favour (see *McGrath v Dawkins*[11]).

Section 1(1)(c) clearly excludes application of the defence once the defend- **6.07** ant has been given notice of the defamatory statement. *Godfrey*,[12] and *Tamiz*,[13] suggest that the defendant loses the ability to rely upon the defence immediately

---

[7] Defamation Act 1996, s 1(3)(c).
[8] Defamation Act 1996, s 1(3)(e).
[9] Defamation Act 1996, s 1(1)(b).
[10] Defamation Act 1996, s 1(1)(c).
[11] [2012] EWHC B3 (QB) at [44].
[12] *Godfrey v Demon Internet Ltd* [2001] QB 201.
[13] *Tamiz v Google Inc* [2013] EWCA Civ 68, [2013] EMLR 14 (p 308) at [44]–[46].

upon receipt of notice. However, where the time between receipt of notice and removal of the offending statement is short, a claim might now be struck out as an abuse of process.[14]

(b) *Electronic Commerce (EC Directive) Regulations 2002*

6.08   These Regulations implement Directive 2000/31. Regulations 17–19 provide defences to persons involved in various different aspects of the publication of material online: reg 17 for conduits (such as an ISP which merely provides customers with access to the internet); reg 18 for caching (storing copies of a web page in order to facilitate faster browsing by users) and reg 19 for storage. These apply only in respect of claims for pecuniary remedies, or in respect of criminal sanctions, but not for claims for injunctions.[15]

6.09   Regulation 19 provides a defence for a person whose involvement consists only in the storage of information provided by another, provided that:

(a) he did not have actual knowledge of the unlawful nature of the information stored, and was not aware of facts and circumstances from which that unlawful nature would have been apparent; or upon gaining such knowledge or awareness, acted 'expeditiously' to remove or disable access to the information; and

(b) the person who provided the information stored was not acting under his authority or control.

This defence is therefore available to website operators in respect of defamatory content posted on their websites by users (not under the authority or control of the operator), so long as the content was created and posted with the operator playing no more than a passive role, ie so that their activity in respect of the content is limited to 'storage',[16] and the operator does not have actual knowledge that the content is libellous, or of facts and circumstances which make that apparent, or has acted expeditiously to remove such material upon gaining such knowledge or awareness.

6.10   The key distinction between this defence and either the common law defence or s 1 of the 1996 Act is that the knowledge that is needed on the part of the website operator in order to render this defence unavailable is knowledge that the statement is unlawful (or of facts and circumstances which make that apparent), rather than that it is simply defamatory. This involves knowing that there is no defence available, and it will be a rare case in which a claimant is able to establish that a defendant has such knowledge, particularly as the defendant is

---

[14]   *Tamiz v Google Inc* [2013] EWCA Civ 68, [2013] EMLR 14 (p 308) at [48]–[50].

[15]   Electronic Commerce (EC Directive) Regulations 2002, SI 2002/2013, reg 20(1)(b).

[16]   *Kaschke v Gray* [2010] EWHC 690 (QB), [2011] 1 WLR 452 at [86].

not required to take a claimant's protestations at face value.[17] The reg 19 defence was therefore widely seen as the most generous available for website operators, at least prior to the coming into force of the 2013 Act.

C. BACKGROUND TO S 5

1. Criticisms of the common law and reform proposals

The Law Commission, in its 2002 scoping paper, *Defamation and the Internet*, **6.11** identified 'the liability of internet service providers (ISPs) for other people's material' as an area of concern.[18] The Commission noted that the safest course for an ISP, upon receiving an allegation that material on a website was defamatory, was to remove the material, whether or not it is true or in the public interest, and concluded that:

> There is a strong case for reviewing the way that defamation law impacts on internet service providers. While actions against primary publishers are usually decided on their merits, the current law places secondary publishers under some pressure to remove material without considering whether it is in the public interest or whether it is true. These pressures appear to bear particularly harshly on ISPs, whom claimants often see as 'tactical targets'. There is a possible conflict between the pressure to remove material, even if true, and the emphasis placed upon freedom of expression under the European Convention of Human Rights.[19]

The Commission suggested suitable reforms might include exempting ISPs from liability entirely (as in the USA), or extending the defence under s 1 of the 1996 Act 'accompanied by clearer guidance to ISPs on how to deal with the practicalities of receiving and responding to complaints, possibly through an industry code'.

No Bill was brought forward following the Commission's scoping paper, and **6.12** the desire for reform in this area may have been quelled by the coming into force on 1 August 2002 of the Electronic Commerce (EC Directive) Regulations 2002, just a few months after the Commission published its paper .

The issue was not mentioned in the House of Commons Culture, Media and **6.13** Sport Committee February 2010 report, *Press Standards, Privacy and Libel*, which was devoted in large part to considering reform of defamation law. Nor did it feature in the Ministry of Justice's *Report of the Libel Working Group*,

---

[17] See the discussion in *Tamiz v Google Inc* [2012] EWHC 449 (QB), [2012] EMLR 24 (p 595) at [57]–[60], overturned by the Court of Appeal on other grounds [2013] EWCA Civ 68, [2013] EMLR 14.

[18] See also the earlier paper: Law Commission, *Aspects of Defamation Procedure: A Scoping Study*, May 2002.

[19] Law Commission, *Defamation and the Internet: A Preliminary Investigation*, Scoping Study No 2, December 2002, para 1.12.

which looked at 'areas in which the case for reform has been urged with particular emphasis in recent times'.

It resurfaced as Recommendation 9 in the Libel Reform Campaign's *Free Speech Is Not for Sale* report[20] to 'Exempt interactive online services and interactive chat from liability'. The report stated:

While the author will always be liable for his or her writing—on a blog or elsewhere—the host should not be liable when material on their site is from a third party. This is an important distinction from traditional publishing and would be an enlightened reform, recognising that internet publishers do not always exercise editorial control but should be treated more like distributors.[21]

Of course, as *Godfrey* and other cases show, internet publishers who did not exercise editorial control were already treated in the same way as distributors.

6.14 Lord Lester's Defamation Bill[22] provided for a two-pronged defence for website operators. Defendants would have a defence if they could establish that either:

(a) their only involvement in the publication of the words complained of was as a 'facilitator', that was 'a person who is concerned only with the transmission or storage of the content of the publication and has no other influence or control over it';[23] or

(b) they were not a 'primary publisher', that is not an author or editor or someone with effective control over the author or editor, unless the claimant could establish:
   (a) that they had served a written notice giving the substance of their complaint;
   (b) fourteen days (or some other period specified by the court) had expired; and
   (c) the statement had not been removed from the publication.

The broad 'facilitator' aspect of this defence would have codified the effect of the decision in *Bunt v Tilley*,[24] that an ISP that merely provided access to the internet was not liable for defamatory messages sent using its services, but would also have reformed the law by providing those merely storing content with an insuperable defence. Those doing more than storing content online, but not having as much involvement as to amount to editing (which would have been a narrowly defined group) would have had a defence so long as they acted within a specified period in response to a properly detailed notice.

---

[20] See para 1.03.
[21] Libel Reform Group, *Free Speech Is Not for Sale*, 6.
[22] See para 1.06.
[23] Clause 9(1) and (6).
[24] [2006] EWHC 407 (QB), [2007] 1 WLR 1243.

No defence along either of these lines was included in the Government's draft   **6.15**
Bill of 2011. Instead, the question of whether greater protection was needed for secondary publishers (particularly those involved in internet publications), or whether
the law should be updated or clarified, was included as an issue upon which views
were sought. The Consultation Paper on the draft Bill noted that ISPs and discussion board operators sought greater protection, while others in the media and
the legal profession sought clarification on how the law applied to different online
activities, and on how 'notice and takedown' procedures should operate.[25]

Responses to the Consultation[26] largely supported greater protection for inter-   **6.16**
net intermediaries and discussion boards, with some support for something akin
to a system utilized in the US for copyright disputes, whereby the intermediary
is given immunity for acting as a liaison between the claimant and the author,
and need only remove the material if the claimant issues proceedings against the
author. Those opposed to greater protection for internet intermediaries emphasized that they were often the only person that could provide the swift removal of
the defamatory material that the claimant desired, and pointed to the difficulties
in identifying and pursuing those responsible for anonymous material.

Picking up on this last theme and tying it to an explicit social aim, the Joint   **6.17**
Parliamentary Committee's Report on the Draft Defamation Bill[27] in 2011 recommended that the law take a different approach depending on whether or not
content was written by an identifiable author: 'we expect, and wish to promote,
a cultural shift towards a general recognition that unidentified postings are not
to be treated as true, reliable or trustworthy'.[28] In cases where the author was
identifiable, the Committee proposed that hosts and service providers could
escape liability by publishing a notice of complaint alongside the material. The
complainant could seek a decision from a court as to whether content should
be entirely removed.[29] However, where the author was not identifiable (and did
not respond promptly to a notice from the host or service provider to identify
themselves), the proposal was that liability should accrue unless the material was
promptly removed; alternatively the host or service provider could seek a 'leave
up' order from a court.[30] The report also emphasized the desirability of hosts
or service providers moderating user-generated content, when the pre-existing
defences provided a disincentive to doing so.[31] It recommended that s 1 of the
1996 Act be amended, and liability determined by the response to the notice of
complaint rather than any involvement at the moderation stage.[32]

---

[25] Ministry of Justice, *Draft Defamation Bill: Consultation*, Consultation Paper CP3/11, March 2011, paras 101–122.
[26] Summary of Responses, 54–62.
[27] HL Paper 203, HC 930-I, 19 October 2011; see paras 1.08 and 1.11.
[28] HL Paper 203, HC 930-I, 19 October 2011, para 103.
[29] HL Paper 203, HC 930-I, 19 October 2011, para 104.
[30] HL Paper 203, HC 930-I, 19 October 2011, para 105.
[31] HL Paper 203, HC 930-I, 19 October 2011, paras 99–100.
[32] HL Paper 203, HC 930-I, 19 October 2011, para 106.

6.18 In its response to the Joint Committee's Report,[33] the Government stated that it agreed in principle with the Committee's aims,[34] but indicated that, having consulted internet organizations, it was concerned by the practical and technical difficulties inherent in requiring a notice of complaint to be published alongside the material complained of, and with the practical issues raised by the idea of the intermediary seeking a 'leave up' order, when the intermediary may have little knowledge of the truth or public interest issues raised by the material.[35] Concerns were also raised as to the drain on court resources, and the feasibility, of having courts as the arbiter of whether material should be permanently removed.[36] Instead, the Government Response favoured the 'liaison' system, in which the intermediary would be required to contact the author about the complaint, and to remove the material if the author consented or could not be contacted, but otherwise be exempted from liability, subject to passing on the author's contact details so that the complainant could pursue them directly. The Government recognized that safeguards would be needed to control the release of the author's details to the complainant to protect, for example, whistleblowers.[37]

2. The Defamation Bill 2012: parliamentary history of s 5

(a) *The Bill*

6.19 The clause in the Bill as presented to Parliament on 10 May 2012 did not explicitly adopt the 'liaison' approach that the Government had suggested it favoured in the response to the Joint Committee's Report. Rather it contained a straightforward immunity for 'operators of websites' in respect of statements posted by identifiable authors, along with a requirement for the operator to comply with regulations (to be made later) in response to a defined 'notice of complaint' in order to have a defence in respect of statements posted by unidentifiable authors. The details of any liaison requirements would, along with the other details of what was required of website operators where the author was unidentifiable, be left to regulations. The clause as introduced was very close to that contained in the eventual Act, save that there was no definition of the crucial term 'identify'; there was no reference to the effect of malice or of moderating; and, in respect of the regulations, there was no suggestion that they may affect what might be treated as a 'notice of complaint'.

---

[33] See para 1.20.

[34] Minsitry of Justice, *The Government's Response to the Report of the Joint Committee on the Defamation Bill* (Cm 8295, February 2012), para 80.

[35] Government Response, paras 78–79.

[36] Government Response, paras 82–84.

[37] Government Response, paras 85–88.

(b) *Commons debates*

The Bill's First Reading was in the House of Commons on 10 May 2012. At the   **6.20**
Second Reading debate on 12 June 2012 the Bill's Commons sponsor, the Lord
Chancellor, the Rt Hon Kenneth Clarke MP, described this clause[38] as 'the most
innovative and difficult part of the Bill'. He said that he was:

... very concerned that our current libel regime is not well suited to dealing with the
internet and modern technology. Legitimate criticism sometimes goes unheard because
the liability of website operators, as providers of the platform on which vast amounts
of information is published by users, puts them in the impossible position of having to
decide when to defend or censor information. Meanwhile, individuals can be the subject
of scurrilous rumour and allegation on the web with little meaningful remedy against the
person responsible.[39]

He went on to refer to the issues to be governed by regulation, stating that there
would be 'a procedure to put complainants in touch with the author'; that the
new defence would ensure 'that material is not taken down without the author
being given an opportunity to defend it', and that steps would be taken to minimize that risk that they might 'inadvertently expose genuine whistleblowers'.[40]

    Sadiq Khan MP broadly welcomed the clause on behalf of the Opposition,   **6.21**
saying that websites would benefit from greater protection 'if they help to identify
those posting defamatory messages' and that he hoped that this would lead to
'greater responsibility' both among those who operate websites and those who
post messages: 'People will know that they when they put a post on a website, it
is possible that their details will be passed on to a potential claimant bringing an
action'.[41] A number of MPs expressed reservations. Helen Goodman MP considered that giving website operators immunity in respect of statements on their websites, and thereby requiring complainants to pursue the originators of the statement was 'unfair'.[42] Robert Flello MP raised his concern that libellous allegations
may remain online if a complainant is unable to take action against the author,
including when some authors are 'impecunious and are out of the jurisdiction'.[43]

    In the Committee debates, Robert Flello MP moved an amendment to cl 5 to   **6.22**
expressly recognize that moderating content would not lead to liability where it
had taken place after publication and had not significantly increased the 'defamatory nature' or extent of publication of the words, or removed from them a
relevant defence.[44] He withdrew the amendment after Jonathan Djanogly MP,
Parliamentary Under-Secretary of State for Justice, stated that a court might

---

[38] *Hansard*, HC Deb, 12 June 2012, Col 177.
[39] *Hansard*, HC Deb, 12 June 2012, Col 177.
[40] *Hansard*, HC Deb, 12 June 2012, Cols 184–185.
[41] *Hansard*, HC Deb, 12 June 2012, Col 192.
[42] *Hansard*, HC Deb, 12 June 2012, Col 201.
[43] *Hansard*, HC Deb, 12 June 2012, Col 262.
[44] *Hansard*, HC Deb, 19 June 2012, Cols 83–86.

consider an operator who moderated a statement so as to change its meaning to make it defamatory or increase the seriousness of the defamation to be a person who had 'posted' the statement for the purposes of subs (2), and as such outside the scope of the defence; and that, further, to allow operators to be protected when they had increased the defamatory nature of a statement, but not significantly, would be to give them an unwarranted level of protection.[45] A similar amendment to make clear that moderating content would not bring with it liability unless the claimant showed that the defendant knew or ought to have known that they were facilitating the publication of unlawful material was withdrawn after Mr Djanogly observed that it would be unfair to put the burden of proving this on claimants. A moderator would escape liability if it complied with the regulations, subject to a court being satisfied that it should not be considered as having posted the statement.[46]

6.23 However, at the Report stage, the Government introduced its own amendment to make clear that moderation alone would not lead to a website operator losing the protection of the defence. In introducing the amendment Jeremy Wright MP, Parliamentary Under-Secretary of State for Justice, commented:

> There might of course be situations when an operator goes too far. They might, for example, moderate content on the website so much as to change the meaning of what the author had posted in a way that makes it defamatory or increases the seriousness of the defamation. In such cases, the courts will have to consider whether the operator's actions were sufficient for them to be regarded as having posted the material.

> We have considered carefully the merits of seeking to prescribe the particular circumstances in which moderation might or might not lead to the operator being regarded as having posted the material. Precisely when an operator should become responsible for a statement they moderate will depend heavily on the individual circumstances of the case. On balance, we think it is right that the courts should have flexibility in making that assessment.[47]

6.24 Paul Farrelly MP also moved an amendment to clarify the meaning of 'identify', by substituting 'sufficient identifying details...so as to be able to serve that person with legal process', but withdrew it after Mr Djanogly in response said:

> the word 'identify' in subsection (3)(a) is intended to mean that the claimant has sufficient information to make contact directly with the individual who posted the material. What constitutes 'sufficient' will obviously depend on the facts of the particular case. On a local discussion forum, where all users are known to one another, a name might in some cases be sufficient form of identification, but on a much larger forum, it is likely that some additional information, such as an e-mail address, might be required. Where an author refuses to engage with the claimant, either when direct contact is made, or by refusing to give

---

[45] *Hansard*, HC Deb, 19 June 2012, Col 86; see also *Hansard*, HC Deb, 21 June 2012, Col 121, and Lord Ahmad in *Hansard*, HL Grand Committee, 15 January 2013, Col GC 191.

[46] *Hansard*, HC Deb, 21 June 2012, Col 120.

[47] *Hansard*, HC Deb, 12 September 2012, Col 310.

consent to the website operator to pass his contact details on to the claimant, a claimant may apply to the court for a *Norwich Pharmacal* order to obtain the information necessary to bring legal proceedings against the author of the defamatory statement...The amendment would effectively require the website operator to provide the claimant with information that they are unlikely to hold, and that they would, in many cases, find difficult to obtain.[48]

At the Report stage, however, the Government introduced its own amendment in very similar terms, which became s 5(4) of the Act.[49] **6.25**

A variety of other amendments were moved, including to define 'operator of a website'. Mr Djanogly rejected this as: **6.26**

...unnecessary and potentially unhelpful. We think the courts will readily understand the term 'operator of a website'. In addition, given the pace at which the internet and technology are developing, to attempt to formulate a precise definition that provides a comprehensive list of the areas covered would run the risk of focusing on technology-specific detail, which could quickly become out of date.[50]

(c) *Lords debates*

In the Lords Grand Committee, Baroness Hayter, with whom Lord Phillips agreed, moved an amendment to replace 'website' with 'an electronic platform'.[51] Lord Ahmad responded that the purpose of cl 5 was 'to provide a defence to website operators that host third party content over which they exercise no editorial control'; and that the definition of 'electronic platform' might be equally problematic.[52] **6.27**

Baroness Hayter and Lord Phillips also moved an amendment to limit the defence to claims for damages rather than claims for injunctions. Lord Ahmed rejected this, noting the court's power under cl 13 to order take down after a successful claim against the author.[53] **6.28**

Lord Phillips moved an amendment to disapply the defence where there was malice or bad faith on the part of the operator. He said this would deal with the situation where an operator 'with an axe to grind against the person who is defamed may even welcome or encourage the posting of the defamations'.[54] Lord Ahmad responded that it was difficult to see how an operator who had complied with the procedure laid down by the regulations could be acting maliciously,[55] but later indicated that he would move a Government amendment to introduce the malice exception,[56] which became s 5(11) of the Act. **6.29**

---

[48] *Hansard*, HC Deb, 21 June 2012, Cols 107–108.
[49] *Hansard*, HC Deb, 12 September 2012, Col 310.
[50] *Hansard*, HC Deb, 21 June 2012, Col 120.
[51] *Hansard*, HL Grand Committee, 19 December 2012, Col GC 565.
[52] *Hansard*, HL Grand Committee, 15 January 2013, Col GC 190.
[53] *Hansard*, HL Grand Committee, 19 December 2012, Col GC 565; *Hansard*, HL Grand Committee, 15 January 2013, Col GC 190.
[54] *Hansard*, HL Grand Committee, 19 December 2012, Col GC 569.
[55] *Hansard*, HL Grand Committee, 15 January 2013, Col GC 195.
[56] *Hansard*, HL Deb, 5 February 2013, Col 208.

D. THE STATUTORY PROVISIONS

6.30 Section 5 provides as follows:

5 Operators of websites

(1) This section applies where an action for defamation is brought against the operator of a website in respect of a statement posted on the website.

(2) It is a defence for the operator to show that it was not the operator who posted the statement on the website.

(3) The defence is defeated if the claimant shows that—
  (a) it was not possible for the claimant to identify the person who posted the statement,
  (b) the claimant gave the operator a notice of complaint in relation to the statement, and
  (c) the operator failed to respond to the notice of complaint in accordance with any provision contained in regulations.

(4) For the purposes of subsection (3)(a), it is possible for a claimant to 'identify' a person only if the claimant has sufficient information to bring proceedings against the person.

(5) Regulations may—
  (a) make provision as to the action required to be taken by an operator of a website in response to a notice of complaint (which may in particular include action relating to the identity or contact details of the person who posted the statement and action relating to its removal);
  (b) make provision specifying a time limit for the taking of any such action;
  (c) make provision conferring on the court a discretion to treat action taken after the expiry of a time limit as having been taken before the expiry;
  (d) make any other provision for the purposes of this section.

(6) Subject to any provision made by virtue of subsection (7), a notice of complaint is a notice which—
  (a) specifies the complainant's name,
  (b) sets out the statement concerned and explains why it is defamatory of the complainant,
  (c) specifies where on the website the statement was posted, and
  (d) contains such other information as may be specified in regulations.

(7) Regulations may make provision about the circumstances in which a notice which is not a notice of complaint is to be treated as a notice of complaint for the purposes of this section or any provision made under it.

(8) Regulations under this section—
  (a) may make different provision for different circumstances;
  (b) are to be made by statutory instrument.

(9) A statutory instrument containing regulations under this section may not be made unless a draft of the instrument has been laid before, and approved by a resolution of, each House of Parliament.

(10) In this section 'regulations' means regulations made by the Secretary of State.

(11) The defence under this section is defeated if the claimant shows that the operator of the website has acted with malice in relation to the posting of the statement concerned.

(12) The defence under this section is not defeated by reason only of the fact that the operator of the website moderates the statements posted on it by others.

E. DISCUSSION

1. The scope of the defence

(a) *An operator of a website who did not post the statement complained of*
The section creates a defence for an 'operator of a website' in respect of a claim **6.31** for defamation over a statement posted on a website, where the operator is able to establish that it was not the operator who 'posted' the statement on the website.

The key terms in the section are not defined, and it will therefore be for the **6.32** courts to interpret them in the ordinary way:

'Website': while this will plainly apply to social networks, review sites and discussion forums, at least in so far as they are accessible by directing an internet browser to a particular URL, the term would appear to exclude the application of the defence to operators of similar services accessible via other means, in particular applications for mobile phones.

'Operator': given the references to moderating and removing content, an 'operator' of a website is presumably a person with effective control over its content. There are different levels of control of a website, and as such there may be more than one 'operator' of any one website. For example a blog site will, it is submitted, be operated by both the blogger and the owner of the website hosting the blog.

'Post': this is presumably intended to have a different meaning to that of 'publish', which occurs elsewhere in the Act (and is said in s 15 to bear the same meaning as it does in law of defamation generally). It may be that the intended distinction is that 'posted' is intended to refer only to the sequence of events leading to the statement becoming available to visitors to the website, as opposed to any steps taken to disseminate it subsequently, and not the general principles of liability for participation in publication.[57]

(b) *Moderation*
Section 5(12) provides that the fact that the operator 'moderates' the statements **6.33** of others posted on the website does not of itself defeat the defence. This is a curious clause, again lacking any definition of the key term ('moderates'), and referring to moderating of statements in general as opposed to the particular statement complained of (compare *Kaschke v Gray*,[58] in the context of the reg 19 defence). In the Lords debates the Government stated that the purpose of the provision was to provide a defence to website operators who 'host third party content over which they exercise no editorial control',[59] but it is difficult to see how moderation is anything other than a form of editorial control. For some websites, moderating involves simply automatically removing or blocking

---

[57] As to which, see, for example, *Gatley on Libel and Slander* (11th edn, 2010) para 6.4.
[58] [2010] EWHC 690 (QB), [2011] 1 WLR 452; see para 6.09.
[59] Lord Ahmad, *Hansard*, HL Grand Committee, 15 January 2013, Col GC 190.

swearwords or spam (see *McGrath v Dawkins*[60]), but for others it will encompass manually monitoring for and removing offensive content, including defamatory statements.

6.34   The parliamentary debates suggest that 'moderation' of a statement which had the effect of turning it from a non-defamatory statement into a defamatory one would attract liability, as would making the defamatory nature of a statement more serious.[61] The question is likely to be whether the process of moderating has involved sufficiently significant changes to the statement to mean that the operator should be regarded as having posted it itself. Despite the removal of uncertainty being one of the drivers behind this provision, this subsection leaves website operators with little indication of what they can or cannot do under the banner of 'moderating', and this is likely to be explored in litigation. Those websites without legally trained staff may therefore prefer not to moderate at all, rather than seek to rely on this uncertain subsection.

2. How a claimant may defeat the defence

(a) *Unidentified author, notice of complaint, and compliance with regulations*
6.35   The defence is defeated if a claimant is able to show that it was not possible for him or her to identify the person who posted the statement, and that the defendant did not respond to a 'notice of complaint' in accordance with regulations.

(i) *Unidentified author*   If it was possible for the claimant to identify the person who posted the statement complained of, without the help of the operator, the operator will have a defence unless the claimant can prove malice. In this situation, the operator does not have to respond to a notice of complaint, in order to preserve the defence. The operator will therefore have what is in effect a qualified privilege defence, virtually unassailable, in respect of posts by sufficiently identifiable authors. This could have provided a strong incentive to operators to ensure that they obtain and present on their websites the real names and/or contact details of the posters of statements, in line with the 'cultural change' away from anonymity that the Joint Committee report indicated desirable.

6.36   However, this virtual immunity will be available 'only if the claimant has sufficient information to bring proceedings against the person'.[62] This will generally require a physical address,[63] although an order for service by an alternative method (such as an email address) may be made by a court.[64] Many claimants will not have the poster's address, and may very well have no contact details at all, prior to contacting the operator, which is when the Government has said that

---

[60] [2012] EWHC B3 (QB); see para 6.06.
[61] See paras 6.22 and 6.23.
[62] Section 5(4).
[63] CPR r 6.6(2).
[64] CPR r 6.15.

the claimant's knowledge is to be judged[65]—after this time, it is the operator's compliance with the regulations that will determine whether it has a defence. It therefore seems likely that the 'identifiable author' defence will not be available even where the poster's real name appears.

This suggests that the purpose of the notice of complaint procedure is simply **6.37** to enable the claimant to obtain from the operator enough information about the poster to enable the claimant to sue them. The reference[66] to a requirement for action relating to the removal of the statement from the website presumably relates to action that would be required, to preserve the defence, if the operator is unable or unwilling to provide that information. This will become clear when the regulations under the section are published.

Where the claimant is unsure of whether the apparent author is in fact the **6.38** person responsible for the statement, for example if the apparent author denied having posted the statement, it would seem likely that, although the burden is on the claimant, they would be able to state that it was not possible for them to identify the author and, in such a case, the operator would be wise to comply with a notice of complaint, giving such information as is necessary to enable the claimant to bring proceedings against the poster.

(ii) *Notice of complaint* Subject to any provision in regulations, a notice of **6.39** complaint for the purposes of the section is a notice which:[67]

(a) specifies the complainant's name,
(b) sets out the statement concerned and explains why it is defamatory of the complainant,
(c) specifies where on the website the statement was posted, and
(d) contains such other information as may be specified in regulations.

It will be noted that the complainant need only show that the statement is defam- **6.40** atory, rather than unlawful. Amendments to change this were resisted in both the Commons and the Lords.

The informal consultation on the regulations issued in December 2012 sug- **6.41** gests that the regulations will require the following further information in a notice of complaint:[68]

(a) the complainant's name and a means of contact (for example, an email address);
(b) specific information to direct the operator to where the post can be found on the website (including a Uniform Resource Locator (URL));
(c) the statement complained of together with an explanation of how the state-ment is defamatory of the complainant, including (as appropriate) details

---

[65] Lord Ahmad, *Hansard*, HL Grand Committee, 15 January 2013, Col GC 193.
[66] In s 5(5)(a).
[67] Section 5(6).
[68] Paragraph 9.

of any factual inaccuracies or unsupportable comment within the words complained of;

(d) an indication of what the complainant takes the statement to mean;

(e) confirmation that the complainant does not have sufficient information to bring proceedings against the poster;

(f) confirmation as to whether the complainant is content for his or her contact details to be passed to the poster.

Since, by virtue of s 1 of the Act, a statement is not defamatory unless it has caused, or is likely to cause, serious harm to the reputation of the claimant, it is suggested that the explanation in a notice of complaint of why the statement is defamatory of the claimant will not comply with s 5(6) if it does not indicate how the statement is said to have caused or be likely to cause serious harm.

6.42   Under s 5(7), the regulations may also make provision for when the court may consider a non-compliant notice to be a proper notice of complaint. There is no indication in the consultation document about this, but presumably this will be a broad discretion for the court depending on all of the circumstances of the case.

6.43   (iii) *Regulations*   Much will depend upon the content of regulations, to be made by the Secretary of State. In addition to provisions as to the notice of complaint,[69] the section specifically provides that such regulations may make provision as to:

(a) the action required to be taken by an operator of a website in response to a notice of complaint (which may in particular include action relating to the identity or contact details of the person who posted the statement and action relating to its removal);

(b) time limits for the taking of any such action, including a discretion for a court to treat action taken after the expiry of a time limit as having been taken before the expiry.[70]

6.44   There are no regulations, even in draft, available at the time of writing. The most detailed indication available is contained in the informal Consultation Paper issued in December 2012, the contents of which are consistent with what was said during parliamentary debate. This suggested that, upon receipt of a valid notice of complaint, the website operator would have a short period, provisionally seventy-two hours,[71] to forward the complaint to the poster, and to ask whether he or she agreed to the statement being removed, and if the poster did not agree, to provide his or her full name and postal address and to indicate

---

[69] See paras 6.39–6.42.
[70] Section 5(5).
[71] Paragraph 12.

whether the poster was content for these details to be passed to the complainant (explaining that the complainant could nevertheless seek a court order for disclosure of those details).[72] The Consultation Paper also envisages that the operator would inform the poster that if he or she did not respond within a short period (provisionally seven days), the statement would be removed.[73]

If the poster refused to provide his or her name and address to the operator, or   **6.45** provided 'clearly false' details, then the operator would need to remove the statement from the website to retain the defence.[74] This highlights the problem that details may be false, but not 'clearly' so. There appears to be no reason why, upon the details turning out to be false, the claimant could not serve another notice of complaint, which should result in the removal of the statement.

The Consultation Paper envisages that where a poster provides the required   **6.46** details but refuses to allow them to be passed to the complainant, and the latter applies for a *Norwich Pharmacal* order against the operator, the operator should inform the poster of such an application, so that the poster may make any submissions he wishes as to why his or her identity should not be revealed.[75]

A procedure that allows a poster to determine whether or not his or her details   **6.47** are to be passed to a complainant may be justified in order to protect whistleblowers, victims of domestic abuse, and other vulnerable persons. However, it is difficult to see why posters would willingly allow their details to be passed to a complainant. The courts might consider providing a disincentive to refusal by ordering the poster to pay the costs of any *Norwich Pharmacal* application, at least where it was clear that a statement was defamatory and there was no legitimate reason for the refusal.

(b) *Malice*

The defence will also be defeated, even in respect of an identifiable author, where   **6.48** the claimant is able to establish that the operator acted with malice in relation to the posting of the statement.[76] This will be a very unusual case. The Explanatory Notes to the Act give as examples of cases in which malice might arise, where the operator 'had incited the poster to make the posting or had otherwise colluded with the poster',[77] but these are surely examples of where the operator might be considered liable because it had posted the statement, rather than as examples of malice.

Malice in defamation cases requires a dominant improper motive—which in   **6.49** practice will only be inferred where the defendant knew the statement was false, or was reckless as to whether or not it was false: *Horrocks v Lowe*.[78] Recklessness is unlikely to be considered a suitable standard for website operators, as they will

---

[72] Paragraph 13.
[73] Paragraph 13.
[74] Paragraph 23.
[75] Paragraph 24.
[76] Section 5(11).
[77] Explanatory Notes, para 42.
[78] [1975] AC 135.

often have no interest in whether a statement on their website is true or false, and it is submitted that they should not be considered 'malicious' simply on that basis or they might be considered malicious in respect of almost everything posted on their sites.

6.50   It will be very difficult to establish actual knowledge of falsity 'in relation to the posting of the statement'. Malice in this sense might have had a useful role to play in circumstances where the statement is demonstrably untrue and the original author is identifiable but impossible to pursue, such as where he or she has died, but the operator simply refuses to take any action. However, this seems ruled out by the clear wording of the subsection that the malice must relate to 'the posting of the statement'.

3. Comparison with s 10 of the 2013 Act and existing defences

6.51   Section 10 of the 2013 Act threatens to render s 5 entirely irrelevant for website operators who do not 'edit' content, as it provides unconditional protection in respect of any statement so long as they are not the 'author, editor or publisher' of the statement, and it is 'reasonably practicable' for the claimant to pursue at least one of those persons.

6.52   The court will naturally wish to avoid a construction of s 10 which has the result that website operators can simply decline to respond to notices of complaint under s 5(3), resting on their defence under s 10. This appears to mean that the court will not hold that it is reasonably practicable for an action to be brought against the author, on the footing that the claimant can obtain the information he or she needed through a *Norwich Pharmacal* action. The s 5 notice of complaint procedure is designed to provide a route by which the claimant may obtain the information, without having to go through a *Norwich Pharmacal* procedure.[79]

6.53   In respect of statements by authors whom the claimant is able to 'identify', the s 5 defence is plainly wider than the pre-existing defences, as only malice will defeat the defence. To this extent the new defence significantly increases the protection for website operators, although, as indicated above, sufficiently identifiable authors are likely to be a narrow class.

6.54   In respect of authors who are not sufficiently identifiable, website operators may prefer not to moderate or engage with the content posted on their websites at all, and instead rely upon reg 19, which protects them until they have actual knowledge of unlawful conduct (or the facts and matters which make that apparent), rather than to engage with the content and risk overstepping the mark on moderation or falling foul of some requirement of the regulations. On the other hand, an operator who wishes to carry out any degree of moderation will welcome the new defence as it will likely have gone beyond merely storing content

---

[79] See further on this, para 11.17.

for the purposes of reg 19, and may have become an 'editor' for the purposes of s 1 of the 1996 Act and s 10 of the 2013 Act. To that extent the defence is likely to further the aim of promoting moderation referred to in the Joint Parliamentary Committee's Report on the Draft Bill. As indicated above, however, the question of when (non-actionable) moderating ends and (actionable) editing begins is left open by the terms of Act.

The defence also provides a greater degree of protection than reg 19 in the **6.55** unusual (and perhaps only theoretical) case in which an operator gains actual knowledge of the unlawful nature of the statement, but does not wish to remove it. Section 5 will provide the operator with a defence so long as it complies with the regulations.

7

PEER-REVIEWED STATEMENTS IN SCIENTIFIC OR ACADEMIC JOURNALS

A. INTRODUCTION

Section 6 of the Act creates a new defence of qualified privilege relating to **7.01** peer-reviewed material in scientific or academic journals.[1] The section did not feature in the Government's draft Defamation Bill,[2] but was inserted as a result of a recommendation from the Joint Committee[3] as part of the pre-legislative scrutiny procedure and introduced by the Government at First Reading. It survived the legislative process as drafted, subject to one small amendment proposed in Grand Committee in the House of Lords clarifying that the privilege extends to electronic journals.

---

[1] Explanatory Notes, para 44.
[2] Ministry of Justice, *Draft Defamation Bill: Consultation*, Consultation Paper CP3/11, March 2011.
[3] HL Paper 203, HC 930-1, 19 October 2011, paras 47–49.

7.02   Whilst the defence may be new, its idea is not. A recommendation for a similar legislative provision was proposed by the Faulks Committee in 1975,[4] but not enacted in any subsequent legislation. Calls for greater protection for scientific and academic discussion featured prominently in the movement for libel reform which led to the 2013 Act and the enactment of the Act as a whole was in no small measure due to the perceived injustice of a handful of cases in this category which became cause célèbres in the campaign and subsequent parliamentary debates.

7.03   Section 6, however, provides additional protection for only one specific aspect of concern to scientists and academics—publications in journals—and would not have been of direct application in any of those cases. It is, however, one of a range of measures in the Act that is intended to increase protection for scientific and academic debate more generally.

B. THE PRE-EXISTING LAW

7.04   There was nothing approximating to s 6 of the Act in the pre-existing law. In one of the principal cases which led to calls for reform, *British Chiropractic Association v Singh*,[5] in which action was brought on a critical report in the *Guardian* newspaper about claims for the effectiveness of chiropractic treatment for various ailments, the Court of Appeal's decision was that whether there was evidence to support such claims was a matter of opinion not fact. Scientific controversy gives rise to divergent views, which may well be defensible as opinion, now under s 3 of the Act. That case would have been unaffected by s 6, and will continue to be of importance. Defamatory statements on scientific or academic matters may need to be defended by a range of defences, including traditional heads of qualified privilege (as to which, see, for example, *Vassiliev v Frank Cass & Co Ltd*[6]) or the public interest defence under s 4 of the Act.

C. BACKGROUND TO S 6

1. Criticisms of the common law and reform proposals

7.05   A number of well-publicized defamation cases from 2008 to 2010 led to widespread expressions of concern that the existing law of libel had the effect of stifling scientific and academic debate. That was one of the main criticisms of libel law made by the Libel Reform Group in its 2009 report *Free Speech Is Not for Sale* published by English PEN, Index on Censorship, and Sense About Science. Amongst the individual campaigners whose names became almost synonymous with the calls for reform were scientists and academics who had faced actual or

---

[4] *Report of the Committee on Defamation* (Cmnd 5909, 1975) para 232.
[5] [2010] EWCA Civ 350, [2011] 1 WLR 133.
[6] [2003] EWHC 1428 (QB), [2003] EMLR 33 (p 461).

prospective defamation actions such as Simon Singh, Peter Wilmshurst, Henrik Thomsen, and Ben Goldacre.

Of these, however, only two cases went to reported hearings[7] and all suc- **7.06** cessfully won their cases when the claim against them was either struck out or withdrawn, sometimes following an interim ruling in their favour under the pre-existing law. Some, however, faced large bills of unrecoverable costs and claimed with some justification[8] that the chilling effect of the proceedings caused them and others to withhold publishing material which they believed to be accurate and in the public interest. The driving force behind reform in this area of the law, therefore, can more accurately be described as the effect of the *threat* of a defamation action, rather than any actual deficiency in the previous substantive law which was ultimately not tested or found to be wanting.[9]

Be that as it may, faced with a rising tide of public opinion, the Government **7.07** agreed that something had to be done to increase protection for scientific and academic debate. In its Consultation Paper published on 15 March 2011, the Ministerial Foreword by then Secretary of State and Lord Chancellor, the Rt Hon Kenneth Clarke MP and Minister of State, Lord McNally stated: 'We are particularly concerned to ensure that the *threat* of libel proceedings is not used to frustrate robust scientific and academic debate'.[10] The Executive Summary noted the concerns raised about the detrimental effect the current law on libel is having on freedom of expression 'particularly in relation to academic and scientific debate'.[11]

Despite this, the draft Bill published alongside the Consultation Paper con- **7.08** tained no express provision relating to scientific or academic journals.[12] The Government's approach initially appears to have been to seek to remove or reduce the threat it had identified through the strengthening of existing defences, in particular the defence of honest opinion. In that regard, the Consultation Paper set out the competing arguments as follows:

Particular concerns have arisen in the context of a number of recent cases involving comment on issues of scientific and academic debate (for example *British Chiropractic Association v Singh* [2010] EWCA Civ 350). The view of those arguing for reform was that

---

[7] *Matthias Roth v (1) Guardian News and Media Ltd (2) Ben Goldacre* [2008] EWHC 398 (QB); *British Chiropractic Association v Singh* [2010] EWCA Civ 350, [2011] 1 WLR 133.

[8] See the intervention of Dr Julian Huppert MP during the Second Reading of the Bill, *Hansard*, HC Deb, 12 June 2012, Cols 238–239, who cited statistics from a survey by Sense About Science in 2010 purporting to show the chilling effect. Contrast this, however, with the evidence published by Tim Wogan in June 2010 (T Wogan, 'A Chilling Effect?' (2010) 328(5984) *Science Magazine* 1348), which found little or no evidence to support this phenomenon.

[9] As has already been said, in the *British Chiropractic Association* case, the Court of Appeal actually found in favour of Dr Simon Singh, and the claimant served notice of discontinuance after it was ruled his words constituted comment and not fact. The claim against Peter Wilmshurst brought by US-based company, NMT Medical, was struck out after the claimant failed to comply with an order to pay £200,000 in security for costs.

[10] Ministry of Justice, *Draft Defamation Bill: Consultation*, Consultation Paper CP3/11, March 2011, 3 (emphasis added).

[11] *Draft Defamation Bill: Consultation*, Consultation Paper CP3/11, March 2011, 5.

[12] Nor indeed had Lord Lester's Bill which had its Second Reading in the House of Lords on 9 July 2010.

legislation would assist in helping achieve greater clarity and earlier resolution of issues around the meaning and the distinction between fact and opinion. Set against this, some concerns were expressed that statutory provisions might add to uncertainty and could lead to disputes becoming more protracted and expensive.[13]

7.09 The Government distinguished its intention to extend qualified privilege to fair and accurate reports of proceedings of a scientific or academic *conference* or a copy of, extract from, or summary of matter published by such a conference[14] (one of the sources of publication in Peter Wilmshurst's case) and concluded that 'this may be helpful together with other proposals in the draft Bill in allaying concerns about the possible chilling effect of the current laws on scientific and academic debate.'[15]

2. The Joint Committee Report on the Draft Defamation Bill

7.10 The genesis of s 6 can be traced to the Joint Committee Report on the Draft Defamation Bill.[16] Describing the Government's proposals for reform as 'modest' the Joint Committee suggested that the Bill should go further to provide for 'improved protection for scientific debates'.[17] Its preferred method for improving this protection was to extend qualified privilege to fair and accurate reports of academic and scientific conferences and also to peer-reviewed articles appearing in journals. It so recommended.[18]

7.11 The reasoning of the Joint Committee was set out in the following paragraphs:

47. It is vital that members of the scientific and academic communities can engage in vigorous and uninhibited debate provided they do so responsibly and honestly, since their work helps to shape every aspect of the world in which we live. This includes medical research into matters of the greatest public importance. Historical examples include the safety of smoking or the risks associated with a drug such as Thalidomide, where the truth emerged over time thanks to persistent and impartial research. A process of critical review is essential through which the work of one person, or group, is published and subsequently challenged by others. It is unavoidable that these efforts to uncover the truth and expand the limits of our understanding sometimes turn out to be wrong or clash with the commercial and personal interests of other individuals and corporate organisations within society. For example, publishing research that reveals a particular product as unsafe or inefficient could seriously damage the business of its manufacturer, but may save lives. There is convincing evidence that defamation law is being used to silence responsible members of the medical and scientific community in order to protect products and profits. In particular, we were informed that 10% of all libel claims involve science and medicine, and that 80% of GPs feel inhibited in discussing medical treatments

---

[13] *Draft Defamation Bill: Consultation*, Consultation Paper CP3/11, March 2011, para 34.

[14] Which became s 7(9) of the Defamation Act 2013.

[15] *Draft Defamation Bill: Consultation*, Consultation Paper CP3/11, March 2011, paras 62–63.

[16] HL Paper 203, HC 930-1, 19 October 2011.

[17] HL Paper 203, HC 930-1, 19 October 2011, 3.

[18] HL Paper 203, HC 930-1, 19 October 2011, para 70.

publicly due to fear of facing a claim. At a cultural and social level, it is also important for historians, geographers, political scientists and other academics similarly to be able to research and publish without undue fear of litigation. We took evidence from various individuals who have first-hand experience of the lengthy and costly trauma of being dragged through the courts. For most academics and scientists defending libel proceedings is unthinkable, with the effect that important issues are either not being discussed publicly or at all.

48. The draft Bill goes some way towards tackling this problem by extending qualified privilege to include fair and accurate reports of what is said at a 'scientific or academic conference'. We welcome this development provided the conference is reputable. However, our inquiry revealed unanimous support for extending protection of qualified privilege to peer-reviewed articles published in scientific or academic journals, as recommended in 1975 by the Faulks Committee when the law of defamation was last reviewed comprehensively. Peer-reviewed articles are arguably the main platform for scientific and academic debate, and more reliable in their quality than conferences. Such articles may, in principle, be protected by other types of legal privilege, including qualified privilege and the so-called Reynolds defence, but the Reynolds defence in particular is often time-consuming and costly to make out. In our view a proper peer review process should lead to the publication being treated as responsible and should have special protection in the public interest without the burden of having to prove 'responsibility' in every individual case. Scientists and academics must not be left in fear of being sued simply for doing their job. **We recommend that a provision is added to the draft Bill extending qualified privilege to peer-reviewed articles in scientific or academic journals.**

49. This raises the question of whether the terms 'scientific or academic conference' and 'peer-reviewed article' should be defined within the Bill in order to provide clear and appropriate boundaries for these new categories of qualified privilege. The Government has stated that it would be difficult to provide a clear and comprehensive definition of 'scientific and academic conference' in statute. We accept that this is correct in principle and note that no witness has suggested a suitable form of words. The same applies to the definition of 'peer-review.' In particular, while the basic elements of peer-review are well established, the precise nature and extent of the process varies between different publications and subjects. Representatives of leading journals did not support attempts to include a precise statutory definition. We accept that leaving it up to the courts to interpret the meaning of these terms would provide greater flexibility for the future, but it would also lead to uncertainty and create greater opportunity for litigation and abuse. We note that the Committee chaired by Mr Justice Faulks proposed a registration system, such that conference reports and peer-reviewed articles appearing in scientific or academic journals would only receive qualified privilege where the organiser or publisher is listed in an official register. We are not convinced by the practicality of this approach due to the large and expanding number of journals in existence (now numbering in their tens of thousands), together with the resources required to determine which journals should receive such protection, and the risk that legitimate publications may be omitted from the list by ignorance or oversight. We are also concerned about the Government being called upon to determine which scientific or academic conferences or journals are more worthy of protection than others. It is preferable for the court to determine in any particular case whether the article or report is protected. In line with our core principle of accessibility and clarity, **we recommend that the Government prepares guidance on the scope of this new type of statutory qualified privilege in consultation with the judiciary and other interested parties.** Our aim is to enhance the protection of free speech by giving certainty to publishers who report on conferences and authors who contribute peer-reviewed articles to journals, but without repealing any part of the existing law.[19]

3. Government response to the Joint Committee Report and Summary of Responses to the Consultation Paper

7.12   The Government gave a sympathetic welcome to the Joint Committee's recommendation in its response to the Joint Committee's Report[20] and stated that it would consider further whether clear protection for peer-reviewed articles published in scientific and academic journals 'can best be achieved through qualified privilege or other means, and how key elements of the peer-review process can be defined to ensure that the scope of any provision is clear'.[21] Referring to the drafting problem identified in para 49 of the Joint Committee's Report, the Government stated that on balance it remained of the view that it was best left to the courts to determine in individual cases whether the defence should extend to the report of a particular conference and, by analogy, which journals should be protected.

7.13   Meanwhile, the Summary of Responses to the Consultation on the Draft Defamation Bill[22] revealed that of the 129 responses received, sixteen were from medical and scientific organizations and a further eight from academics, a combined total representing approximately one fifth of all responses received. The responses received revealed clear support for the proposed enactment of a statutory defence of honest opinion which it was believed would help rectify the position where those offering honest scientific opinions can be threatened by libel actions, especially when coupled with the removal of the public interest requirement.[23]

7.14   There was large support for the proposed new qualified privilege for reports of scientific and academic conferences and three responses supported the extension of privilege to cover peer-reviewed journals 'as these are an equally, if not more, important means of fostering proper scientific discourse and debate'.[24] In contrast, ten responses opposed the extension of qualified privilege to reports of scientific and academic conferences (and by analogy to journals) on the basis that 'not all those with academic tenure or who pursue knowledge through experimentation are reputable or authentic practitioners, nor is it true that all scientific or academic

---

[19] HL Paper 203, HC 930-1, 19 October 2011, paras 47–49.
[20] Ministry of Justice, *The Government's Response to the Report of the Joint Committee on the Defamation Bill* (Cm 8295, February 2012).
[21] Government Response, para 43.
[22] Published by the Ministry of Justice on 24 November 2011.
[23] Summary of Responses to the Consultation, 25.
[24] Summary of Responses, 35.

pursuits are aimed at finding the truth'.[25] Since respondents were not asked whether the peer-review process might overcome the risk of such abuses, it would not be safe to assume that these concerns can automatically be applied to the clause as drafted.

4. The Defamation Bill 2012: parliamentary history of s 6

(a) *The Bill*

The Bill as introduced to Parliament[26] thus contained an entirely new provision at cl 6 headed **'Peer-reviewed statement in scientific or academic journal etc'**. The Government had clearly decided to follow the Joint Committee's recommendation to accord qualified privilege to these types of publications and resolved the question of whether to include a definitive list of protected journals in the negative. However, a number of conditions are attached in order to attract the privilege and the peer-review process is further defined. This section of the Bill remained as drafted throughout its legislative passage through both Houses, subject to one minor clarifying amendment to subs (1), before receiving Royal Assent. 7.15

The Bill was accompanied by Explanatory Notes which confirmed that the defence was new and explained that the term 'scientific journal' would include medical journals. The Explanatory Notes are considered further in Section E of this chapter. 7.16

(b) *Commons debates*

The Bill's First Reading was in the House of Commons on 10 May 2012. At the Second Reading debate on 12 June 2012 the Bill's Commons sponsor, the Lord Chancellor, the Rt Hon Kenneth Clarke MP, opened with reference to freedom of expression being a cornerstone of a democratic society and stated that 'people should be at liberty to debate a subject without fear or favour, whether the matter be political, scientific, academic or anything else'.[27] He went on to state: 'we also want to simplify and clarify the defences available to those accused of libel. As they stand, the defences are sometimes unnecessarily complicated and too narrowly focused on cases relating to mainstream journalism, rather than the online world, NGOs, academics, scientists and so forth'. 7.17

Explaining the principle that underlies privilege, being that there are certain circumstances where a person should be able to speak or write freely and this should override or qualify the protection normally given by the law to reputation, he stated: 7.18

In a further important step forward for the protection of scientists and academics, clause 6 creates a defence of qualified privilege for peer-reviewed material in scientific and academic journals, as recommended by the Joint Committee on the draft Bill. The clause

---

[25] Summary of Responses, 35.
[26] First Reading, House of Commons, 10 May 2012.
[27] *Hansard*, HC Deb, 12 June 2012, Col 177.

defines key elements of the peer-review process to ensure that publications with appropriate procedures will now be given the protection of this new defence.[28]

7.19 Parliamentary Under-Secretary of State, Jonathan Djanogly MP, stated that the protection afforded by cl 6 was important in helping to encourage robust and open scientific and academic debate. He added: 'In drafting the clause, we have given careful consideration to defining key elements of the peer-review process to ensure that the scope of the provisions is clear and appropriate, and we are satisfied that it is'.[29]

7.20 In welcoming the Bill, various Members put on record their thanks to 'certain key people and organisations' who had helped to bring about reform of the libel laws, and the high-profile cases from the scientific and academic community featured prominently in those acknowledgements. Sadiq Kahn MP, Shadow Lord Chancellor, for example, referred to Simon Singh 'whose experiences of struggling with unbalanced and outdated defamation law stimulated a coming together of many scientists, academics, science campaigns, and national academies and institutes. We need to ensure that the threat of libel proceedings is not used to frustrate robust scientific or academic debate or to impede responsible investigative journalism'.[30]

7.21 Sir Peter Bottomley commended the evidence given to the Joint Committee by the editors of *Nature* and the *British Medical Journal* and referred to the case of the cardiologist Dr Peter Wilmshurst 'who faced an unending campaign from a foreign manufacturer of bogus products'.[31] David Lammy MP referred to the cases of Ben Goldacre, a doctor and health writer, and that of Hardeep Singh Kholi, a journalist writing on Sikh issues.[32] Paul Farrelly MP mentioned the same names and added: 'there is concern about the chilling effects of our libel laws on the medical and scientific community, and Sense About Science should be congratulated on bringing these arguments to the fore after several particularly disturbing cases'.[33] The same references were to crop up again and again in the parliamentary debates both in the Commons and the Lords as examples of the outdated English libel laws and the need for reform.

7.22 The problem with these references is that the cases came to represent a general need to reform the law without much clarity as to which areas or why. They conflated a number of different issues which are addressed at various places in the debates and in the resulting Act. Amongst these are: the importance of distinguishing between fact and opinion, the value of an honest opinion defence in scientific and academic matters, the applicability of traditional common law privilege, the raising of the threshold of harm before an action can be brought,

[28] *Hansard*, HC Deb, 12 June 2012, Col 182.
[29] *Hansard*, HC Deb, 12 June 2012, Col 263.
[30] *Hansard*, HC Deb, 12 June 2012, Col 188.
[31] *Hansard*, HC Deb, 12 June 2012, Col 189.
[32] *Hansard*, HC Deb, 12 June 2012, Col 218.
[33] *Hansard*, HC Deb, 12 June 2012, Col 230.

costs and the availability of Conditional Fee Agreements, corporations as claimants in defamation actions, foreign organizations and libel tourism, and the desirability of an early strike out or early resolution procedure. One or more of these factors was an issue in most of what may be described as the 'scientific and academic cases'. Publication in a peer-reviewed journal was not an issue in any of them and the availability of qualified privilege for that category of publication would not have made a difference to their outcome.

Consequently, there was very little focused debate on the details of s 6 itself **7.23** and *Pepper v Hart* material that will be of use to those seeking to discern the parliamentary intention behind its clauses is limited. The first actual dissection of the section itself came on the fourth sitting of the Public Bill Committee on 26 June 2012. Noting the clear consensus on support for the clause, Jonathan Djanogly MP repeated his assertion that 'clause 6 is one of a number of measures in the Bill that are intended to encourage open and robust scientific and academic debate'[34] and shed a little more light on the thinking behind some of its specific provisions:

He explained that the requirements of subss (1), (3) and (8):

stem from discussions we have had with editors of major journals, and they are intended to reflect the core aspects of a responsible peer-review process to ensure that only publications with appropriate procedures are given the protection of the new defence.[35]

In respect of subs (4) he said:

We consider it fair that reviewers participating in the process, who may need to assess the papers submitted by the author and comment on them, and whose assessments are published in the journal, should also be protected.[36]

He explained that subss (6) and (7):

establish that privilege is lost if publication is shown to be made with malice, and that a person who publishes material in a scientific or academic journal is not prevented from relying on other forms of privilege such as that conferred by clause 7(9) on fair and accurate reports of proceedings at a scientific or academic conference.

These ministerial statements do not add much to the Explanatory Notes. In **7.24** response to a question from Robert Flello MP as to whether cl 6 would have availed Simon Singh, in what he described as 'one of the best known examples...of the chilling effect of our current legislation',[37] Mr Djanogly answered 'No'. This is because the publication over which Mr Singh was sued appeared in the *Guardian* and not a peer-reviewed scientific or academic journal.

---

[34] *Hansard*, HC Deb, 12 June 2012, Col 138.
[35] *Hansard*, HC Deb, 12 June 2012, Col 138.
[36] *Hansard*, HC Deb, 12 June 2012, Col 138.
[37] *Hansard*, HC Deb, 12 June 2012, Col 138.

7.25   At Report stage on 12 September 2012, the same scientific and academic cases were again raised in the context of the changes to Conditional Fee Agreements and After The Event insurance under the Legal Aid, Sentencing and Punishment of Offenders Act 2012. It was stated that scientists and academics such as Dr Peter Wilmshurst and Henrik Thomsen would not have been able to defend themselves at all if they had not had the benefit of such arrangements. However, there was no further relevant discussion on cl 6 itself and the Bill passed unamended through Third Reading on 12 September 2012 for consideration in the House of Lords.

(c) *Lords debates*

7.26 The Bill's First Reading was on 8 October 2012. At the Second Reading on 9 October 2012 the Minister of State in the Lords, Lord McNally, opened the debate once again stressing the central part that the desire to strengthen the protection for scientific and academic discussion had played in formulating the legislation. He described cl 6 as 'an important step forward for the protection of scientists and academics'.[38]

7.27   As in the Commons, the Lords welcomed the Bill generally and acknowledged the role of scientists and academics in campaigning for reform. There were a number of informed contributions from, amongst others, Baroness O'Neill (herself a trustee of Sense About Science) on the distinction between anonymized and not easily evaluated content on the internet and peer-reviewed material in journals,[39] Lord Mawhinney, who chaired the Joint Committee, and Lord Bew, who led the discussion in that Committee on the need for what became cl 6. He expressed satisfaction with the method adopted in cl 6 of identifying the correct procedures for running an academic journal and a peer-review process, rather than adopting a list of approved journals.[40]

7.28   The only proposals to change cl 6 came in the third sitting of the Grand Committee on 15 January 2013. Lord Hunt tabled an amendment aimed at extending the protection afforded by the clause to scientific and academic material on the internet. This picked up on a concern expressed by Lord Triesman on Second Reading that the clause in its current form was not 'wholly future-proofed'. He referred to 'a trend towards digital publication and the encouragement of open-source provision of all information in science by the world's leading universities'.[41]

7.29   However, the wording of the amendment, which would have granted qualified privilege to peer-reviewed material 'on a website edited and controlled by a chartered professional or learned body', and another amendment granting

---

[38] *Hansard*, HL Deb, 9 October 2012, Col 934.
[39] *Hansard*, HL Deb, 9 October 2012, Cols 956–957.
[40] *Hansard*, HL Deb, 9 October 2012, Col 980.
[41] *Hansard*, HL Deb, 9 October 2012, Col 970.

similar protection to replies and commentaries on peer-reviewed material (without the requirement that they themselves be peer reviewed), were seen by the Government as going too far. Lord McNally reiterated the cautious approach that was being taken and stated 'we believe that it is important to ensure that only bona fide publications with appropriate procedures are given the protection of the new defence. That is why we have focused the clause on scientific and academic journals, where there is a well established process for peer review'.[42] He reminded the House that the draft clause had been shared with the editors of all the key journals in the scientific community who confirmed that the conditions attached were appropriate to ensure that only material subject to a responsible peer-review process would be protected.

Asked by one peer to reconsider the terminology used, Lord McNally said: 7.30

Let us be clear: right from the start, I wanted to provide protection for genuine academic and scientific debate. I have to say to my noble friend Lord Phillips that 'academic and scientific' is a term that is generally understood—it does not mean the *Beano*. People know one when they see one. Within that, there is also the important context that we are looking for genuine peer review, which, again, is understood.[43]

In the course of his replies to specific questions, Lord McNally confirmed that   7.31 the existing clause would cover peer-reviewed material that was published by such a journal in an electronic form. However, he added that he was willing to examine whether the Government had got its definitions and its scope exactly right, and welcomed the debate that Lord Hunt had provoked with his amendment. On that basis the amendments were withdrawn.

At Report Stage on 5 February 2013, the Government therefore tabled an   7.32 amendment to insert the words '(whether published in electronic form or otherwise)' after 'journal' in subs (1). Speaking to this amendment Lord McNally said that the intention was to confirm, as he had indicated in debate, that the clause did apply to journals published in electronic form 'to avoid any uncertainty on the point and to ensure that the position is clear'.[44]

The Minister also added some helpful clarification on the scope of the clause   7.33 as follows:

I would like to make clear, for the avoidance of doubt, that the term, 'scientific and academic journals' embraces journals in the very important fields of engineering and medicine and that any peer-reviewed material published by scientific and academic bodies in the form of a journal, whether electronic or otherwise, is covered by the clause.[45]

---

[42] *Hansard*, HL Grand Committee, 15 January 2012, Col GC 238.
[43] *Hansard*, HL Grand Committee, 15 January 2012, Col GC 238.
[44] *Hansard*, HL Deb, 5 February 2013, Col 239.
[45] *Hansard*, HL Deb, 5 February 2013, Col 239.

The Explanatory Notes to the Act also state that the term 'scientific journal' would include medical and engineering journals.[46] The Minister concluded:

We think it right that the defence under Clause 6 should be carefully controlled and not extended to discussion on scientific or academic issues more generally. However, we are confident that, in addition to the specific protection provided by the clause, other provisions in the Bill, such as the serious harm test in Clause 1 and the public interest defence in Clause 4, will provide more effective protection of the scientific and academic debate, as well as encouraging freedom of expression in other areas.[47]

D. THE STATUTORY PROVISIONS

7.34   Section 6 provides as follows:

6 Peer-reviewed statement in scientific or academic journal etc

(1) The publication of a statement in a scientific or academic journal (whether published in electronic form or otherwise) is privileged if the following conditions are met.

(2) The first condition is that the statement relates to a scientific or academic matter.

(3) The second condition is that before the statement was published in the journal an independent review of the statement's scientific or academic merit was carried out by—

    (a) the editor of the journal, and

    (b) one or more persons with expertise in the scientific or academic matter concerned.

(4) Where the publication of a statement in a scientific or academic journal is privileged by virtue of subsection (1), the publication in the same journal of any assessment of the statement's scientific or academic merit is also privileged if—

    (a) the assessment was written by one or more of the persons who carried out the independent review of the statement; and

    (b) the assessment was written in the course of that review.

(5) Where the publication of a statement or assessment is privileged by virtue of this section, the publication of a fair and accurate copy of, extract from or summary of the statement or assessment is also privileged.

(6) A publication is not privileged by virtue of this section if it is shown to be made with malice.

(7) Nothing in this section is to be construed—

    (a) as protecting the publication of matter the publication of which is prohibited by law;

    (b) as limiting any privilege subsisting apart from this section.

(8) The reference in subsection (3)(a) to 'the editor of the journal' is to be read, in the case of a journal with more than one editor, as a reference to the editor or editors who were responsible for deciding to publish the statement concerned.

---

[46] Explanatory Notes, para 44.
[47] *Hansard*, HL Deb, 5 February 2013, Col 239.

E. KEY FEATURES OF THE DEFENCE

The wording of the section, together with explanations given in parliamentary   7.35
statements and materials described above, requires little further explanation.

By subs (6) the privilege given by the section is lost if the publication is shown   7.36
to be made with malice. The Explanatory Notes state that 'this reflects the condition attaching to other forms of qualified privilege'.[48] Lord McNally said in
Grand Committee: 'That is, a defendant would forfeit the defence if they could
be shown to have acted with ill will or improper motive'.[49] In other words, malice
will take the form established in common law as defeating qualified privilege.

A difficult question may conceivably arise, as to whether publication of a fair   7.37
and accurate copy of, extract from or summary of the statement or assessment
could be privileged under subs (5), if privilege for publication of the statement
or assessment itself is defeated by malice. Publication of the copy, extract or
summary is, by subs (5), privileged only where publication of the statement or
assessment is itself privileged, and by subs (6), that is not so where publication
of the statement or assessment was malicious. The same point might arise under
subs (4) which protects publication of assessments of the merit of a statement,
but only where publication of the statement was itself privileged.

In the case of privilege for fair and accurate copies, extracts and summaries   7.38
under Sch 1 to the Defamation Act 1996, malice on the part of the person who
made the underlying statement is irrelevant. But it is not a condition of that privilege that publication of the underlying statement should have been privileged.

This situation would have some similarity to that provided for, in relation to the   7.39
defence of honest opinion, by s 3(6) of the Act. The court may consider that persons
who write assessments of the scientific or academic merit of peer-reviewed papers
should not have to concern themselves with the motives of anyone else involved in
the publication of the statement which is being assessed. Likewise, the court may
consider that persons who fairly, accurately, and honestly report peer-reviewed statements or assessments from scientific and academic journals should not have to concern themselves with the motives of those involved in the publication in the journal.
This could perhaps be achieved by construing the requirement that the underlying
statement must be privileged, as meaning privileged in principle, subject to malice.

F. DISCUSSION

As already stated, s 6 provides an entirely new statutory defence for publication   7.40
of scientific and academic matters in peer-reviewed journals as part of a range

---

[48] Explanatory Notes, para 48.
[49] *Hansard*, HL Grand Committee, 15 January 2013, Col GC 239.

of measures in the Act intended to accord greater protection to publications by the scientific and academic community more generally. None of the high-profile cases that gave rise to this section, however, would have benefitted from it as none of them concerned defamatory statements published in peer-reviewed journals. Such statements may also benefit from other defences under the new Act such as truth, honest opinion, or publication on matter of public interest, or traditional duty/interest or reply to an attack qualified privilege at common law.

7.41   Despite the straightforward scheme of the section, a number of its provisions could give rise to questions of interpretation. Perhaps the most significant of these relates to the process of peer review itself. For example:

• What degree of independence is the person who carries out the independent review under subs (3)(b) required to have? Given that one of the persons who is required to carry out an independent review is the editor of the journal, could the other reviewer(s) also be a member(s) of the journal's staff? It is suggested that what the section is aimed at is an expert review which is independent of the authors of the paper being reviewed.

• The subsection requires that the review be as to the 'statement's scientific or academic merit'. What is the position if one or more of the reviewers conclude that the statement is devoid of scientific or academic merit or is otherwise erroneous or misconceived? As it reads, the section purports to accord privilege by the mere completion of the process itself. In practice, this may not arise, since papers which fail the process of peer review do not achieve publication in scientific or academic journals. If a paper is controversial, it may be thought, on the basis of the debates which led to the section, that there is all the more reason for its publication to be protected.

• What degree of expertise is required of the person with 'expertise in the scientific or academic matter concerned'? In an appropriate case, will expert evidence be permitted challenging the expertise of the independent reviewer under subs (3)(b)?

7.42   It was stated in the parliamentary debates that the process of peer review was well understood within the scientific and academic community and that the provisions of the draft section had been shared with the editors of all the key journals who confirmed that the conditions attached were appropriate to ensure that only material subject to a responsible peer-review process would be protected.[50] The courts will have little difficulty in resolving these questions if the Bill's sponsors were correct in their assessment of the common understanding of what the process entails and its accurate transposition into legislative terms.

---

[50] *Hansard*, HL Grand Committee, 15 January 2012, Col GC 238.

8

REPORTS PROTECTED BY PRIVILEGE

A. INTRODUCTION

Section 7 of the Act amends some of the provisions contained within the **8.01** Defamation Act 1996 relating to absolute and qualified privilege. Just as the 1996 Act extended the availability of statutory qualified privilege provided for by the Defamation Act 1952 as a defence to a claim for defamation, the Act further extends the circumstances in which these defences can be utilized.

B. THE PRE-EXISTING LAW

The law recognizes that there are circumstances and occasions where it is in the **8.02** public interest that a person should not be held liable in law for publishing a defamatory statement, irrespective of whether or not he or she can prove the truth of the statement or defend it as honest opinion. Such occasions are said to be privileged, either absolutely privileged or protected by qualified privilege. Absolute privilege attaches to relatively few occasions but, where it does, provides the publisher of a defamatory statement with absolute protection, regardless of the truth or falsity of what has been said and regardless of his or her state of mind. Qualified privilege attaches to a much wider range of circumstances and statements. It is 'qualified' because the defence is defeated if the claimant can prove that the defendant was actuated by malice.

8.03 Absolute privilege and qualified privilege are conferred by both statute and the common law. Most of the law relating to absolute and qualified privilege is unaffected by s 7 of the Act, which amends only ss 14 and 15 of, and Sch 1 to, the Defamation Act 1996. An account and analysis of privilege as a defence to an action for defamation is beyond the scope of this chapter and readers are referred to the established texts on the subject. The changes made by s 7 of the Act, however, are set out and discussed later in this chapter.

8.04 One of the principal statutes conferring privilege upon a large number of specified communications is the Defamation Act 1996. Section 14 of the 1996 Act confers absolute privilege on fair and accurate, contemporaneous reports of court proceedings held in public, with such privilege being limited to UK court proceedings, proceedings of the European Court of Justice, the European Court of Human Rights, and certain international criminal proceedings.[1] Section 7 of the Act significantly widens this privilege so as to make it applicable to court proceedings worldwide, and to *any* court or tribunal established by the Security Council of the United Nations or by international agreement, irrespective of whether the UK is a party. The qualification that the court must be 'exercising the judicial power of the state' is retained.

8.05 Section 15 of the 1996 Act confers qualified privilege on a host of communications listed in Sch 1 to that Act. Part I of Sch 1 lists statements which have qualified privileged 'without explanation or contradiction'; Pt II of Sch 1 lists those which are privileged, 'subject to explanation or contradiction', the difference being that communications listed in Pt II will not be privileged if the claimant can show, '... that the defendant (a) was requested by him to publish in a suitable manner a reasonable letter or statement by way of explanation or contradiction, and (b) refused or neglected to do so'. Section 7 of the Act amends Pt II of Sch 1 so as to widen substantially the availability of qualified privilege subject to explanation or contradiction as a defence to a claim for defamation. Rather than focusing on and being limited to publications principally within the UK and EU Member States, the defence becomes more global in its scope. The law is also clarified in certain respects.

C. BACKGROUND TO S 7

8.06 Lord Lester's Private Member's Defamation Bill [HL] 2010–2011 proposed a number of changes to broaden the scope of the defences of absolute and

---

[1] Any court in the UK, the European Court of Justice or any court attached to that court, the European Court of Human Rights, and any international criminal tribunal established by the Security Council of the United Nations or by an international agreement to which the UK is a party.

qualified privilege. Many of these changes were adopted in similar form in the Government's draft Bill of March 2011. However, rather than repealing and replacing ss 14 and 15 of the 1996 Act, as Lord Lester's Bill had sought to do, the Government decided the most straightforward approach was to amend the 1996 Act.

The Government's proposals were originally set out in cl 5 of its draft Bill. **8.07** Those proposals were broadly welcomed and approved both by respondents to the 2011 consultation and by the Joint Committee.[2] The resulting clause in the Bill introduced to Parliament, cl 7, also had a relatively easy passage through the Commons and Lords. As a result, the wording of s 7 of the Act is very close to that which was originally proposed in cl 5 of the draft Bill, with only a number of relatively small amendments.

1. Absolute privilege

The draft Bill's proposals to extend absolute privilege to fair and accurate, con- **8.08** temporaneous reporting of a wider range of international courts and tribunals were similar to those proposed in Lord Lester's Bill and received strong support from both respondents to the consultation and the Joint Committee. The consultation sought views as to whether or not the Bill should attempt to define the meaning of 'contemporaneous' and, alternatively, as to whether or not the distinction between absolute and qualified privilege in relation to contemporaneous and non-contemporaneous reports should be removed—and, if so, which privilege should apply. Most respondents agreed with the Government's view that attempting to define 'contemporaneous' would be difficult and likely to lead to satellite litigation. Accordingly, the word is not defined in the Act. However, against the tide of submissions of respondents to the consultation, who felt that absolute privilege ought to be available for non-contemporaneous fair and accurate reports of court proceedings as well as contemporaneous ones, the Government decided to maintain the distinction, concluding that absolute privilege should be very carefully proscribed and that a distinction is appropriate primarily because publishers of non-contemporaneous reports have more opportunity to consider what it is they are publishing. Clause 7(1) of the Bill was broadly welcomed by the House, and discussion of the clause was limited.

2. Qualified privilege

Whereas qualified privilege under Pt I of Sch 1 to the 1996 Act extends to fair **8.09** and accurate reports of proceedings in public of a legislature, before a court and in other specific forums anywhere in the world, qualified privilege under Pt II was restricted to the reporting of certain matters taking place within the UK

---

[2] See para 1.08.

and EU Member States. It had been felt for some time that such territorial limitation made little sense in the internet age and that the law in this area needed modernizing.

8.10   The 1996 Act conferred Sch 1 Pt II qualified privilege on the publication of fair and accurate copies of or extracts from notices or other matters issued for the information of the public by or on behalf of legislatures of any Member State, the European Parliament, governments of Member States and the European Commission,[3] and also on fair and accurate copies of or extracts from documents made available by courts in Member States, the European Court of Justice, or by judges or officers of those courts.[4] Similarly, qualified privilege in relation to fair and accurate reporting of proceedings at public meetings and of the findings and decisions of certain associations was, under the 1996 Act, limited to those held within Member States.

8.11   Lord Lester's Bill proposed extending this privilege to publications relating to legislatures, governments, courts, public meetings and associations worldwide. As the Explanatory Notes to Lord Lester's Bill stated:

> There is no good reason why Part 2 qualified privilege should protect publication of a fair and accurate copy of or extract from a notice or other matter issued for the information of the public by or on behalf of the legislature or government of member States of the EEA [European Economic Area], but not of other States...The anomalous scope of Part 2 as it stands is emphasised by the protection given in Part 1 of Schedule 1, without a right to explanation or contradiction, to fair and accurate reports of proceedings in public of a legislature or government anywhere in the world.

In view of this and in response to concerns expressed by organizations that they were often being threatened by libel proceedings for quoting or citing public documents published in non-EU countries, for example in relation to corrupt activity, the Government decided that it would be in the public interest to extend the scope of Pt II qualified privilege to publications beyond the confines of the UK and EU. In this regard, the Government's draft Bill adopted similar proposals to those of Lord Lester's Bill, and including the proposal that qualified privilege should attach to summaries of publications as well as copies and extracts. The vast majority of respondents to the consultation and the Joint Committee strongly supported these changes, as did Parliament.

8.12   Whereas Lord Lester's Bill had included specific provision for the extension of Pt II qualified privilege to the fair and accurate reporting of proceedings at press conferences, the Government decided not to do so in its draft Bill because its view was that a press conference would generally fall within the definition of a 'public meeting' and so would already be protected by qualified privilege under para 12(1) of Sch 1 to the 1996 Act.[5] During the consultation, however, the majority of respondents on this issue supported making explicit reference

---

[3] 1996 Act, Sch 1, Pt II, para 9(1).
[4] 1996 Act, Sch 1, Pt II, para 10.
[5] *McCartan Turkington Breen v Times Newspapers Ltd* [2000] UKHL 57, [2001] 2 AC 277.

to press conferences in the Bill. Whilst most of these respondents believed that press conferences under the existing law would be privileged as public meetings, it was felt that the matter should be left in no doubt. Subsequently, the Bill presented to Parliament inserted a new paragraph in Sch 1—para 11A—making explicit reference to press conferences. Again this was welcomed by both Houses with limited debate on the issue. In the Committee debates Robert Flello MP moved an amendment to make it explicitly clear that privilege would attach to the contents of a press release. However, the amendment was withdrawn when the Government confirmed that the amendment was unnecessary because cl 7(5) was intended to reflect the law as it stands, the courts having recognized that a report based on material handed out to people attending a press conference is still a report of the proceedings at the meeting and thus covered by privilege, even though it may not have been read out during the conference.

3. Companies

In common with Lord Lester's Bill, the Government's draft Bill proposed extending Pt II qualified privilege to fair and accurate reports of proceedings at general meetings of companies worldwide, and in respect of publication of a copy of, extract from, or *summary* of the documents they circulate, rather than restricting the privilege to UK public companies, which had been the position under the 1996 Act. In support of this extension and to highlight what some saw as the unsatisfactory nature of the law, the consultation document gave the example of a case '...where criticisms of named British executives made at a general meeting of a Hong Kong registered public company with substantial interests in the UK could not be reported because they fell outside the ambit of Part 2'. The draft Bill suggested making this change by extending qualified privilege to 'quoted companies', which was to have the same meaning as in s 385(2) of the Companies Act 2006. The vast majority of respondents to the consultation supported the proposal that qualified privilege should be extended to fair and accurate reports of proceedings at general meetings of companies anywhere in the world and to the publication of documents they circulate. However, many felt that the scope of the extension to any 'quoted company' was too narrow, a view shared by the Joint Committee. Accordingly, in the Bill presented to Parliament, the Government changed the definition to any 'listed company', as defined in Pt 12 of the Corporation Tax Act 2009.[6] This extension was welcomed by the House and the provisions were enacted with only one amendment, proposed in the Lords, which extends qualified privilege to a fair and accurate copy of, extract from, or summary of any document circulated to members of a listed company relating to the appointment, resignation, retirement, or dismissal *of the*

8.13

---

[6] Corporation Tax Act 2009, s 1005: '..."listed company" means a company—(a) whose shares are listed on a recognised stock exchange, and (b) which is neither a close company nor a company that would be a close company if it were UK resident'.

auditors of a company, as well as of the directors. The amendment was accepted by the Commons, as it was viewed as being in line with general Government policy to increase the transparency of interactions between companies and their auditors.

4. Academic and scientific conferences

8.14   In response to widespread concerns raised by the science community, and in particular the disquiet expressed in connection with the British Chiropractic Association suing Simon Singh for libel, in respect of an article he had written and which was published in the *Guardian*,[7] the Government's draft Bill sought to introduce provisions which would allay concerns about the perceived chilling effect of UK defamation laws on scientific and academic debate. Accordingly, the draft Bill for the first time explicitly proposed that Pt II qualified privilege be extended to fair and accurate reports of proceedings at academic and scientific conferences, and also to copies of, extracts from, and summaries of matter published at such conferences. In the consultation, the Government conceded that Pt II qualified privilege may already apply to academic and scientific conferences, where they fall into the description of a public meeting or where findings or decisions are published by a scientific or academic association. However, it was felt to be 'helpful' to include specific provision within the Bill. Most respondents to the consultation agreed.

8.15   The Government decided not to attempt to define what constitutes a 'scientific or academic conference', as it was felt that a clear and comprehensive definition would be difficult to achieve and preferred to leave it to the courts to consider in a flexible way whether the defence should be available in the particular circumstances of a case. Again, most respondents to the consultation who expressed a view agreed, as did the Joint Committee.

8.16   The Joint Committee, whilst strongly supporting most of the Government's proposed changes in the draft Bill nevertheless considered that there were areas where the Bill did not go far enough, with academic and scientific debate being one of them. The Joint Committee's response to the draft Bill emphasized what it saw as the vital importance of the scientific and academic communities being able to engage in vigorous and uninhibited debate without the threat of libel proceedings hanging over them. Accordingly, whilst welcoming the extension of Pt II qualified privilege to academic and scientific conferences, the Joint Committee strongly recommended adding a provision to the Bill extending qualified privilege to peer-reviewed articles in scientific or academic journals. This recommendation was accepted by the Government and resulted in cl 6 of the Bill.[8]

---

[7] *British Chiropractic Association v Singh* [2010] EWCA Civ 350, [2011] 1 WLR 133.
[8] See Chapter 7.

D. THE STATUTORY PROVISIONS

As noted above, s 7 of the Act amends only ss 14 and 15 and Pt II of Sch 1 to **8.17**
the 1996 Act. A marked-up copy highlighting the changes to the 1996 Act is
provided in Appendix 2. Section 7 provides as follows:

7 Reports etc protected by privilege
(1) For subsection (3) of section 14 of the Defamation Act 1996 (reports of court proceedings absolutely privileged) substitute—
'(3) This section applies to—
(a) any court in the United Kingdom;
(b) any court established under the law of a country or territory outside the United
Kingdom;
(c) any international court or tribunal established by the Security Council of the
United Nations or by aninternational agreement;
and in paragraphs (a) and (b) "court" includes any tribunal or body exercising the
judicial power of the State.'
(2) In subsection (3) of section 15 of that Act (qualified privilege) for 'public concern'
substitute 'public interest'
(3) Schedule 1 to that Act (qualified privilege) is amended as follows.
(4) For paragraphs 9 and 10 substitute—
'9 (1) A fair and accurate copy of, extract from or summary of a notice or other
matter issued for the information of the public by or on behalf of—
(a) a legislature or government anywhere in the world;
(b) an authority anywhere in the world performing governmental functions;
(c) an international organisation or international conference.
(2) In this paragraph "governmental functions" includes police functions.
10 A fair and accurate copy of, extract from or summary of a document made available by a court anywhere in the world, or by a judge or officer of such a court.'
(5) After paragraph 11 insert—
'11A A fair and accurate report of proceedings at a press conference held anywhere
in the world for the discussion of a matter of public interest.'
(6) In paragraph 12 (report of proceedings at public meetings)—
(a) in sub-paragraph (1) for 'in a member State' substitute 'anywhere in the world';
(b) in sub-paragraph (2) for 'public concern' substitute 'public interest'.
(7) In paragraph 13 (report of proceedings at meetings of public company)—
(a) in sub-paragraph (1), for 'UK public company' substitute 'listed company';
(b) for sub-paragraphs (2) to (5) substitute—
'(2) A fair and accurate copy of, extract from or summary of any document circulated
to members of a listed company—
(a) by or with the authority of the board of directors of the company
(b) by the auditors of the company, or
(c) by any member of the company in pursuance of a right conferred by any
statutory provision.
(3) A fair and accurate copy of, extract from or summary of any document circulated
to members of a listed company which relates to the appointment, resignation,
retirement or dismissal of directors of the company or its auditors.

(4) In this paragraph 'listed company' has the same meaning as in Part 12 of the Corporation Tax Act 2009 (see section 1005 of that Act).'

(8) In paragraph 14 (report of finding or decision of certain kinds of associations) in the words before paragraph (a), for 'in the United Kingdom or another member State' substitute 'anywhere in the world'.

(9) After paragraph 14 insert—

'14A   A fair and accurate—

(a) report of proceedings of a scientific or academic conference held anywhere in the world, or

(b) copy of, extract from or summary of matter published by such a conference.'

(10) For paragraph 15 (report of statements etc by a person designated by the Lord Chancellor for the purposes of the paragraph) substitute—

'15   (1) A fair and accurate report or summary of, copy of or extract from, any adjudication, report, statement or notice issued by a body, officer or other person designated for the purposes of this paragraph by order of the Lord Chancellor.

(2) An order under this paragraph shall be made by statutory instrument which shall be subject to annulment in pursuance of a resolution of either House of Parliament.'

(11) For paragraphs 16 and 17 (general provision) substitute—

'16   In this Schedule—

"court" includes—

(a) any tribunal or body established under the law of any country or territory exercising the judicial power of the State;

(b) any international tribunal established by the Security Council of the United Nations or by an international agreement;

(c) any international tribunal deciding matters in dispute between States;

"international conference" means a conference attended by representatives of two or more governments;

"international organisation" means an organisation of which two or more governments are members, and includes any committee or other subordinate body of such an organisation;

"legislature" includes a local legislature; and

"member State" includes any European dependent territory of a member State.'

E. KEY FEATURES OF THE AMENDMENTS

8.18 Subsection (1) of s 7 of the Act amends and replaces subs (3) of s 14 of the 1996 Act, which concerns the application of absolute privilege to fair and accurate contemporaneous reports of court proceedings. The amendment extends the scope of the defence so that it now covers proceedings in any court established under the law of a country or territory outside the UK, and any international court or tribunal established by the Security Council of the United Nations or by an international agreement, in addition to what was covered previously.[9]

Subsection (2) replaces the expression 'public concern' with the expression **8.19** 'public interest' in s 15(3) of the 1996 Act. Section 15(3) now reads:

This section does not apply to the publication to the public, or a section of the public, of matter which is not of public interest and the publication of which is not for the public benefit.

This is intended to ensure conformity of terminology within the Act and to prevent any possible confusion arising from the use of two different terms with the same meaning in the Act and in the 1996 Act.[10] The same amendment is made by s 7(6)(b) of the Act to para 12(2) of Sch 1 to the 1996 Act in relation to the privilege extended to fair and accurate reports etc of public meetings. Paragraph 12(2) now reads:

In this paragraph 'public meeting' means a meeting bona fide and lawfully held for a lawful purpose and for the furtherance or discussion of a matter of public interest whether admission to the meeting is general or restricted.

Section 7(3)–(10) of the Act amends Pt II of Sch 1 to the 1996 Act, substantially **8.20** extending the circumstances in which qualified privilege as a defence to a claim for defamation is available.

As noted above, s 15 of and Sch 1 to the 1996 Act confer qualified privilege on **8.21** various types of publications, provided they are fair and accurate, on a matter of public concern, and that publication is for the public benefit and not made with malice. Part 2 of Sch 1 sets out categories of publication which are protected by qualified privilege unless the publisher refuses or neglects to publish, in a suitable manner, a reasonable letter or statement by way of explanation or correction when requested to do so. The categories include copies of or extracts from information for the public published by government or authorities performing governmental functions (such as the police)[11] or by courts,[12] reports of proceedings at a range of public meetings,[13] general meetings of UK public companies,[14] and reports of findings or decisions by a range of associations[15] formed in the UK or the EU.

---

[9] Under the 1996 Act, privilege was restricted to fair and accurate reports of proceedings in public before UK courts, the European Court of Justice or any court attached to that court, the European Court of Human Rights, and any international criminal tribunal established by the Security Council of the United Nations or by an international agreement to which the UK is a party.

[10] Explanatory Notes, para 51.

[11] 1996 Act, Sch 1, para 9.

[12] 1996 Act, Sch 1, para 10.

[13] 1996 Act, Sch 1, paras 11–12.

[14] 1996 Act, Sch 1, para 13.

[15] 1996 Act, Sch 1, para 14.

8.22   In addition to qualified privilege attaching to fair and accurate *copies of or extracts from* various types of publication, subss (4), (7)(b), and (10) of s 7 of the Act extend the scope of qualified privilege to cover fair and accurate *summaries* of material.

8.23   As noted above, qualified privilege under Pt II of the 1996 Act only applied to publications arising in the UK and EU Member States. The scope of the defence is now extended by s 7(4), (6)(a), (7), and (8) of the Act to anywhere in the world. For example, para 12 of Sch 1 to the 1996 Act will now read: '(1) A fair and accurate report of proceedings at any public meeting held anywhere in the world . . .'.

8.25   Section 7(5) inserts a new para 11A into Pt II of Sch 1 to the 1996 Act explicitly providing for qualified privilege to extend to a fair and accurate report of proceedings at a press conference held anywhere in the world for the discussion of a matter of public interest. Whilst arguably unnecessary, as most press conferences would, in any event, be protected as public meetings under para 12 of Sch 1 to the 1996 Act, this specific provision was added for clarity.

8.26   The 1996 Act (Sch 1, Pt II, para 13) restricted qualified privilege to fair and accurate reports of proceedings at general meetings and documents circulated by UK public companies only. Section 7(7) extends this to reports relating to companies worldwide whose shares are listed on a recognized stock exchange by extending the provision to 'listed companies'.[16]

8.27   Part II qualified privilege is explicitly extended to fair and accurate reports of proceedings of a scientific or academic conference, and to copies, extracts, and summaries of matter published by such conferences by s 7(9) of the Act, which adds a new paragraph to Pt II of Sch 1 to the 1996 Act—para 14A. Whilst academic and scientific conferences may have been covered in any event under the old law, for example where they fall within para 12 of Sch 1 as a 'public meeting' or where findings or decisions are published by a scientific or academic association (Sch 1, para 14), the amendments were considered to be necessary to ensure that nothing fell through the net. This new provision along with s 6 of the Act fulfils the Government's aim of ensuring that scientific and academic debate is protected and not stifled by what some saw as the UK's overly claimant-friendly libel laws. For a fuller account of the pressure, inside and outside Parliament, for greater protection for scientific and academic debate, see Chapter 7.

8.28   As the Explanatory Notes to s 7 state, 'Subsection (11) substitutes new general provisions in Schedule 1 to reflect the changes that have been made to the substance of the Schedule'.[17]

---

[16] The term 'listed company' is to have the same meaning as in Pt 12 of the Corporation Tax Act 2009, that is '. . . a company— (a) whose shares are listed on a recognised stock exchange, and (b) which is neither a close company nor a company that would be a close company if it were UK resident' (s 1005).

[17] Explanatory Notes, para 59.

F. DISCUSSION

The Government's approach of effecting change by amending parts of the **8.29** Defamation Act 1996, rather than a more radical overhaul and restatement of the entirety of this area of the law in one place, as Lord Lester proposed in his Bill, may attract criticism from some quarters. In addition, the amendments will have done little to appease those who consider Sch 1 to the 1996 Act to be complex and difficult to interpret, especially by non-specialists.

The Act also makes no change to the law relating to the reporting of parlia- **8.30** mentary proceedings, which are protected by a somewhat complex mix of statute, in particular the Parliamentary Papers Act 1840, and the common law. Some no doubt will see this as a missed opportunity. As far back as 1999, the Joint Committee on Parliamentary Privilege commented on the 'somewhat impenetrable early Victorian style' of the Parliamentary Papers Act and recommended that whilst in effect the law be retained, that particular Act should be repealed and the law restated in a modern statute, in a more transparent and accessible manner. Moreover, this recommendation was later endorsed by the House of Commons Culture, Media and Sport Committee in its report *Press Standards, Privacy and Libel* published in 2010. It was certainly Lord Lester's approach in his Bill. However, attempts by him to have such a provision included in the Government's Bill were resisted, the Government deciding to leave parliamentary privilege and associated issues to a Joint Committee currently considering a government Green Paper on more widespread parliamentary privilege reform.

In spite of these limitations, the extension of privilege by s 7 of the Act to **8.31** summaries of material, as well as to reports and copies; the broadening internationally of the scope of the circumstances in which privilege applies; and the clarifications that qualified privilege extends to reports of scientific and academic conferences and of press conferences are widely welcomed. The territorial limitations contained within Pt II of Sch 1 to the 1996 Act were inconsistent with the provisions of Pt I, without any proper justification and seemed simply outdated in today's modern world of global publication. The law is unarguably modernized and clarified in certain important respects.

9

THE SINGLE PUBLICATION RULE

A. INTRODUCTION

9.01 Section 8 of the Act is an example of reform rather than codification of the common law of defamation. It establishes a new rule, the 'single publication rule', aimed at reducing the number of libel actions brought in respect of what might be called stale publications. This replaces the well-established rule of the English common law that each publication of a libel to a third party gives rise to a fresh cause of action, with its own limitation period running from the time of that publication.[1]

9.02 As will be seen, the new rule only applies to material which has already been published to the public or to a section of the public. Furthermore, it does not apply where the statement subsequently published is not substantially the same as the original, or is published in a materially different manner from the original, or is published by someone else. Yet further, the statutory discretion to disapply the one-year limitation period is expressly preserved for cases where the new rule would otherwise work injustice.

---

[1] *Duke of Brunswick v Harmer* (1849) 14 QB 185.

127

B. THE PRE-EXISTING LAW

9.03 The principle of the common law that each publication of defamatory matter constitutes a separate cause of action goes back more than 150 years. In *Duke of Brunswick v Harmer*[2] the plaintiff sent his agent to buy a copy of a newspaper containing an article defamatory of him seventeen years after it had been published. The Court of Queen's Bench rejected the defendant's argument that the limitation period (then six years, now one) should be taken to have run from the original date of publication of the newspaper. The handing over of one back copy of the newspaper to the agent constituted a separate and fresh cause of action upon which proceedings could be brought. This became known as 'the rule in the *Duke of Brunswick*' (described in the Government's Consultation Document and the Explanatory Notes as 'the multiple publication rule').

9.04 This rule was regarded—without criticism—as an established feature of the common law by the House of Lords in *Berezovsky v Michaels*.[3] In *Loutchansky v Times Newspapers Ltd*[4] the Court of Appeal rejected the defendant newspaper's argument that in order to be compatible with Article 10 of the European Convention on Human Rights the common law should develop as it had in the USA, where a single publication rule had been adopted by the majority of state jurisdictions starting in the late 1940s.[5] Interestingly, the court did not regard the social utility of archives as so great as to merit a change in the law. Lord Phillips MR put it this way:

> We accept that the maintenance of archives, whether in hard copy or on the internet, has a social utility, but consider that the maintenance of archives is a comparatively insignificant aspect of freedom of expression. Archive material is stale news and its publication cannot rank in importance with the dissemination of contemporary material. Nor do we believe that the law of defamation need inhibit the responsible maintenance of archives. Where it is known that archive material is or may be defamatory, the attachment of an appropriate notice warning against treating it as the truth will normally remove any sting from the material.[6]

9.05 It is perhaps also worth noting that the defendant's argument in *Loutchansky* expressly recognized that the proposed single publication rule should be subject to certain qualifications, as it was in the USA. Thus, for example, it would apply to all sales of the first edition of a book, but if a new edition were to be published, or a softback edition, or even a reprinting, time would start to run again.[7]

9.06 For completeness, it may also be noted that the newspaper subsequently sought to persuade the European Court of Human Rights that the existing law was

---

[2] (1849) 14 QB 185.
[3] [2000] 1 WLR 2004.
[4] [2001] EWCA Civ 1805, [2002] QB 783.
[5] See, for example, *Gregoire v GP Putnam's Sons* 81 NE2d 45 (1948).
[6] *Loutchansky v Times Newspapers Ltd* [2001] EWCA Civ 1805, [2002] QB 783 at [74].
[7] *Loutchansky v Times Newspapers Ltd* [2001] EWCA Civ 1805, [2002] QB 783 at [63].

contrary to Article 10 of the European Convention on Human Rights. The argument failed.[8] Given the facts of the case, that is perhaps hardly surprising: the newspaper had sought to invoke the single publication rule so as to plead a limitation defence to a second action brought against it one year after the first. But the second claim had only been brought because the newspaper had refused to take down or in any way qualify the text of the original articles. The European Court of Human Rights accepted that newspaper archives constituted an important source for education and historical research, but added that 'the duty of the press to act in accordance with the principles of responsible journalism by ensuring the accuracy of historical, rather than perishable, information published is likely to be more stringent in the absence of any urgency in publishing the material'.[9]

As regards the potential injustice caused by the rule in the *Duke of Brunswick*, **9.07**
the court observed that on the facts no hardship could be said to have been suffered by the newspaper. But it continued:

> The Court would, however, emphasise that while an aggrieved applicant must be afforded a real opportunity to vindicate his right to reputation, libel proceedings brought against a newspaper after a significant lapse of time may well, in the absence of exceptional circumstances, give rise to a disproportionate interference with press freedom under art.10.[10]

Returning to domestic jurisprudence, the rule in the *Duke of Brunswick* was consid- **9.08**
ered again by the Court of Appeal, but left intact, in the landmark case of *Jameel (Yousef) v Dow Jones & Co Inc.*[11] Importantly, however, the court expressed the clear view that the Duke's claim would have been struck out as an abuse of process were it to have been brought in 2005, so technical was the cause of action.

Thus by 2005 the courts already had at their disposal a tool to strike out cases **9.09**
which, although not time-barred because of the common law rule, could properly be described as an abuse of process, on the ground that no real and substantial tort had been committed (or, to use the vernacular expression, the game was not worth the candle). Section 8 now takes the law one step further, by in effect reversing the rule in the *Duke of Brunswick*.

C. BACKGROUND TO S 8

1. Criticisms of the common law and reform proposals

In its 2011 Consultation Paper the Government's position was that the common **9.10**
law rule was not 'suitable for the modern internet age'. It claimed that widespread support for change had been expressed by interested parties in a number

---

[8] *Times Newspapers Ltd v United Kingdom* [2009] EMLR 14 (p 254).
[9] *Times Newspapers Ltd v United Kingdom* [2009] EMLR 14 (p 254) at [45].
[10] *Times Newspapers Ltd v United Kingdom* [2009] EMLR 14 (p 254) at [48].
[11] [2005] EWCA Civ 75, [2005] QB 846.

of different contexts, including the respondents to an earlier consultation carried out by the previous Government in 2009, and the Ministry of Justice Libel Working Group in early 2010.

9.11   Given his unsuccessful attempt to change the law in the *Loutchansky* litigation,[12] it is perhaps no surprise that Lord Lester's Private Member's Defamation Bill [HL] 2010–2011 should have included, at cl 10, a single publication rule to similar effect as the new s 8, albeit structured in a slightly different way. It specifically applied to any publication (such as a book, newspaper, periodical, or material in an archive) which was published by the same person on multiple occasions and on each occasion had the same or substantially the same content. It did not apply where the subsequent publication was made 'in a materially different manner'. The stated objective, explained Lord Lester when introducing the Bill, was to 'allow publishers to retain archives without the fear of open-ended liability, while leaving open the prospect of redress for claimants in appropriate cases'.

2. The Defamation Bill 2012: parliamentary history of s 8

9.12   In its report on the draft Bill, the Joint Parliamentary Committee strongly supported the introduction of a single publication rule, but expressed concern that the proposed rule was too narrow:

> While it protects the individual who originally published the material once the year period has expired, it does not protect anyone else who republishes the same material in a similar manner. For instance, an archive that publishes material written by someone else could be sued successfully, even though the original author could no longer be pursued for continuing to make the material available to readers. A publisher who republishes material previously published by a different person will similarly be exposed.[13]

Accordingly, the Joint Committee recommended[14] that the rule should protect anyone who republishes the same material in a similar manner after it has been in the public domain for more than one year.

9.13   The Government, however, did not accept the Joint Committee's recommendation, saying:

> The Government does not believe that [the Committee's recommendation] would provide adequate protection for claimants. For example, if the claimant were to bring an action in the one year period then they would be prevented from bringing any further action in relation to that material, irrespective of who might republish it. Whilst the claimant may have obtained a court injunction against the original publisher to prevent further publication of the defamatory material, any other publisher would still be free to republish it, and the claimant would have no recourse.[15]

---

[12] See paras 9.04–9.07.
[13] HL Paper 203, HC 930-I, para 59.
[14] HL Paper 203, HC 930-I, para 71.
[15] *The Government's Response to the Report of the Joint Committee on the Defamation Bill* (Cm 8295, February 2012), para 50.

The Government recognized[16] that unfairness could arise where a fair and accurate copy or report of material is published by an archive after one year from first publication, and said that the suggestion that qualified privilege should be available in these circumstances received majority support in the responses to its consultation. The Government said that it would give further consideration to this suggestion, but no such privilege is conferred by the Act.

The version of cl 8 presented to Parliament was unchanged from that contained in the draft Bill. The Bill's First Reading was in the House of Commons on 10 May 2012. At the Second Reading debate on 12 June 2012 the Bill's Commons sponsor, the Lord Chancellor and Secretary of State for Justice, the Rt Hon Kenneth Clarke MP, stated: **9.14**

> A further related proposal to modernise the libel regime is the introduction of a so-called single publication rule. Information online can be copied instantly, stored indefinitely and accessed long after physical forms of publication, yet the current regime allows additional claims for such cases of 'republishing'. The proposed rule seeks to reconcile the need to protect individuals from repeatedly having to face the same defamatory comments with the need to avoid open-ended liability for publishers when old material is accessed years later, which has the potential severely to inhibit freedom of expression. Therefore, the Bill includes a provision that will prevent an action being brought in relation to publication by the same publisher of the same, or substantially the same, material after a one-year limitation period has passed.[17]

The Bill's First Reading in the Lords was on 8 October 2012. At the Second Reading debate on 9 October 2012 there was some criticism of the clause from Lord Black of Brentwood[18] on the ground that the requirement for the manner of subsequent publications not to be 'materially different' from that of the original did not provide sufficient protection to multi-platform news publishers. However, the clause was passed without amendment in either House. **9.15**

D. THE STATUTORY PROVISIONS

Section 8 provides as follows: **9.16**

8 **Single publication rule**
(1) This section applies if a person—
   (a) publishes a statement to the public ("the first publication"), and
   (b) subsequently publishes (whether or not to the public) that statement or a statement which is substantially the same.
(2) In subsection (1) "publication to the public" includes publication to a section of the public.

---

[16] Government Response, para 51.
[17] *Hansard*, HC Deb, 12 June 2012, Col 185.
[18] *Hansard*, HL Deb, 9 October 2012, Col 962.

(3) For the purposes of section 4A of the Limitation Act 1980 (time limit for actions for defamation etc) any cause of action against the person for defamation in respect of the subsequent publication is to be treated as having accrued on the date of the first publication.

(4) This section does not apply in relation to the subsequent publication if the manner of that publication is materially different from the manner of the first publication.

(5) In determining whether the manner of a subsequent publication is materially different from the manner of the first publication, the matters to which the court may have regard include (amongst other matters)—

(a) the level of prominence that a statement is given;

(b) the extent of the subsequent publication.

(6) Where this section applies—

(a) it does not affect the court's discretion under section 32A of the Limitation Act 1980 (discretionary exclusion of time limit for actions for defamation etc), and

(b) the reference in subsection (1)(a) of that section to the operation of section 4A of that Act is a reference to the operation of section 4A together with this section.

E. KEY FEATURES OF THE RULE AND COMMENTARY

1. Section 8(1) and (2): publications covered by the rule

9.17 The new rule confers protection only on defamatory statements that have previously been published 'to the public'. By subs (1)(b) of s 8 that statement need not be identical, as long as it is 'substantially the same' as the first publication; moreover, the subsequent statement need not be published to the public to qualify—it may be a purely private publication. It must, however, be published by the same person.[19]

9.18 As for the extent of publication of the original statement, subs (2) specifically defines 'publication to the public' as including 'publication to a section of the public'. Clearly a publication to only one person would not fall within this definition. But how wide need it be? The Explanatory Notes state[20] that 'the definition is intended to ensure that publications to a limited number of people are covered (for example where a blog has a small group of subscribers or followers)'. It is not clear whether or not publication to a group of friends on, say, a restricted-access Facebook page would come within the definition. It may prove possible to derive assistance from the interpretation of the same phrase in the context of strict liability for 'publications' under s 2(1) of the Contempt of Court Act 1981, as to which see *Arlidge, Eady & Smith on Contempt*[21] where some guidance is tentatively offered. However, the two sections have very different objects, the one being to enlarge liability, the other to reduce it, so some

---

[19] Section 8(1).

[20] At para 61.

[21] (4th edn, 2011) at §§4.39–4.54.

caution is required. It was made clear by the Government in parliamentary debates that the purpose of the phrase in s 2(1) of the 1981 Act was to include meetings and functions *to which the public were invited*. If that is a useful test, then the Facebook page example cited above would not trigger the single publication rule; whilst a tweet on Twitter would surely do so, as a statement published to a section of the public.

2. Section 8(3) and (6): the limitation period

Section 8(3) is at the heart of the new rule: this simply provides that for the purposes of s 4A of the Limitation Act 1980 (which sets a one-year time limit for defamation and similar claims), any cause of action for defamation in respect of the subsequent publication is to be treated as having accrued on the date of the first publication (it being remembered that the rule only applies where both publications were by the same person: see subs (1)). Given the wording of this subsection it seems clear that the rule does not apply to claims for malicious falsehood. **9.19**

Section 8(6) specifically provides that where the new rule applies it does not affect the court's discretion under s 32A of the 1980 Act to disapply the one-year time limit for bringing an action for libel or slander. Section 32A(2) of the 1980 Act requires the court 'to have regard to all the circumstances of the case' and in particular to the length of, and the reasons for, the delay on the part of the claimant, and, where the reason for the delay was ignorance of relevant facts, the date on which the facts did become known to him and the extent to which he acted promptly and reasonably once he knew whether or not the facts might be capable of giving rise to a claim.[22] The Explanatory Notes[23] reiterate that s 32A provides a broad discretion, 'and it is envisaged that this will provide a safeguard against injustice in relation to the application of any limitation issue arising under this section'. **9.20**

It is suggested that in cases where a 'subsequent publication' occurs many years after the date of first publication, but has caused real damage to the claimant's reputation, the court is likely to be sympathetic to applications under s 32A, as long as a claimant has acted promptly and reasonably. In extreme cases, where a defendant is likely to be seriously prejudiced by the passage of time in its defence of a claim, the defendant's interests may nevertheless prevail. **9.21**

3. Section 8(4) and (5): publications outside the scope of the rule

Section 8(4) excludes from the protection of the rule cases where the manner of the subsequent publication is 'materially different' from that of the first publication. Subsection (5) provides that in determining this question the court may **9.22**

---

[22] Limitation Act 1980, s 32(2)(a) and (b).
[23] At para 64.

have regard (amongst other matters) to 'the level of prominence' that a statement is given and 'the extent of the subsequent publication'. The Explanatory Notes[24] give, as a possible example of a materially different manner of publication, 'where a story has first appeared relatively obscurely in a section of a website where several clicks need to be gone through to access it, but has subsequently been promoted to a position where it can be directly accessed from the home page of the site, thereby increasing considerably the number of hits it receives'. Whilst this example seems a little unusual, the court is unlikely to have much difficulty in assessing the question of material difference: what must matter is that the manner of publication of the subsequent publication should be materially different, in its effect or likely effect on harming the claimant's reputation, or in causing damage. The Consultation Paper expressly recognized that the 'materially different' exception 'might also possibly catch a situation where an article is initially published in a subscription based scientific journal with a small readership which is subsequently made available on a free access basis'.[25]

F. DISCUSSION

9.23 It is questionable how far the introduction of a single publication rule really goes. The analogous rule in the USA meets a need which does not arise here, of avoiding a multiplicity of lawsuits in different state jurisdictions. Once it is accepted, as the wording of the new provisions necessarily does, that the social value of archived news materials is not absolute but must in appropriate situations be overridden by the right of individuals to obtain redress for damage to their reputations, and given that the new rule expressly preserves the court's very broad discretion to disapply the limitation period to avoid injustice, then the statutory reform begins to appear more apparent than real.

9.24 It may be that s 8 will have the salutary effect of discouraging a small number of unmeritorious claims that might otherwise have been brought over stale publications with a small circulation, but, as noted above, the courts already have, and have not been shy of using, powers to strike out such claims under the abuse of process doctrine. Those powers can only be enhanced with the new 'substantial harm' test under s 1.

9.25 One situation that the new rule does not specifically address is where there is said to be a need for a final injunction. The courts are already wary of such claims being used to bolster internet libel actions where the damage already done appears spurious—see, for example, *Budu v BBC*.[26] It is furthermore difficult in practice, although perhaps not impossible, to imagine a case where the need for

---

[24] At para 63.
[25] Ministry of Justice, *Draft Defamation Bill: Consultation*, Consultation Paper CP3/11, March 2011, para 77.
[26] [2010] EWHC 616 (Sharp J).

an injunction on a *quia timet* basis would add much to a case for disapplying the limitation period in respect of a subsequent publication that is caught by the single publication rule.

One thing that may be safely predicted, as with other parts of the Act, is that **9.26** the new rule is likely to generate litigation, in particular over the question of what constitutes a 'section of the public' in internet cases, whether the manner of a subsequent publication is 'materially different', and whether or not a case has been made out for disapplying the limitation period.

10

ACTIONS AGAINST
NON-DOMICILED PERSONS

A. INTRODUCTION

Section 9 of the Act creates a new threshold test for acceptance of jurisdiction in **10.01** defamation cases by courts in England and Wales, in cases against non-domiciled persons, ie persons domiciled neither in the UK, nor elsewhere in the EU, nor in a Lugano Convention state. Where the defendant is domiciled in the EU, the EU jurisdiction regime, now found in the Judgments Regulation (referred to in the Act as the Brussels Regulation), applies. A very similar regime applies to European Free Trade Association states, which are parties to the Lugano Convention.

Section 9 provides that in cases against non-domiciled persons, a court in England **10.02** and Wales lacks jurisdiction, unless satisfied that of all the places in the world in which the statement complained of has been published, this jurisdiction is 'clearly the most appropriate place in which to bring an action in respect of the statement'. It is intended to help to deal with the perceived problem of 'libel tourism', in which (mostly) foreign claimants come to this jurisdiction to sue in respect of the relatively insignificant English distribution of foreign publications, because of the perceived advantages of English libel laws, seen as relatively benign to claimants. It seeks to achieve this aim by requiring the court to focus less on the English circulation of the alleged libel, which will be the only cause of action sued on in the action brought in England, and more on the global circulation, and whether, in that context, this jurisdiction is clearly the most appropriate forum for a libel action.

B. THE PRE-EXISTING LAW

10.03   Where the defendant is a non-domiciled person (in the sense described above), the claimant will in almost all cases require permission to serve the claim form out of the jurisdiction under CPR rr 6.36 and 6.37. Where the claim is made in tort, permission may be given where the damage was sustained within the jurisdiction, or the damage resulted from an act committed within the jurisdiction.[1] In libel cases, the damage is sustained at the place or places of publication, which is also where the act is committed. The place of publication is where the statement is seen or received by the persons to whom it is published.[2] Thus print, broadcast, and internet libels are often published in multiple jurisdictions. It is a well-established principle of English libel law that each publication of a libel is a separate tort, so that the publication in England of an internationally disseminated libel constitutes a separate tort (or series of torts).

10.04   Where permission to serve out is required, it can only be given in respect of that part of the global publication of the alleged libel which occurred in England and Wales. In such a case, it is an abuse of the process for the claimant to seek to include in the action matters occurring elsewhere, *Diamond v Sutton*.[3] It follows that, in such a case, the jurisdiction in which the tort was committed will necessarily be this jurisdiction, a fact which has been influential in libel cases in which a question arises as to whether the court should accept jurisdiction, because it was decided by the House of Lords in *Berezovsky v Michaels*[4] that regard must be had to the principle developed in relation to other classes of tort, particularly single jurisdiction torts,[5] that the jurisdiction in which a tort was committed is prima facie the natural forum for the dispute. This has had the tendency to favour the grant of permission to serve out of the jurisdiction in defamation cases. Perhaps the principal effect of s 9 of the Act is to overturn this principle— or at least to change its application—in defamation cases.

10.05   In defamation cases, the usual principles applicable upon applications for permission to serve out of the jurisdiction (or to set aside such service) apply, and will continue to apply, in particular CPR r 6.37(3) which requires that the court must not give permission unless satisfied that England and Wales is the proper place to bring the claim.[6] In particular, in cases not governed by the Judgments Regulation or the Lugano Convention, where permission to serve out of the jurisdiction is required, the onus is on the claimant to satisfy the court that

---

[1] Practice Direction 6B, para 3.1(9).

[2] See *Gatley on Libel and Slander* (11th edn, 2010) para 26.21.

[3] (1866) LR 1 Ex 130 at 132.

[4] [2000] 1 WLR 1004.

[5] *The Albaforth* [1984] 12 Lloyd's Rep 91 line of authority, see Lord Steyn in *Berezovsky v Michaels* [2000] 1 WLR 1004 at 1013–14.

[6] See the notes to CPR r 6.37 in the White Book and *Gatley on Libel and Slander* (11th edn, 2010) paras 26.20 et seq.

England and Wales is clearly the appropriate forum in which the case should be tried in the interests of all the parties and the ends of justice (the principle of *forum conveniens*), a test which, on the face of it, has obvious similarities with that in s 9(2) of the Act.

In *Berezovsky*, the defendants, the editor and publisher of *Forbes* maga- **10.06** zine, which is based and principally circulates in the USA, submitted that in multi-jurisdictional libel cases the court should treat the entire worldwide pub- lication as if it gave rise to a single cause of action, and then ask where such a global cause of action arose, or whether it was clearly best tried in England.[7] This was rejected by the House of Lords, although it accepted that in respect of trans-national libels, the court must consider the global picture.[8]

It has long been established that the libel claimant seeking to establish juris- **10.07** diction in England must show the commission of a real and substantial tort in this jurisdiction, see *Kroch v Rossell.*[9] This clearly did involve comparison of the extent of distribution in England and that in the country of origin of the publi- cation sued on. Scott LJ said:

...it would be ridiculous and fundamentally wrong to have these two cases tried in this country, on a very small and technical publication, when the real grievance of the plain- tiff is a grievance against the widespread publication of the two papers in the respective countries where they are published [France and Belgium].[10]

See also *Berezovsky*, in which consideration was given to the merits of suing in Russia—the claimants were Russians, and the events which were the subject of the alleged libel took place in Russia—and in the USA, where the magazine was published and principally circulated.[11]

C. BACKGROUND TO S 9

1. Criticisms of the common law and reform proposals

Criticism of libel tourism, and of the English courts' supposedly welcoming or **10.08** relaxed attitude to libel tourists, was one of the main planks of the campaign to reform defamation law. For example, in its 2009 report *Free Speech is Not for Sale*, the Libel Reform Group[12] said:

Over the last decade, increasing numbers of foreign claimants have brought libel actions in the English courts, often against defendants who are neither British citizens nor resi- dent in this country. This phenomenon, known as 'libel tourism', has led American states

---

[7] *Berezovsky v Michaels* [2000] 1 WLR 1004 at 1011H and 1012F.
[8] *Berezovsky v Michaels* [2000] 1 WLR 1004 at 1012H–1013C.
[9] [1937] 1 All ER 725.
[10] *Kroch v Rossell* [1937] 1 All ER 725 at 732.
[11] *Berezovsky v Michaels* [2000] 1 WLR 1004 at 1014H–1015B.
[12] English PEN, Index on Censorship, and Sense About Science.

to pass legislation protecting their citizens against the financial consequences of such rulings and the House of Representatives passed a bill this year to protect all US citizens. This has come to be known as 'Rachel's Law', after the American academic Rachel Ehrenfeld who was sued in London by the Saudi businessman Khalid bin Mahfouz over allegations in her book *Funding Evil*. Only 23 copies of the book were available in the UK, but the English Courts still heard the case.[13]

The report did not mention that Dr Ehrenfeld claimed she regarded the action in England as an opportunity to prove the truth of what she had written, and did not take any steps to challenge jurisdiction.[14] The Group's suggested solution to the problem was that libel cases should be heard in the English jurisdiction only if it can be shown that at least 10 per cent of the total number of copies of the publication distributed have been circulated in England and Wales.

10.09 Lord Lester's Private Member's Defamation Bill of May 2010[15] proposed a provision, in cases of publication in more than one jurisdiction (including in cases governed by the Judgments Regulation or Locarno Convention), to the effect that no 'harmful event' should be regarded as having occurred, unless the publication in this jurisdiction caused substantial harm to the claimant's reputation 'having regard to the extent of publication elsewhere'.

10.10 The draft Bill annexed to the Government's Consultation Paper[16] included a clause[17] in the same terms as s 9 of the Act, except that it did not include what is now subs (3), which defines the statement complained of as including statements conveying substantially the same imputation.

10.11 The Joint Parliamentary Committee's report[18] described the concerns which had been expressed about libel tourism, but said:

We found that whilst there have been recent examples of foreigners attempting to use the London courts to pursue libel claims against foreign defendants with little connection to harm suffered in the UK, in reality such cases are extremely rare: no similar cases have proceeded to trial in the last two years. The existing law allows the courts quite wide discretion to refuse to hear cases where another jurisdiction is more appropriate.[19]

The focus of concern had therefore moved to a suggested chilling effect, in which articles in journals published internationally had to be edited or withdrawn because of the risk of legal action in England and Wales. The Joint Committee described evidence for such an effect as convincing, notwithstanding that it had found that in reality there appeared to be no real risk of unwarranted legal action in this country.

---

[13] Libel Reform Group, *Free Speech Is Not for Sale*, 6.
[14] As to the US legislation, see paras 1.01–1.03.
[15] See para 1.06.
[16] See para 1.07.
[17] Clause 7.
[18] HL Paper 203, HC 930-I, 19 October 2011; see para 1.11.
[19] HL Paper 203, HC 930-I, 19 October 2011, para 55.

The Joint Committee was, however, concerned that the Bill made no apparent **10.12** distinction between foreign and English claimants. The focus of the Bill (and the Act) is on non-domiciled defendants. It accordingly recommended:

Foreign parties should not be allowed use of the courts in this country to settle disputes where the real damage is sustained elsewhere or where another jurisdiction is more appropriate. We therefore support the thrust of the Government's proposals but require some modifications, particularly to clarify that residents of England and Wales are not prevented from taking action here against an overseas defendant for damage caused abroad where the current law permits it.[20]

The Joint Committee also recommended that the Government should provide guidance on interpretation, and that, in line with Lord Lester's Bill, the courts should be required to assess the harm caused in England and Wales against that caused in other jurisdictions.[21]

In its response to the Joint Committee's report,[22] the Government said that **10.13** legal advice suggested that amending the clause to exclude claimants domiciled in this jurisdiction could raise difficulties in relation to anti-discrimination principles in European law,[23] but went on to say:

In practice, we consider that if a claimant is domiciled in this jurisdiction the courts are likely to be slow in finding that he or she did not meet the test of England and Wales being clearly the most appropriate place to bring an action, and that it will also often be the case that more harm will have been done here than elsewhere. In view of the difficulties which make a provision on the face of the Bill inappropriate, we propose to clarify in the explanatory notes and during the passage of the Bill that we would normally expect claimants domiciled in England and Wales to satisfy the requirements of the clause.[24]

As regards the Joint Committee's other recommendations, the response said that **10.14** the Government agreed that the extent of harm caused to the claimant in the jurisdiction of England and Wales compared to that suffered elsewhere is a valid consideration when the courts are applying the tests, but it was only one of a range of factors, including, for example, the extent of each party's connection to England and Wales, and whether there is reason to think that the claimant would not receive a fair trial elsewhere.[25] But, since the range of circumstances is diverse, any list of such factors was more appropriate for secondary legislation, and the point would be referred to the Civil Procedure Rule Committee. The Government indicated that it intended amending the clause, along the lines of

---

[20] HL Paper 203, HC 930-I, 19 October 2011, para 56.
[21] HL Paper 203, HC 930-I, 19 October 2011, paras 56 and 72.
[22] Ministry of Justice, *The Government's Response to the Report of the Joint Committee on the Defamation Bill* (Cm 8295, February 2012); see para 1.20.
[23] Government Response, para 56.
[24] Government Response, para 57.
[25] Government Response, para 58.

what became s 9(3) of the Act, the purpose of this being 'to avoid unreasonable arguments that statements published in other jurisdictions should be treated as different publications'.[26]

2. Parliamentary history of s 9

10.15 Introducing the Bill on Second Reading in the Commons, the Lord Chancellor, the Rt Hon Kenneth Clarke MP, said:

Relatively few foreign libel cases ultimately end up in a British courtroom, but I am concerned by the use of threatened proceedings by wealthy foreigners and public figures to stifle investigation and reporting...

It [the clause] should help ensure that powerful interests around the world will not so easily be able to use British justice to gag their critics—a move that I hope will be welcomed across the House...

The problem arises when people come to this country because our system is more generous to their point of view to bring cases that have little or nothing to do with the United Kingdom. I give the example of a Saudi business man, say, threatening an American publication with an action because of an article that has had tiny circulation in the United Kingdom. That is a hypothetical case, but the Saudi would be using the nature of British law to threaten a publication in an entirely different jurisdiction. That is the evil we are trying to address. We are not trying to stop British publications being sued by anybody who can come here and show that we are the right jurisdiction.[27]

10.16 Clearly, the Lord Chancellor was at least as concerned about inappropriate actions by foreign claimants, as with actions against non-domiciled defendants, a point taken up, at Committee stage in the Public Bill Committee, by Robert Flello MP:

The main point that struck me was that despite the talk of tackling libel tourism, the clause, if unamended, would not deal directly with libel tourism—that is, foreign plaintiffs coming to this country to sue because it is a better place for the case to be heard. It covers only libel kidnap when a plaintiff, foreign or not, seeks to serve an action out of jurisdiction on a non-EEA-domiciled person.[28]

The Parliamentary Under-Secretary of State for Justice, Jonathan Djanogly MP, however, explained:

Where a claimant in a case in which the defendant is domiciled outside the UK, EU or Lugano convention state is unable to satisfy the court that, of all the places in which the statement complained of has been published, England and Wales is clearly the most appropriate place to bring an action, he or she should be refused access to our courts and should be required to seek redress abroad.

---

[26] Government Response, para 60.
[27] Hansard, HC Deb, 12 June 2012, Cols 182 and 183.
[28] *Hansard*, Public Bill Committee, 26 June 2012, Cols 153–154.

Such cases are not likely to arise with any frequency, but when they do they give rise to legitimate concerns about libel tourism, which uses up the court's time and resources. We do not believe that the requirement to show that England and Wales is clearly the most appropriate place to bring the claim will cause undue inconvenience to claimants domiciled here who legitimately wish to bring an action in this jurisdiction to protect their reputation.

In most cases where a claimant is domiciled in England and Wales, the clause 9 test is likely to be satisfied, as the main harm to their reputation will have been caused here. In such circumstances, the claimant will readily be able to show that this is the most appropriate place to bring the claim. In cases where the test cannot be satisfied, however, it is right that claimants domiciled here should not be able to use our courts to pursue libel actions that are more appropriately heard elsewhere.[29]

This reassurance about claimants domiciled in England and Wales was repeated, in almost identical terms, by the Minister of State for Justice, Lord McNally, in the Lords Grand Committee.[30] It appears, therefore, to be clear, that although s 9 makes no reference in terms to the domicile or residence of the claimant, application of the test of 'clearly the most appropriate place in which to bring an action' will in practice significantly favour claimants domiciled or resident in England and Wales over foreign claimants, because the main harm to reputation will likely have been suffered in this jurisdiction. An amendment which would have excluded altogether from the ambit of the section cases where the claimant is domiciled in England and Wales was, however, rejected in the Lords Grand Committee. Lord McNally explained: **10.17**

The Government do not consider that narrowing the scope of Clause 9 is appropriate. It would mean, for example, that a Russian oligarch domiciled in England and Wales could sue a person outside the UK/EU in the English courts in circumstances where the alleged main harm to his reputation has occurred in, say, Uzbekistan.[31]

At Committee stage in the Commons, an amendment to require the court to take all relevant factors into consideration and to have regard to the extent of publication outside the jurisdiction was rejected. Jonathan Djanogly MP explained: **10.18**

The Government do not believe that the amendment is necessary because in considering whether the clause 9 test is satisfied, the courts will naturally take all the relevant circumstances into account. In addition, we do not believe that it would be appropriate to single out a specific factor such as the extent of publication.

Extent of publication will, of course, be an important factor. However, the range of circumstances that the court may wish to consider are diverse, and the balance between them will depend on all the circumstances of the case. For example, in addition to the extent of publication, the court may also need to consider factors such as the extent of

---

[29] *Hansard*, Public Bill Committee, 26 June 2012, Cols 154–155.
[30] *Hansard*, HL Grand Committee, 17 January 2013, Col GC 340.
[31] *Hansard*, HL Grand Committee, 17 January 2013, Col GC 339.

each party's connection to England and Wales, the extent of the claimant's reputation here and whether the claimant would receive a fair trial elsewhere. We do not consider it appropriate to give greater weight to a particular factor by including it in the Bill.[32]

D. THE STATUTORY PROVISIONS

10.19 Section 9 provides as follows:

9 Action against a person not domiciled in the UK or a Member State etc

(1) This section applies to an action for defamation against a person who is not domiciled—
   (a) in the United Kingdom;
   (b) in another Member State; or
   (c) in a state which is for the time being a contracting party to the Lugano Convention.

(2) A court does not have jurisdiction to hear and determine an action to which this section applies unless the court is satisfied that, of all the places in which the statement complained of has been published, England and Wales is clearly the most appropriate place in which to bring an action in respect of the statement.

(3) The references in subsection (2) to the statement complained of include references to any statement which conveys the same, or substantially the same, imputation as the statement complained of.

(4) For the purposes of this section—
   (a) a person is domiciled in the United Kingdom or in another Member State if the person is domiciled there for the purposes of the Brussels Regulation;
   (b) a person is domiciled in a state which is a contracting party to the Lugano Convention if the person is domiciled in the state for the purposes of that Convention.

(5) In this section—
   'the Brussels Regulation' means Council Regulation (EC) No 44/2001 of 22nd December 2000 on jurisdiction and the recognition and enforcement of judgments in civil and commercial matters, as amended from time to time and as applied by the Agreement made on 19th October 2005 between the European Community and the Kingdom of Denmark on jurisdiction and the recognition and enforcement of judgments in civil and commercial matters (OJ No L299 16.11.2005 at p 62);
   'the Lugano Convention' means the Convention on jurisdiction and the recognition and enforcement of judgments in civil and commercial matters, between the European Community and the Republic of Iceland, the Kingdom of Norway, the Swiss Confederation and the Kingdom of Denmark signed on behalf of the European Community on 30th October 2007.

---

[32] *Hansard*, Public Bill Committee, 26 June 2012, Col 155.

E. KEY FEATURES OF THE SECTION

The test, for the court to have jurisdiction to hear and determine an action **10.20** against a non-domiciled defendant, is that the court must be satisfied that 'of all the places in which the statement complained of has been published, England and Wales is clearly the most appropriate place' for an action. It appears that the court must focus on the global publication of the alleged libel ('all the places' in which it has been published), and decide which is the most appropriate place in which to bring an action in respect of the publication. The Explanatory Notes to the Act say that the statutory test 'means that in cases where a statement has been published in this jurisdiction and also abroad, the court will be required to consider the overall global picture to consider where it would be most appropriate for a claim to be heard'.[33] Only if England and Wales emerges as clearly the most appropriate place, should jurisdiction be accepted.

The relative size of the publication in England and Wales and in other jurisdic- **10.21** tions will clearly be an important factor. Even a large circulation in England and Wales may not be enough, if publication was mainly abroad. The Explanatory Notes give the example of a statement published 100,000 times in Australia and only 5,000 times in England, saying that would be a good basis on which to conclude that the most appropriate jurisdicton in which to bring an action in respect of the statement was Australia rather than England.[34] It is clear that the extent to which harm to the claimant's reputation, and other damage, has been suffered, or is likely to be suffered, in the English jurisdiction may be a critical factor, and in many cases of greater weight than the mere relative size of circulation in England and Wales and abroad. For this reason, as is clear from the parliamentary history of the section, English claimants have a good chance of clearing the hurdle set by the section.

As has already been suggested,[35] one of the most important effects of the sec- **10.22** tion will be to remove the focus on the circulation of the alleged libel in this jurisdiction (and on the harm caused thereby). This came about, because the cause of action sued on is, in these cases, confined to the tort committed in England and Wales, and because of the principle that the jurisdiction where the tort was committed is prima facie the natural forum for the dispute. It is clear that, under the section, there is no such presumption.

Subsection (3) of s 9 is included to preclude technical arguments based on **10.23** insubstantial differences in the alleged libel, as published in the English jurisdiction and elsewhere, where the imputation (or meaning) is the same or substantially the same.[36]

---

[33] Explanatory Notes, para 66.
[34] Explanatory Notes, para 66.
[35] See para 10.04.
[36] See para 10.14.

F. DISCUSSION

10.24 There appear to be two main potential difficulties of construction which may arise in practice. The first is the question whether the section in effect allows for only one action in respect of the global circulation of the alleged libel, either in England and Wales or abroad, or whether there are circumstances in which the court could be permitted to contemplate more than one action, one in England and Wales and another abroad—in other words whether there could ever be two 'most appropriate places' in which to bring an action.

10.25 It is obvious that the wording of the section, requiring that 'England and Wales is clearly the most appropriate place in which to bring an action' favours a construction in which the court can contemplate only one action being appropriate in respect of the global circulation. But it does not appear to be so straightforward. An example is a case in which emails are sent by a non-domiciled defendant to the claimant's two principal customers, one in England, and the other in another jurisdiction. The email contains a serious and false libel, which foreseeably causes both customers to withdraw their custom. Must the claimant choose which publication to sue on? And how would the court decide which jurisdiction was the more appropriate in which to bring an action?

10.26 There may also be cases in which the remedy which the claimant most needs is an injunction to prevent threatened publications, perhaps in more than one jurisdiction. The section does not in terms contemplate such a situation, since it refers to 'all the places in which the statement complained of *has been published*'.

10.27 In such cases, it is suggested that Articles 8 and 6 of the European Convention on Human Rights may enable the court to cut the knot. Personal reputation is recognized as a Convention right under Article 8,[37] and Article 6 mandates access to justice for the protection of a person's civil rights, including the right to reputation under the English law of defamation. There may be cases in which access to justice in this jurisdiction cannot be denied, even though there is another jurisdiction in which the case for access to justice is at least as compelling. There may, exceptionally, be two places which are clearly the most appropriate in which to bring an action.

10.28 Apart from exceptional cases, the court appears to be required to identify the single most appropriate place for an action. This may have the effect that the claimant cannot be compensated for injury to his or her reputation in this jurisdiction, where he or she has suffered greater injury elsewhere, and where the foreign court has jurisdiction only in respect of publication in its territory. The problem may be more apparent than real. Parliament may be taken to have contemplated that the principal objective of libel litigation, in cases where the publication has already taken place, is vindication, and that, for that purpose,

---

[37] See, for example, *Re Guardian News and Media Ltd* [2010] UKSC 1, [2010] 2 AC 697.

more than one lawsuit is generally superfluous. If that is right, an important factor in the court's consideration may be to identify the place where the claimant may most effectively achieve vindication.

The second main question of construction which may arise relates to the **10.29** fairly common situation in which a defamatory story about a celebrity is picked up and and repeated around the world, each of the stories conveying the same or substantially the same imputation, so as to amount to the same statement complained of, by virtue of subs (3). Where the claimant chooses to sue a non-domiciled defendant in respect of publication in the English jurisdiction, could it be said that the most appropriate place to bring an action is against a quite different defendant who published a more widely circulated and/or more damaging story in another jurisdiction?

It is suggested that this is not a possible construction of the section. The 'state- **10.30** ment complained of', referred to in subs (2), must mean the statement published by the non-domiciled defendant against whom the action has been brought, referred to in subs (1). The purpose of subs (3) is to give an expanded definition to the 'statement complained of', as referred to in subs (2). Subsection (3) must therefore likewise refer to statements published by the non-domiciled defendant. It is therefore suggested that the section does not cover separate statements conveying the same imputation published by separate defendants. The alternative construction would be a radical change, and nothing in the parliamentary history or the Explanatory Notes suggests that it was intended.

The libel claimant seeking to establish jurisdiction in England and Wales must, **10.31** under the pre-existing law, show a real and substantial tort in this jurisdiction.[38] It may be asked whether the effect of s 1 of the Act is to replace that test with a higher one, requiring the claimant to show, as a threshold test, that publication has caused or is likely to cause serious harm to his or her reputation *in this jurisdiction.* It is suggested that that cannot be so. Section 1 goes to the question whether the statement is defamatory. There is a conceptual difficulty about the same statement being, in English law, defamatory when published in France, but not defamatory, because of its more limited circulation or the claimant's more limited reputation, when published in England. Possibly, this conceptual difficulty is already inherent in s 1. In practice, however, the claimant will have to show that the publication of the statement globally has caused or is likely to cause serious harm, otherwise he or she will fail to show that the statement is defamatory, and there will be an evident difficulty about the claimant satisfying the test in s 9(2), if he or she cannot show serious harm, or the likelihood of serious harm, in England and Wales.

---

[38] See also para 10.07.

11

ACTIONS AGAINST SECONDARY PUBLISHERS AND ORDERS TO REMOVE THE STATEMENT OR CEASE DISTRIBUTING

A. INTRODUCTION

Section 10 of the Act provides that the court has no jurisdiction to entertain an action against a secondary publisher, that is, a person who is not the author, editor, or commercial publisher of the statement as defined in s 1 of the Defamation Act 1996, unless it is not reasonably practicable for an action to be brought against a primary publisher. **11.01**

Section 13 provides that, where a successful action for defamation has been brought by a claimant, usually that is against a primary publisher, the court may order (a) the operator of a website on which the statement was posted to remove it, or (b) a secondary publisher to stop distributing, selling, or exhibiting material containing the statement. **11.02**

These sections are linked, because s 13 was introduced to remedy a potential problem to which s 10 (and/or, in the case of the operator of a website, s 5 of the Act) could give rise, where the claimant had successfully sued the author of the statement, but, without s 13, would be unable to prevent the continued dissemination of the statement, for example by the operator of a website or a distributor of printed material containing the statement. **11.03**

11.04   It appears to be envisaged that a s 13 order would be made 'during or shortly after the conclusion of proceedings' against the primary publisher, 'or on a separate application under Part 23 of the Civil Procedure Rules', for which purpose it seems that a supplementary rule of court is contemplated.[1]

B. THE PRE-EXISTING LAW

11.05   Under the common law, a secondary publisher was a proper defendant to defamation proceedings, subject to having a defence of innocent dissemination at common law, or under s 1 of the Defamation Act 1996, or under the Electronic Commerce (EC Directive) Regulations 2002,[2] all of which remain in force, but will be of much reduced use following the introduction of s 10.

11.06   'Author', 'editor', and 'publisher'—that is, persons referred to in this chapter as primary publishers—are defined in s 1 of the Defamation Act 1996 as:

- 'author' means the originator of the statement, but does not include a person who did not intend that his or her statement be published at all;
- 'editor' means a person having editorial or equivalent responsibility for the content of the statement or the decision to publish it; and
- 'publisher' means a commercial publisher, that is a person whose business is issuing material to the public, or a section of the public, who issues material containing the statement in the course of that business.

Section 1(3) of the 1996 Act gives examples of persons who are not to be considered as primary publishers, for example persons only involved as printers, producers, distributors, or sellers of printed material, or operators of communications systems by means of which the statement is transmitted or made available by a person over whom they have no effective control.

C. BACKGROUND TO SS 10 AND 13

1. Criticisms of the pre-existing law and reform proposals

11.07   The draft Bill annexed to the Government's Consultation Paper[3] contained nothing corresponding to either s 10 or s 13. What became s 10 originated in a submission to the Joint Parliamentary Committee[4] by the Booksellers Association, which was concerned that s 1 of the Defamation Act 1996 had *reduced* the

---

[1] Lord Ahmad in the House of Lords: *Hansard*, HL Grand Committee, 17 January 2013, Col GC 357.

[2] SI 2002/2013; see *Gatley on Libel and Slander* (11th edn, 2010) paras 6.19–6.31.

[3] Ministry of Justice, *Draft Defamation Bill: Consultation*, Consultation Paper CP3/11, March 2011; see para 1.07.

[4] See para 1.08.

protection for secondary publishers, in providing that such publishers lose their protection if they know or have reason to believe that the publication contains any defamatory statement. Under the common law defence of innocent dissemination, the Association said, there was a defence if the secondary publisher reasonably believed there to be a good defence, for example of justification. As a result, a claimant could effectively prevent the sale or distribution of a book, simply by having a letter written to the bookseller threatening proceedings unless it was withdrawn.[5] Whether the Association was correct in its view of the effect of the common law of innocent dissemination, or in its view that s 1 superseded the common law defence, was at best contentious.

Nevertheless, the Joint Committee recommended that the Government should **11.08** amend the innocent dissemination defence in order to provide secondary publishers with the same level of protection that existed before s 1 of the 1996 Act was introduced.[6] In its Response, the Government said:

We share the Committee's concern that the position of offline intermediaries such as booksellers should be adequately protected. Alongside the development of a new system relating to online publication we will consider how offline intermediaries can best be protected and will ensure that any provisions which are included in the Bill take their concerns properly into account.[7]

As a result, the Bill introduced into the Commons contained cl 10, in identical **11.09** terms to the section which emerged as s 10 of the Act.

2. Parliamentary history of ss 10 and 13

Jonathan Djahogly MP, Parliamentary Under-Secretary of State for Justice, **11.10** explained in the Commons Public Bill Committee,[8] having referred to the concerns of secondary publishers, and to consultation:

The respondents on that point in the consultation, and the Joint Committee, argued that the Government should include a provision in the Bill to offer booksellers and other secondary publishers greater protection. In the light of that, and in accordance with our aim of ensuring that secondary publishers are not unfairly targeted and that action is taken against the primary publisher wherever possible, Clause 10 removes the possibility of an action for defamation being brought against a secondary publisher, except where it is not reasonably practicable for the claimant to bring the action against the author, editor or commercial publisher of the material.

. . .

---

[5] Report of the Joint Parliamentary Committee, HL Paper 203, HC 930-I, 19 October 2011, para 60, footnote 109.

[6] Report of the Joint Parliamentary Committee, 8 and para 60.

[7] Ministry of Justice, *The Government's Response to the Report of the Joint Committee on the Defamation Bill* (Cm 8295, February 2012), para 89.

[8] *Hansard,* Public Bill Committee, 26 June 2012, Cols 162–163.

There are differing views about whether section 1 [of the 1996 Act] was more restrictive than the common law defence that was previously available. We decided that it would not be appropriate to provide a complete bar against any action against a secondary publisher, for example by introducing a requirement for knowledge that the statement is libellous for the defence to fail, as that could provide an incentive for website operators not to comply with the clause 5 procedure,[9] in the knowledge that they would be likely to succeed in the other defence.

11.11   Significant points were raised, in amendments proposed or questions asked in the Commons Public Bill Committee. Paul Farrelly MP raised the point[10] that, as it stood, 'clause 10 would provide a complete defence to website operators in relation to any case where the author, etc., was reasonably identifiable, and the sensible clause 5 notice procedures would be redundant'. Jonathan Djanogly MP explained:[11]

> ... if a website operator were to fail to follow the clause 5 process and then attempted to rely on clause 10,[12] on the basis that they are not the author, editor or commercial publisher of the third party material, it would be for the court to decide whether the fact that they had failed to follow the process set out in clause 5 meant that it was not reasonably practicable for the claimant to pursue the primary publisher.

> For example, where the author of the third party material is posting anonymously, the website operator's failure to follow the process designed to assist the claimant in identifying the author would make it significantly more difficult for the claimant to pursue the author. If a court judged that it no longer made pursuing the author 'reasonably practicable', it could allow the claimant to bring an action against the website operator in respect of the third-party material.'

11.12   Mr Farrelly also raised the point[13] that cl 10 would have the effect that a secondary publisher could carry on disseminating defamatory material, even if the author, editor, or publisher was successfully sued. He therefore proposed[14] an amendment to the effect that s 10 should not prevent a court from granting an injunction against a secondary publisher. Mr Djanogly was concerned that this would expose secondary publishers to lawsuits or the threat of lawsuits, when the purpose of the clause was to reduce the likelihood of that. He said that the Government would give further consideration to Mr Farelly's point. The same point was raised in the Lords Grand Committee.[15] This was the origin of s 13 of the Act.

---

[9] Now s 5 of the Act.
[10] *Hansard*, Public Bill Committee, 26 June 2012, Col 158.
[11] *Hansard*, Public Bill Committee, 26 June 2012, Col 158.
[12] *Hansard* says 'clause 1', but this is clearly a mistake.
[13] *Hansard*, Public Bill Committee, 26 June 2012, Col 157.
[14] *Hansard*, Public Bill Committee, 26 June 2012, Col 160.
[15] *Hansard*, HL Grand Committee, 17 January 2013, Col GC 344.

Mr Djanogly was asked about the circumstances in which it would not be 11.13
reasonably practicable for the claimant to take action against the author, editor,
or publisher, and responded:

We do not believe that it is appropriate to prescribe in secondary legislation circumstances
in which it would not be reasonably practicable for the claimant to pursue the primary
publisher, as that will be for the court to determine in each individual case.[16]

At the Report stage, the Government introduced a new provision corresponding 11.14
to s 13(1)(a) of the Act, that is the power to order a website operator to remove
the statement, but not (at that stage) any other secondary publisher. The new
Parliamentary Under-Secretary of State for Justice, Jeremy Wright MP, said:

[The] new clause...deals with an issue raised in Committee by the hon. Member for
Newcastle-under-Lyme (Paul Farrelly). He was concerned that circumstances could arise
in which a claimant who had successfully brought an action against the author of defamatory material online could be left unable to secure the removal of the material. That situation might arise as a result of the fact that an author might not always be in a position
to remove material that had been found to be defamatory from a website, while the new
defence in clause 5 might prevent the website operator from being required to do so. The
Government indicated in Committee that we would consider whether anything further
was needed to address such situations.

We have concluded that although such situations are likely to be rare, it would be appropriate to include a provision in the Bill to ensure that claimants in such cases do not experience any difficulty in securing the removal of material that has been found to be defamatory. [The] new clause...therefore provides that where a court gives a judgment for the
claimant in a defamation action, it may order the operator of a website on which the
defamatory statement is posted to remove that statement. Such an order could be made
either during proceedings or on a separate application. New clause 1(2)[17] ensures that the
provision does not have any wider effect on the inherent jurisdiction of the High Court.[18]

At Report stage in the Lords, the Government introduced an amendment to deal 11.15
with the situation in which a claimant had successfully sued an offline primary
publisher, but a secondary publisher refused to stop disseminating the statement,
thus adding s 13(1)(b) and (2).[19]

D. THE STATUTORY PROVISIONS

Sections 10 and 13 provide as follows: 11.16

10 **Action against a person who was not the author, editor etc**
(1) A court does not have jurisdiction to hear and determine an action for defamation
brought against a person who was not the author, editor or publisher of the statement

---

[16] *Hansard*, Public Bill Committee, 26 June 2012, Col 163.
[17] Now s 13(3) of the Act.
[18] *Hansard*, HC Deb, 12 September 2012, Col 309.
[19] *Hansard*, HL Deb, 5 February 2013, Col 249.

complained of unless the court is satisfied that it is not reasonably practicable for an action to be brought against the author, editor or publisher.

(2) In this section 'author', 'editor' and 'publisher' have the same meaning as in section 1 of the Defamation Act 1996.

13 Order to remove statement or cease distribution etc

(1) Where a court gives judgment for the claimant in an action for defamation the court may order—

    (a) the operator of a website on which the defamatory statement is posted to remove the statement, or

    (b) any person who was not the author, editor or publisher of the defamatory statement to stop distributing, selling or exhibiting material containing the statement.

(2) In this section 'author', 'editor' and 'publisher' have the same meaning as in section 1 of the Defamation Act 1996.

(3) Subsection (1) does not affect the power of the court apart from that subsection.

E. DISCUSSION

11.17 Questions will arise about when it will be 'not reasonably practicable' for an action to be brought against a primary publisher. It would appear that a secondary publisher could not claim that the claimant can obtain sufficient information about a primary publisher, by using the *Norwich Pharmacal* jurisdiction, to make it reasonably practicable to bring an action against him, at least if the secondary publisher is a website operator served with a notice of complaint under s 5. That would risk making the s 5 notice procedures redundant, as Paul Farrelly MP feared.[20] It is inherent in the Minister's answer to Mr Farrelly that a website operator could not normally stand on its s 10 defence to avoid responding to a notice of complaint in accordance with regulations.

11.18 So far as concerns offline publications, a secondary publisher which was threatened with suit, would be wise to provide the claimant with the details which would make it practicable for action to be brought against the author (or other primary publisher). It is unlikely, but possible, that a claimant might sue an offline secondary publisher, without taking the necessary steps to make it practicable to sue the author (or other primary publisher), including making a *Norwich Pharmacal* application. The court might then decline to accept jurisdiction, at least if the person sued was not in a position to supply information about the author (or other primary publisher) to enable the claimant to sue them, but the information could without much difficulty be obtained from someone else, if necessary through *Norwich Pharmacal*. In theory, this could lead to some difference in treatment between online and offline publications. But that would merely be the consequence of the court ensuring that the statutory procedures and defences work as Parliament intended.

---

[20] See para 11.11.

What if the author and commercial publisher are bankrupt? Would that have **11.19** the result that it was 'not reasonably practicable' to sue them, so that the claimant could, for example, sue the distributor if it was continuing to disseminate the book containing the defamatory statement? If the author and publisher appeared malicious, intransigent, and determined to inflict maximum damage on the claimant, it might be hard to deny the claimant a remedy against the distributor which persisted in disseminating the book. In general, it is suggested that the impecuniosity of the author and publisher would, by itself, make it unappealing and costly to bring an action against them, rather than 'not reasonably practicable' to do so. But 'reasonably practicable' is a flexible test, which will normally enable the court to meet the justice of the case.

An order against a non-party that it should take down the statement com- **11.20** plained of, or cease disseminating it, is a novelty at the conclusion of an action against someone else. Section 13 clearly gives the court discretion as to whether such an order should be made. If the respondent to an application for such an order wishes to raise a defence not raised by the defendant in the action in which the claimant has obtained judgment, Article 10 of the European Convention on Human Rights considerations will come into play, and the court may decline to make the order.

12

TRIAL TO BE WITHOUT A JURY UNLESS THE COURT ORDERS OTHERWISE

A. INTRODUCTION

Section 11 of the Act abolishes the presumption that all defamation cases are to be tried by jury. **12.01**

B. THE PRE-EXISTING LAW

The presumption, which was perhaps more accurately described as a constitu- **12.02**
tional right as to the mode of trial—although the Court of Appeal accepts the
'right' is qualified in nature[1]—was contained in s 69 of the Senior Courts Act
1981 and s 66 of the County Courts Act 1984 (there being no material difference between the two provisions). While trial by jury required an application by
any party to the action, the court was obliged to order the proceedings be tried
by jury (assuming it was satisfied it was a claim in respect of libel or slander)
'unless the court is of opinion that the trial requires any prolonged examination
of documents or accounts or any scientific or local investigation which cannot
conveniently be made with a jury'. Recent case law had established that if application for trial by jury was not made within twenty-eight days from service of

---

[1] *Fiddes v Channel Four Television Corporation* [2010] EWCA Civ 730, [2010] 1 WLR 2245 at [9]
(Lord Neuberger MR, Kay LJ, and Sedley LJ).

the defence, as required by CPR r 26.11, the right to trial by jury was lost, and the issue became a matter for the court's discretion.[2]

12.03 The threshold question under s 69 of the 1981 Act and s 66 of the 1984 Act—whether the claim was one in respect of libel or slander—conferred no discretion on the court. It was the qualifying words[3] which conferred the discretion on the court to disallow a jury trial.

12.04 While it was traditionally accepted by the Court of Appeal that the exercise of the discretion 'will depend substantially on the circumstances of each individual case',[4] that court has also recognized that the effect of s 69 is that the emphasis—and general trends of the modern era—is now against trial by jury.[5]

12.05 The historic rationale underlying the presumption in favour of trial by jury was, as Nourse LJ identified it in *Goldsmith v Pressdram Ltd*,[6] premised on the theory that 'whether someone's reputation has or has not been falsely discredited ought to be tried by other ordinary men and women and, as Lord Camden said, it is the jury who are the people of England'. Also, ordinary men and women are perhaps better placed to determine whether or not the words complained of are in fact defamatory, given that the accepted test of whether or not something is defamatory depends upon the view of 'right-thinking members of society generally' or 'reasonable people generally'.[7]

C. BACKGROUND TO S 11

12.06 The traditional view became more artificial given the increasing complexity of the law of defamation. Modern practicalities, including judicial time and the costs of trial, have in part contributed to the abolition of juries. This much was acknowledged by the Lord Chancellor, the Rt Hon Kenneth Clarke MP, during the Second Reading of the Bill in the House of Commons[8] and Lord Browne of Eaton-under-Heywood in the House of Lords.[9]

12.07 The decisive argument against retention of jury trial, which was set out in para 23 of the Joint Parliamentary Committee's report,[10] was that key issues of fact, such as the defamatory meaning of the statement complained of, and whether it is fact or opinion, are jury questions, which in practice made it impossible to have these issues decided at an early stage. A judge could pre-empt the decision

---

[2] *Thornton v Telegraph Media Group Ltd* [2011] EWCA Civ 748, [2011] EMLR 29.

[3] As set out in para 12.02.

[4] *Aitken v Preston* [1997] EMLR 415 at 421–2 (Lord Bingham CJ).

[5] *Aitken v Preston* [1997] EMLR 415 at 422; *Goldsmith v Pressdram* [1988] 1 WLR 64.

[6] [1988] 1 WLR 64 at 74.

[7] *Skuse v Granada Television* [1996] EMLR 278 at 286 (Lord Bingham MR).

[8] *Hansard*, HC Deb, 12 June 2012, Cols 185, 186.

[9] *Hansard*, HL Deb, 17 January 2013, Col GC 351.

[10] Report of the Joint Parliamentary Committee, HL Paper 203, HC 930-I, 19 October 2011; see para 1.11.

of a jury only in a case where there is but one answer that could be given by a non-perverse jury. This often prolonged cases and greatly increased costs. Early resolution of key issues would, in many cases, simplify and reduce the issues, by making it clear whether truth or honest opinion was the appropriate defence, or by ruling out justification of any other meaning than the one which the statement had been found to bear. The Lord Chancellor said at Second Reading:

Many basic legal issues that could otherwise quickly be sorted out by a judge sitting alone, such as deciding the meaning that allegedly defamatory material can have, cannot be resolved until full trial, whether or not a jury is ultimately used. That causes unnecessary delay and expense, to everyone's detriment.[11]

What s 11 does not do is elucidate the circumstances in which the mode of trial **12.08** should be by jury. The heading to s 11 indicates that the court retains a discretion to order trial by jury but is silent as to what circumstances would justify such a course and, perhaps most importantly, the criteria the court should apply when considering whether or not to exercise the discretion and order trial by jury.

In the Second Reading of the Bill in the House of Lords, Lord Browne of **12.09** Ladyton called for 'detailed guidance relating to the criteria for the judge to consider when deciding whether a jury trial should be ordered'.[12] At one stage during the course of debates a proposed addition to the Bill was sought to be introduced which would have allowed a court to order trial by jury 'in a case involving a senior figure in public life and when that person's credibility is at stake'.[13] That proposal was considered unnecessary. Indeed in the Government's Response to the Joint Committee's report, it was indicated that to introduce statutory guidelines 'could be too prescriptive and could generate disputes' and that 'there would also be a risk that detailed provisions setting out when jury trial may be appropriate could inadvertently have the effect of leading to more cases being deemed suitable for a jury than at present, which would work against the Committee's view (which the Government shares) that jury trial should be exceptional'.[14]

D. DISCUSSION

The absence of any guidelines or criteria as to when it will be appropriate for **12.10** a claim to be tried by jury is unfortunate and leaves scope for arguments as to when it will be appropriate for the new presumption against jury trials to be displaced. Under the old body of cases which examined the operation of s 69 of

---

[11] *Hansard*, HC Deb, 12 June 2012, Col 186.
[12] *Hansard*, HL Deb, 9 October 2012, Col 940.
[13] See proposed Amendment 51, moved by Lord Mawhinney, *Hansard*, HL Grand Committee, 17 January 2013, Col GC 350.
[14] Ministry of Justice, *The Government's Response to the Report of the Joint Committee on the Defamation Bill* (Cm 8295, February 2012), para 62.

the 1981 Act, two factors were traditionally considered relevant to and favouring trial by jury. The factors were cases which involved: (1) prominent figures in public life and questions of great national interest;[15] and (2) issues of credibility and an attack on the honour and integrity of a claimant.[16] Neither feature was considered to be decisive.

12.10   The absence of criteria guiding the s 11 discretion makes it difficult to predict the attitude the courts will take to applications for trial by jury. Parties may well seek to rely on the factors set out in the old case law, indeed it was those factors which informed the content of the proposed Amendment 51. What success a party seeking trial by jury will have remains to be seen. However, what is clear, and clear beyond doubt, is that s 11 operates as a presumption against jury trials and that the intention of Parliament in enacting the provision was to make trial by jury an exception to the rule. The practical effect may well be that trial by jury will be a wholly exceptional occurrence and one which will be rarely seen if at all.

12.11   Abolition of the presumption of trial by jury will have a transformative effect on the conduct of some, perhaps many, defamation cases. Key issues will be resolved at an early stage, possibly before service of defence, with substantial knock-on effects on the defences that can be run at trial.[17] In some cases, early resolution of key issues will rule out any defence. In many cases, it will promote settlement. See Chapter 3[18] for discussion of the consequences of abolition of the presumption on the defence of truth.

---

[15] *Aitken v Preston* [1997] EMLR 415 at 422, as cited in *Fiddes v Channel Four Television Corporation* [2010] EWCA Civ 730, [2010] 1 WLR 2245 at [15].

[16] *Goldsmith v Pressdram* [1988] 1 WLR 64 at 71H, as cited in *Fiddes v Channel Four Television Corporation* [2010] EWCA Civ 730, [2010] 1 WLR 2245 at [15].

[17] See para 12.07.

[18] At para 3.39.

13

COURT'S POWER TO ORDER
A SUMMARY OF ITS JUDGMENT
TO BE PUBLISHED

A. INTRODUCTION

Section 12 of the Act empowers the court, where it gives judgment for the claim- **13.01** ant, to order the defendant to publish a summary of the judgment, and contains provisions for settling the wording of the summary and the mode of publication.

B. THE PRE-EXISTING LAW

At common law, the court had no power to order a defendant to publish any cor- **13.02** rection or apology, or to publicize a judgment in favour of a defamation claimant. The court's powers to give relief were limited to the usual common law and equitable remedies, principally damages and injunction. There is a constitutional dimension to any jurisdiction to make orders as to what the press must publish, and the role of the jury was an obstacle to any such power. A jury is not suited to giving a narrative verdict, and the jury's view of the facts, particularly the extent to which the libel complained of may have been proved to be true, had to be discerned from the size of its award of damages. Vindication for the claimant was provided by a suitably large award of damages, in relation to the seriousness of the libel.

13.03   Those publications which signed up to the Press Complaints Commission Code of Practice, however, undertook an obligation under para 1(iv) of the Code to 'report fairly and accurately the outcome of an action for defamation to which it has been a party, unless an agreed settlement states otherwise, or an agreed statement is published'.

13.04   The breach in the principle that the court made no orders of this kind came with the summary disposal provisions of the Defamation Act 1996 (ss 8 and 9), which enabled the court to give summary judgment in defamation claims and provided for the grant of summary relief to claimants, including 'an order that the defendant publish or cause to be published a suitable correction and apology'. Failing agreement between the parties on content of the correction and apology, s 9(2) of the 1996 Act empowered the court to direct the defendant to publish a summary of the court's judgment. Failing agreement on mode of publication, the court was empowered to 'direct the defendant to taken such reasonable and practicable steps as the court considers appropriate'.

13.05   Section 12 of the 2013 Act clearly builds on these provisions. Summary disposal is, by s 8(5) of the 1996 Act, without a jury, which removed the obstacle referred to in para 13.02. Abolition of the presumption of trial by jury of defamation actions by s 11 of the 2013 Act now removes the obstacle to the grant of relief of this kind at trial.

C. BACKGROUND TO S 12

13.06   Neither Lord Lester's Bill, nor the Bill published by the Ministry of Justice with its Consultation Paper[1] contained any provision to the effect of s 12. The provision was not therefore considered by the Joint Parliamentary Committee or in the Government's Response. Clause 12, which became s 12, was included in the Bill introduced into the House of Commons in May 2012. On Second Reading, the Lord Chancellor, the Rt Hon Kenneth Clarke MP, said:

> Alongside these adjustments in the law to help support freedom of expression, I want to ensure that effective remedies are available for those defamed. Often what most concerns claimants is not financial compensation, but meaningful public clarification that the story was wrong. We have therefore included provisions in clause 12 extending existing powers to enable the court to order publication of a summary of its judgment. Parties will be encouraged to reach agreement, where possible, on the contents of the summary and issues such as where, when and how it is to be published. However, in the absence of agreement, the court will be empowered to settle the wording of the summary and give directions on those other matters.[2]

13.07   The provision generated little debate. On Second Reading in the Lords, Lord Black of Brentwood, a former director of the Press Complaints Commission, raised the constitutional dimension referred to in para 13.02:

---

[1] See paras 1.06–1.07.
[2] *Hansard*, HC Deb, 12 June 2012, Cols 183–184.

Clause 12 hands to the courts the power to order the publication of the summary of a judgment. This is potentially tantamount to giving judges the power to dictate the content of a newspaper or magazine front page or the running order of the 10 o'clock news, and is inimical to any basic concept of editorial and press freedom or indeed of an independent media...The clause is both otiose and odious, and it should go.[3]

In Grand Committee, however, no amendment was proposed to cl 12, which was agreed without debate.

D. THE STATUTORY PROVISIONS

Section 12 provides as follows: **13.08**

12 Power of court to order a summary of its judgment to be published
(1) Where a court gives judgment for the claimant in an action for defamation the court may order the defendant to publish a summary of the judgment.
(2) The wording of any summary and the time, manner, form and place of its publication are to be for the parties to agree.
(3) If the parties cannot agree on the wording, the wording is to be settled by the court.
(4) If the parties cannot agree on the time, manner, form or place of publication, the court may give such directions as to those matters as it considers reasonable and practicable in the circumstances.
(5) This section does not apply where the court gives judgment for the claimant under section 8(3) of the Defamation Act 1996 (summary disposal of claims).

E. DISCUSSION

Orders under s 12 may be expected to become standard where judgment is given   **13.09**
for the claimant, if the claimant asks for it, and where it is not impractical to require the defendant to publish a summary. The constitutional objection considered earlier in this chapter may be regarded as having been disposed of by Parliament, and the court may be expected to have little time for any objection by the defendant on grounds of free speech or unwillingness to comply.

This form of relief may have a knock-on effect, perhaps substantial, on the   **13.10**
size of defamation damages. The summary of the judgment to be published by the defendant will no doubt be drafted to produce the full appropriate vindication, and may be regarded as replacing the vindication element in defamation damages, substantially or wholly, leaving damages for injury to reputation and feelings.

---

[3] *Hansard*, HL Deb, 9 October 2012, Col 963.

14

SPECIAL DAMAGE

A. THE STATUTORY PROVISIONS

Section 14 provides as follows: **14.01**

14 Special damage

(1) The Slander of Women Act 1891 is repealed.
(2) The publication of a statement that conveys the imputation that a person has a contagious or infectious disease does not give rise to a cause of action for slander unless the publication causes the person special damage.

B. BACKGROUND TO S 14

There was no clause corresponding to this section in the Bill put out for consul- **14.02**
tation by the Government, and the Joint Committee said nothing about it.[1] The
Government's response,[2] in the section on other issues arising from consultation
where the Committee had not made specific recommendations, said:

In the case of slander, the presumption of damage does not apply, and some special
damage must be proved to flow from the statement complained of unless the publication
falls into certain specific categories. The consultation paper sought views on whether one
such category contained in the Slander of Women Act 1891 relating to words imputing unchastity or adultery to any woman or girl, and a common law category relating
to imputations that a person is suffering from a communicable disease such as venereal
disease, leprosy or the plague, should be repealed through the Repeals Bill, on the basis

---

[1] See paras 1.07 and 1.11.
[2] Ministry of Justice, *The Government's Response to the Report of the Joint Committee on the Defamation Bill* (Cm 8295, February 2012); see para 1.20.

that they are outdated and potentially discriminatory. There was overwhelming support for this in consultation responses, and on reflection we have decided to include a provision repealing these provisions in the Defamation Bill rather than the Repeals Bill.[3]

14.03 A clause in the terms which emerged as s 14 was therefore included in the Bill introduced into the Commons. It did not generate any controversy or debate during the Bill's passage through Parliament.

C. DISCUSSION

14.04 There is nothing to add to the explanation of the reform in the Government's response. The effect of s 14 is that, in all cases of slander save two, a person defamed can only succeed on proof of special damage[4] arising as the direct and natural and reasonable result of the publication of the words. The two remaining exceptions, in which the slander is actionable per se, are:

(1) where the words impute a crime for which the claimant can be made to suffer physically by way of punishment, and
(2) where the words are calculated to disparage the claimant in any office, profession, calling, trade, or business held or carried on by him at the time of publication.[5]

---

[3] Government Response, para 99.
[4] For what constitutes special damage, see *Gatley on Libel and Slander* (11th edn, 2010) para 5.2.
[5] Defamation Act 1952, s 2.

APPENDIX 1

Defamation Act 2013 and Explanatory Notes

CONTENTS

Slander

General provisions

An Act to amend the law of defamation   [25th April 2013]

BE IT ENACTED by the Queen's most Excellent Majesty, by and with the advice and consent of the Lords Spiritual and Temporal, and Commons, in this present Parliament assembled, and by the authority of the same, as follows:—

Requirement of serious harm

1   Serious harm

(1)   A statement is not defamatory unless its publication has caused or is likely to cause serious harm to the reputation of the claimant.

(2)   For the purposes of this section, harm to the reputation of a body that trades for profit is not 'serious harm' unless it has caused or is likely to cause the body serious financial loss.

Defences

2   Truth

(1)   It is a defence to an action for defamation for the defendant to show that the imputation conveyed by the statement complained of is substantially true.

(2)   Subsection (3) applies in an action for defamation if the statement complained of conveys two or more distinct imputations.

(3)   If one or more of the imputations is not shown to be substantially true, the defence under this section does not fail if, having regard to the imputations which are shown to be substantially true, the imputations which are not shown to be substantially true do not seriously harm the claimant's reputation.

(4)   The common law defence of justification is abolished and, accordingly, section 5 of the Defamation Act 1952 (justification) is repealed.

3   Honest opinion

(1)   It is a defence to an action for defamation for the defendant to show that the following conditions are met.

(2)   The first condition is that the statement complained of was a statement of opinion.

(3)   The second condition is that the statement complained of indicated, whether in general or specific terms, the basis of the opinion.

(4)   The third condition is that an honest person could have held the opinion on the basis of—

(a)   any fact which existed at the time the statement complained of was published;

(b)   anything asserted to be a fact in a privileged statement published before the statement complained of.

(3) The second condition is that before the statement was published in the journal an independent review of the statement's scientific or academic merit was carried out by—
   (a) the editor of the journal, and
   (b) one or more persons with expertise in the scientific or academic matter concerned.

(4) Where the publication of a statement in a scientific or academic journal is privileged by virtue of subsection (1), the publication in the same journal of any assessment of the statement's scientific or academic merit is also privileged if—
   (a) the assessment was written by one or more of the persons who carried out the independent review of the statement; and
   (b) the assessment was written in the course of that review.

(5) Where the publication of a statement or assessment is privileged by virtue of this section, the publication of a fair and accurate copy of, extract from or summary of the statement or assessment is also privileged.

(6) A publication is not privileged by virtue of this section if it is shown to be made with malice.

(7) Nothing in this section is to be construed—
   (a) as protecting the publication of matter the publication of which is prohibited by law;
   (b) as limiting any privilege subsisting apart from this section.

(8) The reference in subsection (3)(a) to 'the editor of the journal' is to be read, in the case of a journal with more than one editor, as a reference to the editor or editors who were responsible for deciding to publish the statement concerned.

7 Reports etc protected by privilege

(1) For subsection (3) of section 14 of the Defamation Act 1996 (reports of court proceedings absolutely privileged) substitute—

   '(3) This section applies to—
      (a) any court in the United Kingdom;
      (b) any court established under the law of a country or territory outside the United Kingdom;
      (c) any international court or tribunal established by the Security Council of the United Nations or by an international agreement;
   and in paragraphs (a) and (b) "court" includes any tribunal or body exercising the judicial power of the State.'

(2) In subsection (3) of section 15 of that Act (qualified privilege) for 'public concern' substitute 'public interest'.

(3) Schedule 1 to that Act (qualified privilege) is amended as follows.

(4) For paragraphs 9 and 10 substitute—

   '9 (1) A fair and accurate copy of, extract from or summary of a notice or other matter issued for the information of the public by or on behalf of—
      (a) a legislature or government anywhere in the world;
      (b) an authority anywhere in the world performing governmental functions;
      (c) an international organisation or international conference.

(2) In this paragraph "governmental functions" includes police functions.

10 A fair and accurate copy of, extract from or summary of a document made available by a court anywhere in the world, or by a judge or officer of such a court.'

(5) After paragraph 11 insert—

'11A A fair and accurate report of proceedings at a press conference held anywhere in the world for the discussion of a matter of public interest.'

(6) In paragraph 12 (report of proceedings at public meetings)—
    (a) in sub-paragraph (1) for 'in a member State' substitute 'anywhere in the world';
    (b) in sub-paragraph (2) for 'public concern' substitute 'public interest'.

(7) In paragraph 13 (report of proceedings at meetings of public company)—
    (a) in sub-paragraph (1), for 'UK public company' substitute 'listed company';
    (b) for sub-paragraphs (2) to (5) substitute—

'(2) A fair and accurate copy of, extract from or summary of any document circulated to members of a listed company—
    (a) by or with the authority of the board of directors of the company,
    (b) by the auditors of the company, or
    (c) by any member of the company in pursuance of a right conferred by any statutory provision.

(3) A fair and accurate copy of, extract from or summary of any document circulated to members of a listed company which relates to the appointment, resignation, retirement or dismissal of directors of the company or its auditors.

(4) In this paragraph "listed company" has the same meaning as in Part 12 of the Corporation Tax Act 2009 (see section 1005 of that Act).'

(8) In paragraph 14 (report of finding or decision of certain kinds of associations) in the words before paragraph (a), for 'in the United Kingdom or another member State' substitute 'anywhere in the world'.

(9) After paragraph 14 insert—

'14AA fair and accurate—
    (a) report of proceedings of a scientific or academic conference held anywhere in the world, or
    (b) copy of, extract from or summary of matter published by such a conference.'

(10) For paragraph 15 (report of statements etc by a person designated by the Lord Chancellor for the purposes of the paragraph) substitute—

'15 (1) A fair and accurate report or summary of, copy of or extract from, any adjudication, report, statement or notice issued by a body, officer or other person designated for the purposes of this paragraph by order of the Lord Chancellor.

(2) An order under this paragraph shall be made by statutory instrument which shall be subject to annulment in pursuance of a resolution of either House of Parliament.'

(11) For paragraphs 16 and 17 (general provision) substitute—

'16 In this Schedule—
"court" includes—
  (a) any tribunal or body established under the law of any country or territory exercising the judicial power of the State;
  (b) any international tribunal established by the Security Council of the United Nations or by an international agreement;
  (c) any international tribunal deciding matters in dispute between States;
"international conference" means a conference attended by representatives of two or more governments;
"international organisation" means an organisation of which two or more governments are members, and includes any committee or other subordinate body of such an organisation;
"legislature" includes a local legislature; and
"member State" includes any European dependent territory of a member State.'

Single publication rule

8 Single publication rule

(1) This section applies if a person—
  (a) publishes a statement to the public ('the first publication'), and
  (b) subsequently publishes (whether or not to the public) that statement or a statement which is substantially the same.
(2) In subsection (1) 'publication to the public' includes publication to a section of the public.
(3) For the purposes of section 4A of the Limitation Act 1980 (time limit for actions for defamation etc) any cause of action against the person for defamation in respect of the subsequent publication is to be treated as having accrued on the date of the first publication.
(4) This section does not apply in relation to the subsequent publication if the manner of that publication is materially different from the manner of the first publication.
(5) In determining whether the manner of a subsequent publication is materially different from the manner of the first publication, the matters to which the court may have regard include (amongst other matters)—
  (a) the level of prominence that a statement is given;
  (b) the extent of the subsequent publication.
(6) Where this section applies—
  (a) it does not affect the court's discretion under section 32A of the Limitation Act 1980 (discretionary exclusion of time limit for actions for defamation etc), and
  (b) the reference in subsection (1)(a) of that section to the operation of section 4A of that Act is a reference to the operation of section 4A together with this section.

Jurisdiction

9 Action against a person not domiciled in the UK or a Member State etc

(1) This section applies to an action for defamation against a person who is not domiciled—

(a) in the United Kingdom;

(b) in another Member State; or

(c) in a state which is for the time being a contracting party to the Lugano Convention.

(2) A court does not have jurisdiction to hear and determine an action to which this section applies unless the court is satisfied that, of all the places in which the statement complained of has been published, England and Wales is clearly the most appropriate place in which to bring an action in respect of the statement.

(3) The references in subsection (2) to the statement complained of include references to any statement which conveys the same, or substantially the same, imputation as the statement complained of.

(4) For the purposes of this section—

(a) a person is domiciled in the United Kingdom or in another Member State if the person is domiciled there for the purposes of the Brussels Regulation;

(b) a person is domiciled in a state which is a contracting party to the Lugano Convention if the person is domiciled in the state for the purposes of that Convention.

(5) In this section—

"the Brussels Regulation" means Council Regulation (EC) No 44/2001 of 22nd December 2000 on jurisdiction and the recognition and enforcement of judgments in civil and commercial matters, as amended from time to time and as applied by the Agreement made on 19th October 2005 between the European Community and the Kingdom of Denmark on jurisdiction and the recognition and enforcement of judgments in civil and commercial matters (OJ No L299 16.11.2005 at p 62);

"the Lugano Convention" means the Convention on jurisdiction and the recognition and enforcement of judgments in civil and commercial matters, between the European Community and the Republic of Iceland, the Kingdom of Norway, the Swiss Confederation and the Kingdom of Denmark signed on behalf of the European Community on 30th October 2007.

10 Action against a person who was not the author, editor etc

(1) A court does not have jurisdiction to hear and determine an action for defamation brought against a person who was not the author, editor or publisher of the statement complained of unless the court is satisfied that it is not reasonably practicable for an action to be brought against the author, editor or publisher.

(2) In this section 'author', 'editor' and 'publisher' have the same meaning as in section 1 of the Defamation Act 1996.

Trial by jury

11 Trial to be without a jury unless the court orders otherwise

(1) In section 69(1) of the Senior Courts Act 1981 (certain actions in the Queen's Bench Division to be tried with a jury unless the trial requires prolonged examination of documents etc) in paragraph (b) omit 'libel, slander,'.

(2) In section 66(3) of the County Courts Act 1984 (certain actions in the county court to be tried with a jury unless the trial requires prolonged examination of documents etc) in paragraph (b) omit 'libel, slander,'.

Summary of court judgment

12 Power of court to order a summary of its judgment to be published

(1) Where a court gives judgment for the claimant in an action for defamation the court may order the defendant to publish a summary of the judgment.

(2) The wording of any summary and the time, manner, form and place of its publication are to be for the parties to agree.

(3) If the parties cannot agree on the wording, the wording is to be settled by the court.

(4) If the parties cannot agree on the time, manner, form or place of publication, the court may give such directions as to those matters as it considers reasonable and practicable in the circumstances.

(5) This section does not apply where the court gives judgment for the claimant under section 8(3) of the Defamation Act 1996 (summary disposal of claims).

Removal, etc of statements

13 Order to remove statement or cease distribution etc

(1) Where a court gives judgment for the claimant in an action for defamation the court may order—

(a) the operator of a website on which the defamatory statement is posted to remove the statement, or

(b) any person who was not the author, editor or publisher of the defamatory statement to stop distributing, selling or exhibiting material containing the statement.

(2) In this section 'author', 'editor' and 'publisher' have the same meaning as in section 1 of the Defamation Act 1996.

(3) Subsection (1) does not affect the power of the court apart from that subsection.

Slander

14 Special damage

(1) The Slander of Women Act 1891 is repealed.

(2) The publication of a statement that conveys the imputation that a person has a contagious or infectious disease does not give rise to a cause of action for slander unless the publication causes the person special damage.

General provisions

15 Meaning of 'publish' and 'statement'

In this Act—

"publish" and "publication", in relation to a statement, have the meaning they have for the purposes of the law of defamation generally;

"statement" means words, pictures, visual images, gestures or any other method of signifying meaning.

16 Consequential amendments and savings etc

(1) Section 8 of the Rehabilitation of Offenders Act 1974 (defamation actions) is amended in accordance with subsections (2) and (3).

(2) In subsection (3) for 'of justification or fair comment or' substitute 'under section 2 or 3 of the Defamation Act 2013 which is available to him or any defence'.

(3) In subsection (5) for 'the defence of justification' substitute 'a defence under section 2 of the Defamation Act 2013'.

(4) Nothing in section 1 or 14 affects any cause of action accrued before the commencement of the section in question.

(5) Nothing in sections 2 to 7 or 10 has effect in relation to an action for defamation if the cause of action accrued before the commencement of the section in question.

(6) In determining whether section 8 applies, no account is to be taken of any publication made before the commencement of the section.

(7) Nothing in section 9 or 11 has effect in relation to an action for defamation begun before the commencement of the section in question.

(8) In determining for the purposes of subsection (7)(a) of section 3 whether a person would have a defence under section 4 to any action for defamation, the operation of subsection (5) of this section is to be ignored.

17 Short title, extent and commencement

(1) This Act may be cited as the Defamation Act 2013.

(2) Subject to subsection (3), this Act extends to England and Wales only.

(3) The following provisions also extend to Scotland—
    (a) section 6;
    (b) section 7(9);
    (c) section 15;
    (d) section 16(5) (in so far as it relates to sections 6 and 7(9));
    (e) this section.

(4) Subject to subsections (5) and (6), the provisions of this Act come into force on such day as the Secretary of State may by order made by statutory instrument appoint.

(5) Sections 6 and 7(9) come into force in so far as they extend to Scotland on such day as the Scottish Ministers may by order appoint.

(6) Section 15, subsections (4) to (8) of section 16 and this section come into force on the day on which this Act is passed.

Defamation Act 2013 Explanatory Notes

2013 CHAPTER 26

Introduction

1. These explanatory notes relate to the Defamation Act 2013, which received Royal Assent on 25 April 2013. They have been prepared by the Ministry of Justice in order to assist the reader in understanding the Act. They do not form part of the Act and have not been endorsed by Parliament.

2.The notes need to be read in conjunction with the Act. They are not, and are not meant to be, a comprehensive description of the Act. So where a section or part of a section does not seem to require any explanation or comment, none is given.

Summary

3. The Defamation Act 2013 reforms aspects of the law of defamation. The civil law on defamation has developed through the common law over a number of years, periodically being supplemented by statute, most recently the Defamation Act 1952 ('the 1952 Act') and the Defamation Act 1996 ('the 1996 Act').

Background

4. The Government's Coalition Agreement gave a commitment to review the law of defamation, and on 9 July 2010 the Government announced its intention to publish a draft Defamation Bill. The Draft Defamation Bill (Cm 8020) was published for full public consultation and pre-legislative scrutiny on 15 March 2011.

5. The public consultation closed on 10 June 2011. The Ministry of Justice received 129 responses from a range of interested parties. A comprehensive summary of the responses received was published on 24 November 2011 (Draft Defamation Bill Summary of Responses to Consultation CP(R) 3/11). In addition to the Government consultation, pre-legislative scrutiny of the draft Bill was undertaken by a Parliamentary Joint Committee. The committee held oral evidence sessions between April and July 2011 and its final report was published on 19 October 2011 (The Joint Committee on the Draft Defamation Bill Report Session 2010-2012, HL 203, HC 930-I).

6. The Government response to the Joint Committee's report was published on 29 February 2012 (The Government's Response to the Report of the Joint Committee on the Draft Defamation Bill Cm 8295) and set out the Government's conclusions including on certain matters raised in the public consultation but not specifically addressed in the Committee's report.

Territorial Extent and Application

7. Most of the Act's provisions extend to England and Wales only, but certain provisions also extend to Scotland:

- Section 6 relates to the publication of peer-reviewed statements in scientific or academic journals.
- Section 7(9) extends qualified privilege to fair and accurate reports of proceedings of a scientific or academic conference.
- Section 15 defines the terms 'publish' and 'statement'.
- Section 16(5) is a saving provision which relates in part to sections 6 and 7(9).
- Section 17 determines the extent and commencement of the Act.

8. In relation to Wales, the Act does not relate to devolved matters or confer functions on the Welsh Ministers.

9. The Act amends a number of enactments which extend to Scotland and Northern Ireland as well as to England and Wales. These amendments, apart from that made by section 7(9) which extends to Scotland, will extend to England and Wales only.

Commentary on Sections

Section 1: Serious harm

10. Subsection (1) of this section provides that a statement is not defamatory unless its publication has caused or is likely to cause serious harm to the reputation of the claimant. The provision extends to situations where publication is likely to cause serious harm in order to cover situations where the harm has not yet occurred at the time the action for defamation is commenced. Subsection (2) indicates that for the purposes of the section, harm to the reputation of a body that trades for profit is not 'serious harm' unless it has caused or is likely to cause the body serious financial loss.

11. The section builds on the consideration given by the courts in a series of cases to the question of what is sufficient to establish that a statement is defamatory. A recent example is *Thornton v Telegraph Media Group Ltd*[1] in which a decision of the House of Lords in *Sim v Stretch*[2] was identified as authority for the existence of a 'threshold of seriousness' in what is defamatory. There is also currently potential for trivial cases to be struck out on the basis that they are an abuse of process because so little is at stake. In *Jameel v Dow Jones & Co*[3] it was established that there needs to be a real and substantial tort. The section raises the bar for bringing a claim so that only cases involving serious harm to the claimant's reputation can be brought.

12. Subsection (2) reflects the fact that bodies trading for profit are already prevented from claiming damages for certain types of harm such as injury to feelings, and are in practice likely to have to show actual or likely financial loss. The requirement that this be serious is consistent with the new serious harm test in subsection (1).

---

[1] [2010] EWHC 1414.
[2] [1936] 2 All ER 1237.
[3] [2005] EWCA Civ 75.

Section 2: Truth

13. This section replaces the common law defence of justification with a new statutory defence of truth. The section is intended broadly to reflect the current law while simplifying and clarifying certain elements.

14. Subsection (1) provides for the new defence to apply where the defendant can show that the imputation conveyed by the statement complained of is substantially true. This subsection reflects the current law as established in the case of *Chase v News Group Newspapers Ltd*,[4] where the Court of Appeal indicated that in order for the defence of justification to be available 'the defendant does not have to prove that every word he or she published was true. He or she has to establish the "essential" or "substantial" truth of the sting of the libel'.

15. There is a long-standing common law rule that it is no defence to an action for defamation for the defendant to prove that he or she was only repeating what someone else had said (known as the 'repetition rule'). Subsection (1) focuses on the imputation conveyed by the statement in order to incorporate this rule.

16. In any case where the defence of truth is raised, there will be two issues: i) what imputation (or imputations) are actually conveyed by the statement; and ii) whether the imputation (or imputations) conveyed are substantially true. The defence will apply where the imputation is one of fact.

17. Subsections (2) and (3) replace section 5 of the 1952 Act (the only significant element of the defence of justification which is currently in statute). Their effect is that where the statement complained of contains two or more distinct imputations, the defence does not fail if, having regard to the imputations which are shown to be substantially true, those which are not shown to be substantially true do not seriously harm the claimant's reputation. These provisions are intended to have the same effect as those in section 5 of the 1952 Act, but are expressed in more modern terminology. The phrase 'materially injure' used in the 1952 Act is replaced by 'seriously harm' to ensure consistency with the test in section 1 of the Act.

18. Subsection (4) abolishes the common law defence of justification and repeals section 5 of the 1952 Act. This means that where a defendant wishes to rely on the new statutory defence the court would be required to apply the words used in the statute, not the current case law. In cases where uncertainty arises the current case law would constitute a helpful but not binding guide to interpreting how the new statutory defence should be applied.

Section 3: Honest opinion

19. This section replaces the common law defence of fair comment[5] with a new defence of honest opinion. The section broadly reflects the current law while simplifying and clarifying certain elements, but does not include the current requirement for the opinion to be on a matter of public interest.

20. Subsections (1) to (4) provide for the defence to apply where the defendant can show that three conditions are met. These are condition 1: that the statement complained of was a statement of opinion; condition 2: that the statement complained of indicated, whether in general or specific terms, the basis of the opinion; and condition 3: that an honest person could have held the opinion on the basis of any fact which existed at the

---

[4] [2002] EWCA Civ 1772 at para 34.
[5] The Supreme Court in *Spiller v Joseph* [2010] UKSC 53 referred to this as honest comment.

time the statement complained of was published or anything asserted to be a fact in a privileged statement published before the statement complained of.

21. Condition 1 (in subsection (2)) is intended to reflect the current law and embraces the requirement established in *Cheng v Tse Wai Chun Paul*[6] that the statement must be recognisable as comment as distinct from an imputation of fact. It is implicit in Condition 1 that the assessment is on the basis of how the ordinary person would understand it. As an inference of fact is a form of opinion, this would be encompassed by the defence.

22. Condition 2 (in subsection (3)), reflects the test approved by the Supreme Court in *Joseph v Spiller*[7] that 'the comment must explicitly or implicitly indicate, at least in general terms, the facts on which it is based'. Condition 2 and Condition 3 (in subsection (4)) aim to simplify the law by providing a clear and straightforward test. This is intended to retain the broad principles of the current common law defence as to the necessary basis for the opinion expressed but avoid the complexities which have arisen in case law, in particular over the extent to which the opinion must be based on facts which are sufficiently true and as to the extent to which the statement must explicitly or implicitly indicate the facts on which the opinion is based. These are areas where the common law has become increasingly complicated and technical, and where case law has sometimes struggled to articulate with clarity how the law should apply in particular circumstances. For example, the facts that may need to be demonstrated in relation to an article expressing an opinion on a political issue, comments made on a social network, a view about a contractual dispute, or a review of a restaurant or play will differ substantially.

23. Condition 3 is an objective test and consists of two elements. It is enough for one to be satisfied. The first is whether an honest person could have held the opinion on the basis of any fact which existed at the time the statement was published (in subsection (4)(a)). The subsection refers to 'any fact' so that any relevant fact or facts will be enough. The existing case law on the sufficiency of the factual basis is covered by the requirement that 'an honest person' must have been able to hold the opinion. If the fact was not a sufficient basis for the opinion, an honest person would not have been able to hold it.

24. The second element of condition 3 (in subsection (4)(b)) is whether an honest person could have formed the opinion on the basis of anything asserted to be a fact in a 'privileged statement' which was published before the statement complained of. For this purpose, a statement is a 'privileged statement' if the person responsible for its publication would have one of the defences listed in subsection (7) of the section if an action was brought in respect of that statement. The defences listed are the defence of absolute privilege under section 14 of the 1996 Act; the defence of qualified privilege under section 15 of that Act; and the defences in sections 4 and 6 of the Act relating to publication on a matter of public interest and peer-reviewed statements in a scientific or academic journal.

25. Subsection (5) provides for the defence to be defeated if the claimant shows that the defendant did not hold the opinion. This is a subjective test. This reflects the current law whereby the defence of fair comment will fail if the claimant can show that the statement was actuated by malice.

26. Subsection (6) makes provision for situations where the defendant is not the author of the statement (for example where an action is brought against a newspaper editor in

---

[6] (2000) 10 BHRC 525.
[7] [2010] UKSC 53 (at para 105).

respect of a comment piece rather than against the person who wrote it). In these circumstances the defence is defeated if the claimant can show that the defendant knew or ought to have known that the author did not hold the opinion.

27. Subsection (8) abolishes the common law defence of fair comment. Although this means that the defendant can no longer rely on the common law defence, in cases where uncertainty arises in the interpretation of section 3, case law would constitute a helpful but not binding guide to interpreting how the new statutory defence should be applied.

28. Subsection (8) also repeals section 6 of the 1952 Act. Section 6 provides that in an action for libel or slander in respect of words consisting partly of allegations of fact and partly of expression of opinion, a defence of fair comment shall not fail by reason only that the truth of every allegation of fact is not proved if the expression of opinion is fair comment having regard to such of the facts alleged or referred to in the words complained of as are proved. This provision is no longer necessary in light of the new approach set out in subsection (4). A defendant will be able to show that conditions 1, 2 and 3 are met without needing to prove the truth of every single allegation of fact relevant to the statement complained of.

Section 4: Publication on matter of public interest

29. This section creates a new defence to an action for defamation of publication on a matter of public interest. It is based on the existing common law defence established in *Reynolds v Times Newspapers*[8] and is intended to reflect the principles established in that case and in subsequent case law. Subsection (1) provides for the defence to be available in circumstances where the defendant can show that the statement complained of was, or formed part of, a statement on a matter of public interest and that he reasonably believed that publishing the statement complained of was in the public interest. The intention in this provision is to reflect the existing common law as most recently set out in *Flood v Times Newspapers*.[9] It reflects the fact that the common law test contained both a subjective element—what the defendant believed was in the public interest at the time of publication—and an objective element—whether the belief was a reasonable one for the defendant to hold in all the circumstances.

30. In relation to the first limb of this test, the section does not attempt to define what is meant by 'the public interest'. However, this is a concept which is well-established in the English common law. It is made clear that the defence applies if the statement complained of 'was, or formed part of, a statement on a matter of public interest' to ensure that either the words complained of may be on a matter of public interest, or that a holistic view may be taken of the statement in the wider context of the document, article etc in which it is contained in order to decide if overall this is on a matter of public interest.

31. Subsection (2) requires the court, subject to subsections (3) and (4), to have regard to all the circumstances of the case in determining whether the defendant has shown the matters set out in subsection (1).

32. Subsection (3) is intended to encapsulate the core of the common law doctrine of 'reportage' (which has been described by the courts as 'a convenient word to describe the neutral reporting of attributed allegations rather than their adoption by the newspaper'[10]).

---

[8] [2001] 2 AC 127.
[9] [2012] UKSC 11. See, for example, the judgement of Lord Brown at 113.
[10] Per Simon Brown in *Al-Fagih* [2001] EWCA Civ 1634.

In instances where this doctrine applies, the defendant does not need to have verified the information reported before publication because the way that the report is presented gives a balanced picture. In determining whether for the purposes of the section it was reasonable for the defendant to believe that publishing the statement was in the public interest, the court should disregard any failure on the part of a defendant to take steps to verify the truth of the imputation conveyed by the publication (which would include any failure of the defendant to seek the claimant's views on the statement). This means that a defendant newspaper for example would not be prejudiced for a failure to verify where subsection (3) applies.

33. Subsection (4) requires the court, in considering whether the defendant's belief was reasonable, to make such allowance for editorial judgement as it considers appropriate. This expressly recognises the discretion given to editors in judgments such as that of *Flood*, but is not limited to editors in the media context.

34. Subsection (5) makes clear for the avoidance of doubt that the defence provided by this section may be relied on irrespective of whether the statement complained of is one of fact or opinion.

35. Subsection (6) abolishes the common law defence known as the Reynolds defence. This is because the statutory defence is intended essentially to codify the common law defence. While abolishing the common law defence means that the courts would be required to apply the words used in the statute, the current case law would constitute a helpful (albeit not binding) guide to interpreting how the new statutory defence should be applied. It is expected the courts would take the existing case law into consideration where appropriate.

Section 5: Operators of websites

36. This section creates a new defence for the operators of websites where a defamation action is brought against them in respect of a statement posted on the website.

37. Subsection (2) provides for the defence to apply if the operator can show that they did not post the statement on the website. Subsection (3) provides for the defence to be defeated if the claimant can show that it was not possible for him or her to identify the person who posted the statement; that they gave the operator a notice of complaint in relation to the statement; and that the operator failed to respond to that notice in accordance with provision contained in regulations to be made by the Secretary of State. Subsection (4) interprets subsection (3)(a) and explains that it is possible for a claimant to 'identify' a person for the purposes of that subsection only if the claimant has sufficient information to bring proceedings against the person.

38. Subsection (5) provides details of provision that may be included in regulations. This includes provision as to the action which an operator must take in response to a notice (which in particular may include action relating to the identity or contact details of the person who posted the statement and action relating to the removal of the post); provision specifying a time limit for the taking of any such action and for conferring a discretion on the court to treat action taken after the expiry of a time limit as having been taken before that expiry. This would allow for provision to be made enabling a court to waive or retrospectively extend a time limit as appropriate. The subsection also permits regulations to make any other provision for the purposes of this section.

39. Subsection (6) sets out certain specific information which must be included in a notice of complaint. The notice must specify the complainant's name, set out the statement concerned and where on the website the statement was posted and explain why it is

defamatory of the complainant. Regulations may specify what other information must be included in a notice of complaint.

40. Subsection (7) permits regulations to make provision about the circumstances in which a notice which is not a notice of complaint is to be treated as a notice of complaint for the purpose of the section or any provision made under it.

41. Subsection (8) permits regulations under this section to make different provision for different circumstances.

42. Subsection (11) provides for the defence to be defeated if the claimant shows that the website operator has acted with malice in relation to the posting of the statement concerned. This might arise where, for example, the website operator had incited the poster to make the posting or had otherwise colluded with the poster.

43. Subsection (12) explains that the defence available to a website operator is not defeated by reason only of the fact that the operator moderates the statements posted on it by others

Section 6: Peer-reviewed statement in scientific or academic journal etc

44. This section creates a new defence of qualified privilege relating to peer-reviewed material in scientific or academic journals (whether published in electronic form or otherwise). The term 'scientific journal' would include medical and engineering journals.

45. Subsections (1) to (3) provide for the defence to apply where two conditions are met. These are condition 1: that the statement relates to a scientific or academic matter; and condition 2: that before the statement was published in the journal an independent review of the statement's scientific or academic merit was carried out by the editor of the journal and one or more persons with expertise in the scientific or academic matter concerned. The requirements in condition 2 are intended to reflect the core aspects of a responsible peer-review process. Subsection (8) provides that the reference to 'the editor of the journal' is to be read, in the case of a journal with more than one editor, as a reference to the editor or editors who were responsible for deciding to publish the statement concerned. This may be relevant where a board of editors is responsible for decision-making.

46. Subsection (4) extends the protection offered by the defence to publications in the same journal of any assessment of the scientific or academic merit of a peer-reviewed statement, provided the assessment was written by one or more of the persons who carried out the independent review of the statement, and the assessment was written in the course of that review. This is intended to ensure that the privilege is available not only to the author of the peer-reviewed statement, but also to those who have conducted the independent review who will need to assess, for example, the papers originally submitted by the author and may need to comment.

47. Subsection (5) provides that the privilege given by the section to peer-reviewed statements and related assessments also extends to the publication of a fair and accurate copy of, extract from or summary of the statement or assessment concerned.

48. By subsection (6) the privilege given by the section is lost if the publication is shown to be made with malice. This reflects the condition attaching to other forms of qualified privilege. Subsection (7)(b) has been included to ensure that the new section is not read as preventing a person who publishes a statement in a scientific or academic journal from relying on other forms of privilege, such as the privilege conferred under section 7(9) to fair and accurate reports etc of proceedings at a scientific or academic conference.

Section 7: Reports etc protected by privilege

49. This section amends the provisions contained in the 1996 Act relating to the defences of absolute and qualified privilege to extend the circumstances in which these defences can be used.

50. Subsection (1) replaces subsection (3) of section 14 of the 1996 Act, which concerns the absolute privilege applying to fair and accurate contemporaneous reports of court proceedings. Subsection (3) of section 14 currently provides for absolute privilege to apply to fair and accurate reports of proceedings in public before any court in the UK; the European Court of Justice or any court attached to that court; the European Court of Human Rights; and any international criminal tribunal established by the Security Council of the United Nations or by an international agreement to which the UK is a party. Subsection (1) replaces this with a new subsection, which extends the scope of the defence so that it also covers proceedings in any court established under the law of a country or territory outside the United Kingdom, and any international court or tribunal established by the Security Council of the United Nations or by an international agreement.

51. Subsection (2) amends section 15(3) of the 1996 Act by substituting the phrase 'public interest' for 'public concern', so that the subsection reads 'This section does not apply to the publication to the public, or a section of the public, of matter which is not of public interest and the publication of which is not for the public benefit'. This is intended to prevent any confusion arising from the use of two different terms with equivalent meaning in this Act and in the 1996 Act. Subsection (6)(b) makes the same amendment to paragraph 12(2) of Schedule 1 to the 1996 Act in relation to the privilege extended to fair and accurate reports etc of public meetings.

52. Subsections (3) to (10) make amendments to Part 2 of Schedule 1 to the 1996 Act in a number of areas so as to extend the circumstances in which the defence of qualified privilege is available. Section 15 of and Schedule 1 to the 1996 Act currently provide for qualified privilege to apply to various types of report or statement, provided the report or statement is fair and accurate, on a matter of public concern, and that publication is for the public benefit and made without malice. Part 1 of Schedule 1 sets out categories of publication which attract qualified privilege without explanation or contradiction. These include fair and accurate reports of proceedings in public, anywhere in the world, of legislatures (both national and local), courts, public inquiries, and international organisations or conferences, and documents, notices and other matter published by these bodies.

53. Part 2 of Schedule 1 sets out categories of publication which have the protection of qualified privilege unless the publisher refuses or neglects to publish, in a suitable manner, a reasonable letter or statement by way of explanation or correction when requested to do so. These include copies of or extracts from information for the public published by government or authorities performing governmental functions (such as the police) or by courts; reports of proceedings at a range of public meetings (e.g. of local authorities) general meetings of UK public companies; and reports of findings or decisions by a range of associations formed in the UK or the European Union (such as associations relating to art, science, religion or learning, trade associations, sports associations and charitable associations).

54. In addition to the protection already offered to fair and accurate copies of or extracts from the different types of publication to which the defence is extended, amendments are made by subsections (4), (7)(b) and (10) of the section to extend the scope of

qualified privilege to cover fair and accurate summaries of the material. For example, subsection (4) extends the defence to summaries of notices or other matter issued for the information of the public by a number of governmental bodies, and to summaries of documents made available by the courts.

55. Currently qualified privilege under Part 1 of Schedule 1 extends to fair and accurate reports of proceedings in public of a legislature; before a court; and in a number of other forums anywhere in the world. However, qualified privilege under Part 2 only applies to publications arising in the UK and EU member states. Subsections (4), (6)(a), (7), and (8) extend the scope of the defence to cover the different types of publication to which the defence extends anywhere in the world. For example, subsection (6) does this for reports of proceedings at public meetings, and subsection (8) for reports of certain kinds of associations.

56. Subsection (5) provides for qualified privilege to extend to a fair and accurate report of proceedings at a press conference held anywhere in the world for the discussion of a matter of public interest. Under the current law as articulated in the case of *McCartan Turkington Breen v Times Newspapers Ltd*,[11] it appears that a press conference would fall within the scope of a 'public meeting' under paragraph 12 of Schedule 1 to the 1996 Act. This provision has been included in the Act to clarify the position.

57. Currently Part 2 qualified privilege extends only to fair and accurate reports of proceedings at general meetings and documents circulated by UK public companies (paragraph 13). Subsection (7) of the section extends this to reports relating to public companies elsewhere in the world. It achieves this by extending the provision to 'listed companies' within the meaning of Part 12 of the Corporation Tax Act 2009 with a view to ensuring that broadly the same types of companies are covered by the provision in the UK and abroad. It also extends a provision in the 1996 Act (which provides for qualified privilege to be available in respect of a fair and accurate copy etc of material circulated to members of a listed company relating to the appointment, resignation, retirement or dismissal of directors of the company) to such material relating to the company's auditors.

58. Subsection (9) inserts a new paragraph into Schedule 1 to the 1996 Act to extend Part 2 qualified privilege to fair and accurate reports of proceedings of a scientific or academic conference, and to copies, extracts and summaries of matter published by such conferences. It is possible in certain circumstances that Part 2 qualified privilege may already apply to academic and scientific conferences (either where they fall within the description of a public meeting in paragraph 12, or where findings or decisions are published by a scientific or academic association (paragraph 14)). The amendments made by subsection (9) will however ensure that there is not a gap.

59. Subsection (11) substitutes new general provisions in Schedule 1 to reflect the changes that have been made to the substance of the Schedule. It also removes provisions allowing for orders to be made by the Lord Chancellor identifying 'corresponding proceedings' for the purposes of paragraph 11(3) of the Schedule, and 'corresponding meetings and documents' for the purposes of paragraph 13(5). The provision relating to paragraph 13(5) no longer has any application in the light of the amendments made to that paragraph by subsection (7), while the power in relation to paragraph 11(3) has never been exercised and the amendment leaves the provision to take its natural meaning.

---

[11] [2001] 2 AC 277.

Section 8: Single publication rule

60. This section introduces a single publication rule to prevent an action being brought in relation to publication of the same material by the same publisher after a one year limitation period from the date of the first publication of that material to the public or a section of the public. This replaces the longstanding principle that each publication of defamatory material gives rise to a separate cause of action which is subject to its own limitation period (the 'multiple publication rule').

61. Subsection (1) indicates that the provisions apply where a person publishes a statement to the public (defined in subsection (2) as including publication to a section of the public), and subsequently publishes that statement or a statement which is substantially the same. The aim is to ensure that the provisions catch publications which have the same content or content which has changed very little so that the essence of the defamatory statement is not substantially different from that contained in the earlier publication. Publication to the public has been selected as the trigger point because it is from this point on that problems are generally encountered with internet publications and in order to stop the new provision catching limited publications leading up to publication to the public at large. The definition in subsection (2) is intended to ensure that publications to a limited number of people are covered (for example where a blog has a small group of subscribers or followers).

62. Subsection (3) has the effect of ensuring that the limitation period in relation to any cause of action brought in respect of a subsequent publication within scope of the section is treated as having started to run on the date of the first publication.

63. Subsection (4) provides that the single publication rule does not apply where the manner of the subsequent publication of the statement is 'materially different' from the manner of the first publication. Subsection (5) provides that in deciding this issue the matters to which the court may have regard include the level of prominence given to the statement and the extent of the subsequent publication. A possible example of this could be where a story has first appeared relatively obscurely in a section of a website where several clicks need to be gone through to access it, but has subsequently been promoted to a position where it can be directly accessed from the home page of the site, thereby increasing considerably the number of hits it receives.

64. Subsection (6) confirms that the section does not affect the court's discretion under section 32A of the Limitation Act 1980 to allow a defamation action to proceed outside the one year limitation period where it is equitable to do so. It also ensures that the reference in subsection (1)(a) of section 32A to the operation of section 4A of the 1980 Act (section 4A concerns the time limit applicable for defamation actions) is interpreted as a reference to the operation of section 4A together with section 8. Section 32A provides a broad discretion which requires the court to have regard to all the circumstances of the case, and it is envisaged that this will provide a safeguard against injustice in relation to the application of any limitation issue arising under this section.

Section 9: Action against a person not domiciled in the UK or a Member State etc

65. This section aims to address the issue of 'libel tourism' (a term which is used to apply where cases with a tenuous link to England and Wales are brought in this jurisdiction). Subsection (1) focuses the provision on cases where an action is brought against a person who is not domiciled in the UK, an EU Member State or a state which is a party to the

Lugano Convention. This is in order to avoid conflict with European jurisdictional rules (in particular the Brussels Regulation on jurisdictional matters[12]).

66. Subsection (2) provides that a court does not have jurisdiction to hear and determine an action to which the section applies unless it is satisfied that, of all the places in which the statement complained of has been published, England and Wales is clearly the most appropriate place in which to bring an action in respect of the statement. This means that in cases where a statement has been published in this jurisdiction and also abroad the court will be required to consider the overall global picture to consider where it would be most appropriate for a claim to be heard. It is intended that this will overcome the problem of courts readily accepting jurisdiction simply because a claimant frames their claim so as to focus on damage which has occurred in this jurisdiction only. This would mean that, for example, if a statement was published 100,000 times in Australia and only 5,000 times in England that would be a good basis on which to conclude that the most appropriate jurisdiction in which to bring an action in respect of the statement was Australia rather than England. There will however be a range of factors which the court may wish to take into account including, for example, the amount of damage to the claimant's reputation in this jurisdiction compared to elsewhere, the extent to which the publication was targeted at a readership in this jurisdiction compared to elsewhere, and whether there is reason to think that the claimant would not receive a fair hearing elsewhere.

67. Subsection (3) provides that the references in subsection (2) to the statement complained of include references to any statement which conveys the same, or substantially the same, imputation as the statement complained of. This addresses the situation where a statement is published in a number of countries but is not exactly the same in all of them, and will ensure that a court is not impeded in deciding whether England and Wales is the most appropriate place to bring the claim by arguments that statements elsewhere should be regarded as different publications even when they are substantially the same. It is the intention that this new rule will be capable of being applied within the existing procedural framework for defamation claims.

Section 10: Action against a person who was not the author, editor etc

68. This section limits the circumstances in which an action for defamation can be brought against someone who is not the primary publisher of an allegedly defamatory statement.

69. Subsection (1) provides that a court does not have jurisdiction to hear and determine an action for defamation brought against a person who was not the author, editor or publisher of the statement complained of unless it is satisfied that it is not reasonably practicable for an action to be brought against the author, editor or publisher.

70. Subsection (2) confirms that the terms 'author', 'editor' and 'publisher' are to have the same meaning as in section 1 of the 1996 Act. By subsection (2) of that Act, 'author' means the originator of the statement, but does not include a person who did not intend that his statement be published at all; 'editor' means a person having editorial or equivalent responsibility for the content of the statement or the decision to publish it; and 'publisher' means a commercial publisher, that is, a person whose business is issuing material to the public, or a section of the public, who issues material containing the statement in

---

[12] Council Regulation (EC) 44/2001 on jurisdiction and the recognition and enforcement of judgments in civil and commercial matters.

the course of that business. Examples of persons who are not to be considered the author, editor or publisher are contained in subsection (3) of section 1 of the 1996 Act.

Section 11: Trial to be without a jury unless the court orders otherwise

71. This section removes the presumption in favour of jury trial in defamation cases.

72. Currently section 69 of the Senior Courts Act 1981 and section 66 of the County Courts Act 1984 provide for a right to trial with a jury in certain civil proceedings (namely malicious prosecution, false imprisonment, fraud, libel and slander) on the application of any party, 'unless the court considers that the trial requires any prolonged examination of documents or accounts or any scientific or local investigation which cannot conveniently be made with a jury'.

73. Subsection (1) and subsection (2) respectively amend the 1981 and 1984 Acts to remove libel and slander from the list of proceedings where a right to jury trial exists. The result will be that defamation cases will be tried without a jury unless a court orders otherwise.

Section 12: Power of court to order a summary of its judgment to be published

74. In summary disposal proceedings under section 8 of the 1996 Act the court has power to order an unsuccessful defendant to publish a summary of its judgment where the parties cannot agree the content of any correction or apology. The section gives the court power to order a summary of its judgment to be published in defamation proceedings more generally.

75. Subsection (1) enables the court when giving judgment for the claimant in a defamation action to order the defendant to publish a summary of the judgment. Subsection (2) provides that the wording of any summary and the time, manner, form and place of its publication are matters for the parties to agree. Where the parties are unable to agree, subsections (3) and (4) respectively provide for the court to settle the wording, and enable it to give such directions in relation to the time, manner, form or place of publication as it considers reasonable and practicable. Subsection (5) disapplies the section where the court gives judgment for the claimant under section 8(3) of the 1996 Act. The summary disposal procedure is a separate procedure which can continue to be used where this is appropriate.

Section 13: Order to remove statement or cease distribution etc

76. This section relates to situations where an author may not always be in a position to remove or prevent further dissemination of material which has been found to be defamatory. Subsection (1) provides that where a court gives judgment for the claimant in an action for defamation, it may order the operator of a website on which a defamatory statement is posted to remove the statement, or require any person who was not the author, editor or publisher of the statement but is distributing, selling or exhibiting the material to cease disseminating it. This will enable an order for removal of the material to be made during or shortly after the conclusion of proceedings.

77. Subsection (3) ensures that the provision does not have any wider effect on the jurisdiction of the court to grant injunctive relief.

Section 14: Actions for slander: special damage

78. This section repeals the Slander of Women Act 1891 and overturns a common law rule relating to special damage.

79. In relation to slander, some special damage must be proved to flow from the statement complained of unless the publication falls into certain specific categories. These include a provision in the 1891 Act which provides that 'words spoken and published...which impute unchastity or adultery to any woman or girl shall not require special damage to render them actionable'. Subsection (1) repeals the Act, so that these circumstances are not exempted from the requirement for special damage.

80. Subsection (2) abolishes the common law rule which provides an exemption from the requirement for special damage where the imputation conveyed by the statement complained of is that the claimant has a contagious or infectious disease. In case law dating from the nineteenth century and earlier, the exemption has been held to apply in the case of imputations of leprosy, venereal disease and the plague.

Section 15: Meaning of 'publish' and 'statement'

81. This section sets out definitions of the terms 'publish', 'publication' and 'statement' for the purposes of the Act. Broad definitions are used to ensure that the provisions of the Act cover a wide range of publications in any medium, reflecting the current law.

Section 16: Consequential amendments and savings etc

82. Subsections (1) to (3) make consequential amendments to section 8 of the Rehabilitation of Offenders Act 1974 to reflect the new defences of truth and honest opinion. Section 8 of the 1974 Act applies to actions for libel or slander brought by a rehabilitated person based on statements made about offences which were the subject of a spent conviction.

83. Subsections (4) to (8) contain savings and interpretative provisions.

Section 17: Short title, extent and commencement

84. This section sets out the territorial extent of the provisions and makes provision for commencement.

Commencement

85. Section 15, the savings related provisions in subsections (4) to (8) of section 16 and section 17 (short title, commencement and extent) come into force on the day on which the Act is passed. Otherwise, the Act will come into force on such day as the Secretary of State may specify by order (section 17(4)) or, in so far as provisions extend to Scotland, on such day as the Scottish Ministers may by order appoint (section 17(5)).

Hansard References

86. The following table sets out the dates and Hansard references for each stage of the Act's passage through Parliament.

Stage	Date	Hansard reference
House of Commons		
Introduction	10 May 2012	Vol. 545 Col. 164 http://www.publications.parliament.uk/pa/cm201213/ cmhansrd/cm120510/debtext/120510-0001. htm#12051029000012
Second Reading	12 June 2012	Vol. 546 Cols. 177-267 http://www.publications.parliament.uk/pa/cm201213/ cmhansrd/cm120612/debtext/120612-0001. htm#12061240000002
Committee	19 June 2012 21 June 2012 26 June 2012	Public Bill Committee: Defamation Bill
Report and Third Reading	12 September 2012	Vol. 505 Cols. 309-381 http://www.publications.parliament.uk/pa/cm201213/ cmhansrd/cm120912/debtext/120912-0002. htm#12091223000002
House of Lords		
Introduction	8 October 2012	Vol. 739 Col. 828 http://www.publications.parliament.uk/pa/ld201213/ ldhansrd/text/121008-0001.htm#1210084000451
Second Reading	9 October 2012	Vol. 739 Cols. 932-986 http://www.publications.parliament.uk/pa/ld201213/ ldhansrd/text/121009-0001.htm#12100930000316
Committee	17 December 2012 19 December 2012 15 January 2013 17 January 2013	Vol. 741 Cols. GC413-GC468 Vol. 741 Cols. GC521-GC578 Vol. 742 Cols. GC181-GC240 Vol. 742 Cols. GC307-GC372
Report	5 February 2013	Vol. 743 Cols. 140-254 http://www.publications.parliament.uk/pa/ld201213/ ldhansrd/text/130205-0001.htm#13020546001351
Third Reading	25 February 2013	Vol. 743 Cols. 848-852 http://www.publications.parliament.uk/pa/ld201213/ ldhansrd/text/130225-0001.htm#13022512000429
Ping Pong		
Commons Consideration of Lords Amendments	16 April 2013	Commons: Vol. 561 Cols. 266-288 http://www.publications.parliament.uk/pa/cm201213/ cmhansrd/cm130416/debtext/130416-0003. htm#13041655000001
Lords Consideration of Commons Reasons	23 April 2013	Lords: Vol. 744 Cols. 1362-1387 http://www.publications.parliament.uk/pa/ld201213/ ldhansrd/text/130423-0001.htm#13042379000292
Consideration of Lords message	24 April 2013	Vol. 561 Cols. 913-923 http://www.publications.parliament.uk/pa/cm201213/ cmhansrd/cm130424/debtext/130424-0002. htm#13042446000003
Royal Assent	25 April 2013	http://www.publications.parliament.uk/pa/ld201213/ ldhansrd/text/130425-0001.htm#13042554000435 http://www.publications.parliament.uk/pa/cm201213/ cmhansrd/cm130425/debtext/130425-0002. htm#13042550000004

Defamation Act 1996, Sch 1 (as Amended by the Defamation Act 2013)

SCHEDULE 1

Qualified Privilege

Part I: Statements Having Qualified Privilege without Explanation or Contradiction

1   A fair and accurate report of proceedings in public of a legislature anywhere in the world.
2   A fair and accurate report of proceedings in public before a court anywhere in the world.
3   A fair and accurate report of proceedings in public of a person appointed to hold a public inquiry by a government or legislature anywhere in the world.
4   A fair and accurate report of proceedings in public anywhere in the world of an international organisation or an international conference.
5   A fair and accurate copy of or extract from any register or other document required by law to be open to public inspection.
6   A notice or advertisement published by or on the authority of a court, or of a judge or officer of the court, anywhere in the world.
7   A fair and accurate copy of or extract from matter published by or on the authority of a government or legislature anywhere in the world.
8   A fair and accurate copy of or extract from matter published anywhere in the world by an international organisation or an international conference.

Part II: Statements Privileged Subject to Explanation or Contradiction

9   (1)   [...] *A fair and accurate copy of, extract from or summary of a notice or other matter issued for the information of the public by or on behalf of—*
       (a)   *a legislature or government anywhere in the word;*
       (b)   *an authority anywhere in the world performing governmental functions;*
       (c)   *an international organisation or international conference.*
    (2)   *In this paragraph 'government functions' includes police functions.*
10   [...] *A fair and accurate copy of, extract from or summary of a document made available by any court anywhere in the world, or by a judge or officer of such a court.*

11 (1) A fair and accurate report of proceedings at any public meeting or sitting in the United Kingdom of—

    (a) a local authority, local authority committee or in the case of a local authority which are operating executive arrangements the executive of that authority or a committee of that executive;

    (b) a justice or justices of the peace acting otherwise than as a court exercising judicial authority;

    (c) a commission, tribunal, committee or person appointed for the purposes of any inquiry by any statutory provision, by Her Majesty or by a Minister of the Crown, a member of the Scottish Government, the Welsh Ministers or the Counsel General to the Welsh Assembly Government or a Northern Ireland Department;

    (d) a person appointed by a local authority to hold a local inquiry in pursuance of any statutory provision;

    (e) any other tribunal, board, committee or body constituted by or under, and exercising functions under, any statutory provision.

(1A) In the case of a local authority which are operating executive arrangements, a fair and accurate record of any decision made by any member of the executive where that record is required to be made and available for public inspection by virtue of section 22 of the Local Government Act 2000 or of any provision in regulations made under that section.

(2) In sub-paragraphs (1)(a) and (1A)—

'local authority' means—

    (a) in relation to England and Wales, a principal council within the meaning of the Local Government Act 1972, any body falling within any paragraph of section 100J(1) of that Act or an authority or body to which the Public Bodies (Admission to Meetings) Act 1960 applies,

    (b) in relation to Scotland, a council constituted under section 2 of the Local Government etc. (Scotland) Act 1994 or an authority or body to which the Public Bodies (Admission to Meetings) Act 1960 applies,

    (c) in relation to Northern Ireland, any authority or body to which sections 23 to 27 of the Local Government Act (Northern Ireland) 1972 apply; and

'local authority committee' means any committee of a local authority or of local authorities, and includes—

    (a) any committee or sub-committee in relation to which sections 100A to 100D of the Local Government Act 1972 apply by virtue of section 100E of that Act (whether or not also by virtue of section 100J of that Act), and

    (b) any committee or sub-committee in relation to which sections 50A to 50D of the Local Government (Scotland) Act 1973 apply by virtue of section 50E of that Act.

(2A) In sub-paragraphs (1) and (1A)—

'executive' and 'executive arrangements' have the same meaning as in Part II of the Local Government Act 2000;

(3) A fair and accurate report of any corresponding proceedings in any of the Channel Islands or the Isle of Man or in another member State.

11A *A fair and accurate report of proceedings at a press conference held anywhere in the world for the discussion of a matter of public interest.*

12 (1) A fair and accurate report of proceedings at any public meetings held [...] *anywhere in the world.*

    (2) In this paragraph a 'public meeting' means a meeting bona fide and lawfully held for a lawful purpose and for the furtherance or discussion of a matter of [...] *public interest,* whether admission to the meeting is general or restricted.

13 (1) A fair and accurate report of proceedings at a general meeting of a [...] *listed company.*

    (2) *[...] A fair and accurate copy of or extract from or summary of any document circulated to members of a listed company –*

        (a) *by or with the authority of the board of directors of the company,*

        (b) *by the auditors of the company, or*

        (c) *by any member of the company in pursuance of a right conferred by any statutory provision*

    (3) *[....] A fair and accurate copy of, extract from or summary of any document circulated to members of a listed company which relates to the appointment, resignations, retirement or dismissal of directors of the company or its auditors.*

    (4) *[...] In this paragraph 'listed company' has the same meaning as in Part 12 of the Corporation Tax Act 2009 (see section 1005 of that Act).*

    (5) *[...]*

14 A fair and accurate report of any finding or decision of any of the following descriptions of association, formed [...] *anywhere in the world,* or of any committee or governing body of such an association –

    (a) an association formed for the purpose of promoting or encouraging the exercise of or interest in any art, science, religion or learning, and empowered by its constitution to exercise control over or adjudicate on matters of interest or concern to the association, or the actions or conduct of any person subject to such control or adjudication;

    (b) an association formed for the purpose of promoting or safeguarding the interests of any trade, business, industry or profession, or of the persons carrying on or engaged in any trade, business, industry or profession, and empowered by its constitution to exercise control over or adjudicate upon matters connected with that trade, industry, or profession, or the actions or conduct of those persons;

    (c) an association formed for the purpose of promoting or safeguarding the interests of a game, sport or pastime to the playing or exercise of which members of the public are invited or admitted, and empowered by its constitution to exercise control over or adjudicate upon persons connected with or taking part in the game, sport or pastime;

    (d) an association formed for the purpose of promoting charitable objects or other objects beneficial to the community and empowered by its constitution to exercise control over or to adjudicate on matters of interest or concern to the association, or the actions or conduct of any person subject to such control or adjudication.

14A *A fair and accurate—*

    (a) report of proceedings of a scientific or academic conference held anywhere in the world, or

    (b) copy of, extract from or summary of matter published by such a conference.

15 (1) *[...] A fair and accurate report or summary of, or copy of or extract from, any adjudication, report, statement or notice issued by a body, officer or other person designated for the purposes of this paragraph by order of the Lord Chancellor.*

(2) *An order under this paragraph shall be made by statutory instrument which shall be subject to annulment in pursuance of a resolution of either House of Parliament.*

Part III: Supplementary Provisions

16 [...] *In this Schedule—*
'court' includes:
(a) any tribunal or body established under the law of any country or territory exercising the judicial power of the state;
(b) any international tribunal established by the Security Council of the United Nations or by an international agreement;
(c) any international tribunal deciding matters in dispute between states
'international conference' means a conference attended by representatives of two or more governments;
'international organisation' means an organisation of which two or more governments are members, and includes any committee or other subordinate body of such an organisation;
'legislature' includes a local legislature; and
'member State' includes any European dependent territory of a member State.

17 [...]

Index